COMMANDO

The Elite Fighting Forces of the Second World War

SALLY DUGAN

First published 2001 by Channel 4 Books
an imprint of Macmillan Publishers Ltd
25 Eccleston Place London SW1W 9NF
Basingstoke and Oxford

www.macmillan.com

Associated companies throughout the world

ISBN 07522 6143 6

1 3 5 7 9 8 6 4 2

A CIP catalogue record for this book is available from the British Library.

Designed and typeset by seagulls
Printed and bound by Mackays of Chatham, plc, Chatham, Kent

Picture credits
While every effort has been made to trace copyright holders for
photographs featured in this book, the publishers will be glad to make
proper acknowledgements in future editions in the event that any
regrettable omissions have occurred at the time of going to press.

Bundesarchiv: Page 2 (bottom), Page 3 (top left and right); Ian Chard
(Photograph from Harry Chard): Page 6 (bottom); Imperial War Museum:
Page 1 (top), Page 5 (top), Page 6 (top), Page 7, Page 8; Rupert Harding-Newman
Museum: Page 4 (centre); Topham Picturepoint: Page 1 (bottom), Page 2 (top),
Page 3 (bottom), Page 4 (top and bottom), Page 5 (bottom).

This book accompanies the television series
'Commando' made by Windfall Films for Channel 4.
Producers: Kate Barker & Henry Chancellor
Executive Producers: Ian Duncan & Oliver Morse

ACKNOWLEDGEMENTS

The idea for *Commando* came during filming for a previous Windfall Films series, *Colditz*. Many commandos demonstrated the qualities for which they had originally been selected by ending up in this supposedly escape-proof camp. As they talked, it became clear that there was another story to be told beyond the barbed wire.

This book would not have been possible without the enthusiasm and helpfulness of the many survivors of Second World War special forces operations who agreed to be interviewed. Windfall Films would like to thank the St-Nazaire, Commando, Long Range Desert Group, LRDG (NZ) and Special Air Service Regimental Associations for providing access to their members; also the Parachute 2 Club, X Troop 11 SAS, and Brendan O'Carroll. Staff at the Imperial War Museum gave helpful direction in their library and archives, and Peter Hearn kindly commented on the parachuting section (although any unintentional mistakes are not his).

At Windfall Films, special thanks are due to Kate Barker and Henry Chancellor, the series' producers, for finding time to read the manuscript in the middle of a busy filming schedule. Marisa Verazzo, the production manager, patiently answered apparently endless queries, and David Coward and Sascha Olofson provided valuable research. Executive producers Ian Duncan and Oliver Morse helped to get the project off the ground, and the Windfall office staff, Val Prodromou and Lucinda Emmett, gave very effective moral and practical support. Daphne Walsh's highly efficient transcription service was invaluable in helping to meet what seemed like an impossible deadline. Finally, the Channel 4 Books team – Charlie Carman, Sandy Holton and Verity Willcocks, together with her assistant, Kate Neil – showed faith in the project. Without this – and their editorial skills – there would have been no book.

CONTENTS

INTRODUCTION

On 24 May 1940 the German general Erwin Rommel wrote confidently to his wife: 'My estimate is that the war will be won in a fortnight.' It is easy to see why he was so sure. British and French soldiers were being hastily evacuated from Dunkirk, and the Germans had Paris in their sights.

However – as is well known – the Second World War was not won by anybody in a fortnight. One of the many reasons for this lay in an idea hatched by Winston Churchill within the two weeks that followed Rommel's pronouncement. On 3 June 1940 he wrote to his military chiefs of staff instructing them to prepare 'specially trained troops of the hunter class, who can develop a reign of terror on the "butcher and bolt" policy'.

These were the elite fighting forces that were to carry out daring hit-and-run raids and gather intelligence behind enemy lines in the desert, in the air, and from the sea. As commander of the Afrika Korps, Rommel himself was to experience the disconcerting effect of unpredictable sabotage attacks by phantom raiders who came apparently from nowhere.

War is a messy business, and contributions to victory – or defeat – cannot be worked out in clinically exact percentage terms. An audit of the number of soldiers killed, military installations damaged, or aircraft destroyed would tell less than half the story. Some of the raids described in these pages were successful; some were fiascos. All were high-risk. For this reason, many conventional soldiers regarded special forces with suspicion. However, they provided one thing that could not be measured in concrete terms: hope for the future.

The youthful enthusiasm, bravery and single-mindedness of Churchill's raiders captured newspaper headlines, raising morale at a time when Hitler seemed to be having everything his way. There were colourful characters like Jack Churchill (no relation), the ex-Brylcreem boy who led his troops with a tune on his bagpipes. There was David Stirling, nicknamed 'The Phantom Major', and described by Montgomery as being 'quite, quite mad'.

This book – and the television series it accompanies – contains the testimonies of Second World War veterans who fought with the Army Commandos, the Long Range Desert Group, the Special Air Service, and the Parachute Regiment. It does not pretend to be a comprehensive survey of the role of special forces in the Second World War. Other organizations, such as the Special Operations Executive, the Special Boat Service and the Royal Marine Commandos have already had both books and television series to themselves.

In the Second World War, soldiers fought supported by tanks, artillery and aircraft. A supply system provided food, medical care, transport and letters from home. However, those who volunteered to fight with special forces had to be self-sufficient. They knew that if they were wounded, they might well simply be left behind to face possible torture and execution.

Many survivors claim that at the time they were young and never thought they would not survive. Young men signed up for parachuting who had never even been in an aircraft, let alone jumped out of one. They embarked on troopships for the desert when the only sand they had seen had been on bucket and spade holidays. Although some were career soldiers, or had served in the Territorials, most were simply civilians in uniform. They were trained to be killers without knowing how they would react when faced with the reality of bloodshed. Their motives for volunteering for these dangerous missions were as different as the individuals themselves. John Smale, who served with the Army Commandos, recalled:

It's difficult to understand the feeling in the country at the time. It was felt that the Germans were going to invade any minute, that [they] were just waiting to come over. This seemed a marvellous opportunity to have a go at them.

Londoner Burt Shipton, whose family suffered badly in the Blitz, had more personal reasons for wanting to get at the Germans: 'They destroyed my home, my father was killed, my mother was left on her own and I couldn't do much about that – but I could do a little bit towards the overall defeat of the Germans.'

Dick Bradley – whose original surname was Goebbels – found himself taking up arms against his own country. He recalled:

Being brought up as a good Catholic, I thought it was my duty to fight Hitlerism, because the Catholic Church was persecuted by Hitler almost as much as the Jewish population – maybe not to a similar degree, but they certainly had a very, very rough time.

Some were attracted by the comradeship and lack of starchiness. As Bill 'Tiger' Watson put it: 'There was very little 'sir'-ing or saluting. There didn't need to be. It sounds rather sentimental, but you were a band of brothers.' Others liked the idea of the relative freedom, and the scope for individual feats of daring. New Zealander Alf Saunders, one of the first to volunteer for service with the Long Range Desert Group, recalled:

I didn't have any great patriotic feelings of fighting for king and country. I just wanted a change, and I wanted some adventure, and I thought: 'This is the cheapest way I can get overseas.' It was as simple as that.

The reality of these operations – some of which were little more than suicide missions – meant that many volunteers got rather more 'adventure' than they had expected.

PART ONE

Ungentlemanly Warfare

THE GUERNSEY FIASCO

Desperation was in the air. Churchill had been Prime Minister for less than a month. He had told the members of his new government: 'I have nothing to offer but blood, toil, tears and sweat.' Britain was filling up with exiled monarchs, ousted from their countries by the apparently unstoppable German advance.

In this climate, Churchill wanted to be able to offer something positive. That something turned out to be the Commandos – shock troops on the model of the Boer *kommandos*, who had so effectively raided behind British cavalry lines in the Boer War.

Churchill knew more about the *kommandos* than most, as he had been captured by them while acting as a war correspondent. As a soldier, too, he had seen the daring and success of their horseback hit-and-run sabotage attacks. The *kommandos* got their name because they were 'commandeered' from among eligible citizens. Churchill's idea was for small, highly trained groups that could carry out raids like the Boers – but they would be volunteers.

An urgent call was sent out for forty officers and 5,000 other ranks to train as a self-sufficient, mobile force. They were to be ready to strike wherever and whenever they were needed.

Some volunteers were already at hand, formed into independent companies that had been supposed to carry out ship-borne raids on the Norwegian coast. However, at least half of them had simply spent their time waiting around in frustration.

Proper Commando training for these, and the new volunteers, would take time. Churchill badly needed a quick morale-booster. He told his Chief of Staff, General Hastings Ismay, on 5 June 1940: 'It is essential to get out of our minds the idea that the Channel ports and all the country in between them are enemy territory.'

So it was that, in less than three weeks after the evacuation of Dunkirk, a shambolic party of men crossed the Channel, travelling in tiny motorboats originally designed to pick up ditched RAF pilots. They were trained as soldiers, but not as commandos. The plan was to check out the defences at key points along the French coast and generally harass the Germans. The reality was rather different.

One group never landed at all, having been unable to get off their waterlogged boat. The commanding officer of another group was about to shoot at some German cyclists when the magazine fell off his sub-machine gun. The cyclists – who were as surprised as he was – simply turned round and went the other way.

The third group had planned to throw some hand grenades into a hotel at Le Touquet, which was supposed to be harbouring German soldiers. However, it turned out that the hotel was boarded up. They did kill two Germans on the way back – but when they got to their prearranged pick-up point, they found their boat was too far out at sea to be contacted and they were forced to make a swim for it.

Chaotic though the raid was, they had at least proved that such exercises were possible – and they had come back unharmed. Churchill was encouraged and, after the German invasion of the Channel Islands, he planned to use Commandos to retaliate. This was Operation Ambassador, which took place on 14 July 1940.

The commander of the first Commando unit – rather confusingly called Number 3 Commando, even though at the time there was neither a Number 1 nor a Number 2 – was John Durnford-Slater. He was appointed on 28 June; within a week, he had managed to raise a unit of some 500 men and thirty-five officers – all volunteers. In his autobiography, *Commando*, he recalled:

> I wanted cheerful officers, not groaners. A good physique was important, but size was not. I looked for intelligence and keenness.
>
> I travelled and interviewed, interviewed and travelled non-stop, until, finally, I had the officers I needed. Then I sent them out in teams of three to comb the command for other ranks. I gave them four days to select their men and get them to Plymouth.

The men were given a subsistence allowance of 6s. 8d. a day and told to find their own billets. Meanwhile, Durnford-Slater was called up to Combined Operations headquarters in London to help plan the Guernsey raid. One of those who helped to brief him was the film star David Niven.

As preparation for Operation Ambassador, several Guernseymen were taken to the island by submarine. One managed to get in touch with the baker who had the contract for supplying bread to the German garrison, and reported that the island was occupied by 469 Germans, with the main body of troops centred in St Peter Port. Accordingly, plans were laid for an attack on an aerodrome, with a diversionary raid elsewhere. However, bad weather delayed the operation – and at the last moment one of the landing places was changed as the Germans had reinforced the original site. There was no way of telling the Guernseymen what had happened.

Other practical problems included a severe shortage of weapons, because so much had been left in France after the evacuation of Dunkirk. John Smale, who was in Number 3

Commando recalled:

> We in my own particular troop had been quite lucky, in that we'd been told that there was a supply of proper rifles, Lee Enfields, in a certain out-of-the-way place near Plymouth. I remember going down and seeing these marvellous pre-war rifles there, beautifully oiled, in lovely condition, and we'd got permission to take them.
>
> But then for the raid, somehow or other they managed to get some Tommy guns, and of course everybody was talking about Tommy guns at the time – they thought they were marvellous.

Tommy guns – Thompson sub-machine guns – were the weapons of choice of American gangsters. They were heavy but devastatingly effective. At the time there were only nine of them in the country; seven were specially lent to the Commandos for the raid.

Preparations were carried out at the Royal Naval College, Dartmouth. Here, the commandos were briefed on the details of the operation, given a meal and told to collect their weapons. These were laid out in the college gym, as John Smale recalled:

> I came into the main hall where the troop was waiting, and where they were told that they'd got to load their magazines, and I was horrified to find these little naval cadets of fifteen coming round the soldiers and saying: 'Let's have a go at it – I'll do that for you, corporal.' These little boys who'd probably never touched a weapon before were loading these magazines before they were going into action. Well, of course, you've got to know what you're doing, because if you don't do it right you'll get stoppages. We had to knock that one on the head pretty quick, but I've often wondered whether the Duke of Edinburgh was one of the little boys or not at the time.

Anyway, having eventually reloaded the magazines, we went off on a destroyer. We had several RAF crash boats, which were coming along behind us. Now, after being at sea for a bit, one of these crash boats had developed engine trouble. I was amazed at the ease with which the captain of the destroyer said: 'You'll have to put an explosive charge in it and sink it' – an expensive thing like that. I shudder to think what the cost of it was, but there was nothing else they could do. They couldn't leave it floating about at sea.

So we went on with one less crash boat, and then this particular ship that I was on missed Guernsey – or was missing it. Durnford-Slater was on the bridge with the captain and said to him, 'Look – there's an island over there. I suppose that's not our island, is it?', and he said, 'My God! You're right – it is,' and he did a sharp turn left and we managed to find our way to Guernsey.

The main group – which had been supposed to raid the aerodrome – missed Guernsey altogether and ended up on Sark, as John Smale recalled:

We were given to understand that the reason the Navy was incapable of navigating from Dartmouth to the Channel Islands – which sounds unbelievable – was because the ships had just been what they call degaussed [demagnetized to protect them from mines]. Because there was the danger of mines at sea, a method of avoiding mines and saving the ships had been devised whereby they put an electric current around the steel body of the ship. What they didn't realize, because it was such early days of this particular method, was that this upset the compass. They assumed that their compass was correct, but it wasn't – and, of course, that ruined the raid.

However, at the time, Durnford-Slater's group had no way of finding out that the main raid was not going ahead. The men simply concentrated on getting themselves ashore while they still had the cover of darkness. The Navy found the landing place relatively easily, as it was near a prominent landmark. This was the 100-foot-high Doyle Monument, built to commemorate a former governor of Guernsey. John Smale:

> We spotted the Doyle Monument all right, and we approached the land. Of course, we were all tensed up and keeping quiet – and then, out of all the quietness, the Navy were calling out their naval expressions: 'Hard a-port' or something, whatever it was they had to call out. Then the chap at the back would shout, 'Hard a-port,' and the fellow in the front would repeat it in loud language. There were we, wretched soldiers, whispering away... anyway, they got us in. I think we had to wade a little, but not much.
>
> We had a very, very steep cliff to climb up. Fortunately, it wasn't mined, but we had no end of a job clambering up this with all our weapons, and we also had coils of concertina wire. Anyway, we got to the top all right. There was a bungalow at the top, so we thought, 'Well, we'd better see who's in that, in case there are any Germans billeted in it.' So we went in there, and there was one old man there. I've always felt so very sorry for him, particularly now I'm the age that I am, and I think what it could have been like if I'd been in his position, that in the middle of the night his bungalow is invaded by a crowd of people armed to the teeth. He was absolutely terrified, and our troop commander said: 'Oh, he's mad.' Well, I'm sure he wasn't mad; he was just scared out of his wits completely, poor chap. Anyway, we locked him in the lavatory, and there he stayed as far as I know.

Durnford-Slater took a group down to the barracks, where they imagined there was a German garrison. John Smale and his commandos had the job of blocking the main road between the barracks and the airport. They created a roadblock by moving stones from a nearby garden and surrounding them with wire. However, they were a little hazy about what else to do.

> We'd only been together for maybe three weeks. We were all completely raw. I believe we did some sort of rehearsal for it, but then the scheme was changed anyway, so it wasn't of any value. We were told briefly before we started what to expect, but it was all pretty amateurish.
>
> I remember we were told there was a telephone line, and that we'd got to try and tear the line down. We didn't know how to start on it. There was one of our Royal Engineer NCOs [Non-Commissioned Officers]: because he was a Royal Engineer, they thought he must know about telephones. I think he did get in touch with the telephone company in Plymouth, but we didn't really know what we were up to. He took along some rope with something on the end of it and tried to throw it over the top, but of course he should have had clamping irons and gone up the pole, but he didn't.

Meanwhile, they stayed by their makeshift wall of rockery stones and stood guard on the road.

> Of course, we had sentries out, and we'd been told by Durnford-Slater that if anybody came back along that path we could assume that they were Germans and we must shoot them. Well, after a bit, sure enough, we heard footsteps coming. So the sentries called me up, and rather faded into the background themselves. They thought, 'Well, that's what he's paid for,' I suppose. So I thought, 'Well, now, do I shoot this chap out of hand, or what happens next?'
>
> We'd been given a password, which was 'Desmond'. We didn't know it at the time, but there was a chap called Desmond Mulholland who was a Guernseyman in the British Army who'd been put ashore to contact us. He hadn't been able to contact us because at the last minute they'd changed the plan. He was waiting where he was told we would be

coming, which was several miles up the coast, so he wasn't able to help us. We didn't know that this password tied up with him, but of course it would have done the trick all right, because if he heard his own Christian name being called out, he'd have been quite happy, I expect.

Anyway, I challenged this chap and got the password, Desmond, and it turned out that it was one of our officers. Durnford-Slater had sent him back to tell us that the place was empty.

With still no sign of any Germans, the commandos made their way back down some concrete steps to the beach, where they had arranged to be picked up. John Durnford-Slater was last down from the clifftop. In his haste, he tripped and fell head over heels. He had been carrying his cocked revolver at the ready – and in his fall, it went off. The sound of the explosion echoing round the cliffs alerted the Germans, and machine guns started firing.

The tide had come in, there was a heavy swell, and the waiting crash boats could not get near enough to the beach to take the men off. They made several trips with a dinghy for the weapons, but on the last trip it was picked up and smashed against the rocks. The weapons went to the bottom of the sea. John Durnford-Slater told his troops they would have to swim for it – but there was a problem. Three of the men turned out to be non-swimmers, even though the original letter calling for Commando volunteers had specifically mentioned that they had to be able to swim. John Smale recalled:

We did a swimming test at Plymouth before we left, but somehow or other they must have fudged that swimming test. Durnford-Slater told them, rightly or wrongly, that he would try to get a submarine sent over the next night. Well, whether they would have sent a submarine over for three private soldiers is a matter of working out, but I'm sure they wouldn't. One of them was a chap whom I knew fairly well,

Corporal Dumper. I remember the rather odd expression –
he said: 'Well, I'm not sweating on it, sir.' How true it was.

Fred Drain – who had been on the raid with his brother, Pat, who
could swim – remembered being left with just a torch to signal
for the submarine that never came. The non-swimmers – and the
Guernseymen who had waited in vain to help them in their raid
on the island – were all eventually taken prisoner by the
Germans. Meanwhile, the rest of the group swam out to the crash
boats. In his autobiography, John Durnford-Slater recalled:

> Some of the men, with more wisdom than modesty,
> preferred to swim naked. I had the added handicap of senti-
> ment. In my right hand I carried a silver cigarette case which
> my wife had given me; in my left a spirit flask which had
> been my father's. It took, I suppose, seven or eight minutes
> to swim out, but it seemed hours and I was exhausted. As a
> sailor bent down from the launch to drag me aboard, the
> final effort of helping him, to my great annoyance, made me
> let go of the flask and the case.

It looked for a while as if they were going to have to make a
very seasick journey in these small launches, one of which had
broken down and was being taken in tow. Daylight was not far
off, and there was the ever-present danger of the *Luftwaffe*,
which had bases nearby. The commandos were late for their
rendezvous with the destroyer, and they were worried she
would have turned round and be heading for home. Luckily
for them, however, the captain had decided to do one last
sweep before giving up on them. John Smale recalled:

> Fortunately, somebody had a torch – I think it was Durnford-
> Slater – and he flashed this torch and they managed to spot
> it. We were in wet battledress, and we were given what they
> call slops, which was, I think, the naval word for clothing that
> they kept for survivors from shipwrecks and that sort of

thing. So we had to change into these football jerseys, odd things like that.

John Durnford-Slater, who had abandoned his battledress on the beach, gratefully accepted the captain's offer of a loan of his tunic to cover his bare top. It was only as they approached Dartmouth that the captain casually mentioned that he had been suffering from scabies (a contagious skin disease causing itching, which was a common problem among the commandos). Durnford-Slater took a hasty hot bath.

Meanwhile, his own tunic, which had his name sewn into the collar, was picked up next morning by the Germans on the beach. Several Durnfords living on the Channel Islands found themselves harassed by the Gestapo, under suspicion of harbouring the fugitive Commando.

John Smale recalled:

> We got off on leave very soon. I must say that was one of the things Durnford-Slater was very, very good about. He took the attitude that if there was nothing going on you might just as well be on leave, and by that time with any luck he would have got something else which you'd be training for.
>
> I was home within a day or so, and I remember my mother saying to me: 'Where have you been? What have you been up to?' So I said: 'Oh, I was in Guernsey last night.' The horror on her face!

Churchill was furious when he received the report on Operation Ambassador. He wrote: 'Let there be no more silly fiascos like those perpetrated at Guernsey.' As a result, Admiral Sir Roger Keyes – a veteran of the First World War – was appointed the first Director of Combined Operations. Tough Commando training was instigated, and the force was reorganized.

John Smale felt that some important lessons had been learned at Guernsey, especially about the need for proper communication.

It's been thought that it was an Army failure. Well, it wasn't an Army failure; it was the fault of the Navy, who couldn't get there, and of the planners, who changed their plan at the last minute and who left these people there with no contact, and who were liable to be shot as spies. It was a terrible state of affairs, really.

Operation Ambassador was by no means the last planning disaster. However, communication was to improve as wireless technology developed, and the Army and Navy became more used to working together. Without both these things, Combined Operations could be little more than a grand-sounding title.

For the commandos, the main lesson of Operation Ambassador was a simple one: they still had a lot to learn. As John Durnford-Slater put it in *Commando*:

Looking back, I can see that under such rushed conditions, with no experience, no proper landing craft and inadequate training, this first operation was foredoomed to failure. Later, the very word 'Commando' was to become synony-mous with perfectly trained, tough, hard-fighting and skilled specialists. You don't achieve that overnight.

THUGS WITH
CAULIFLOWER EARS

Most of those who volunteered for the Commandos were in their late teens or early twenties. They were young, fit and keen to have a go at the enemy. Some had been rugby players and boxers; some were ex-convicts. However, the stereotypical picture of the typical commando as a hulking great thug with cauliflower ears is rather wide of the mark. Apart from the fact that there was no such thing as a 'typical' commando, some of the most successful commandos were rather small.

The commandos were a collection of individuals – sometimes distinctly eccentric individuals – and they were given much more freedom than they would have enjoyed in other parts of the Army. Bill 'Tiger' Watson recalled one particularly colourful character known as Hoppy:

> He was a lovely man – he's unfortunately gone the way we all go eventually – but he was a small officer. He looked a bit like one of the Marx brothers – the one with a big moustache. He would read poetry on a night march, much to the anger and ire of the person marching in front, because he would walk into the back of their heels and he'd say, 'Oh, I'm terribly sorry', you know.

He remembered one occasion when Hoppy turned up late for a training session:

> The colonel said: 'There's one thing I absolutely insist upon, gentlemen, and that is punctuality.' At that moment the door opened and in came Hoppy, peering through his thick spectacles. The colonel said: 'You – you're late.' Hoppy looked at his watch and said: 'Oh, am I, sir? I thought I was just on time.' The colonel said: 'Just sit down, Mr Hopwood.' You know, he was vague in that way – but not when it came to action, oh, no.
>
> He made a good commando because he'd got a lot of imagination. He could be decisive when he wanted to be. He was the sort of person who, if nothing was going on, would switch off and do his own thing. I think his vagueness was simply because he was interested in something else, not because he wasn't with it. We had everything from people who became high-powered businessmen to people who were schoolmasters.

One thing they all had in common was enthusiasm. As Bob Hoyle put it:

> We'd come together from all sorts of regiments – Scottish, English, Irish, Welsh. We'd come from all corners to be part of it. We were all reckless. I suppose you would say, in the modern idiom, we were all up for it.

In his autobiography *Commando*, John Durnford-Slater explained his selection process:

> I always avoided anyone who talked too much, and soon learned a lesson in this when a fine athletic-looking fellow who had taken part in many sports proved to be useless and boastful and had to be discharged. We never enlisted anybody who looked like the tough-guy criminal type, as I considered that this sort of man would be a coward in battle.

Durnford-Slater himself was a quiet man, as John Smale recalled:

> He had a very strange way of talking, which people would mimic, but he had a great personality, which reflected on the soldiers, and he was very well respected. Now and again, when we were training, he'd get the whole Commando together and just talk to us and give us his ideas. That went down very well. I remember one big meeting that was held in one of the Largs hotels. I can't remember whether it was just a social affair or whether there'd been a formal meeting before it, but at the end of it we sat there with our glasses of beer and had a singsong. From regular army ways of going on it seems most extraordinary, but it was very good for morale. We went away singing one of the popular songs of the time – 'She'll Be Wearing Pink Pyjamas When She Comes', I think it was.
>
> One of the things that impressed me very much was when he died, which was about thirty years ago now. I went to his funeral. One of the wreaths was from a couple of soldiers who'd served with him, and it just said: 'To Colonel Durnford-Slater, the man who made Number 3 what it was, from Len and Ginger, Number 5 Troop.' I thought, 'Well, that says everything, really.'

Following the Guernsey fiasco, the commandos did joint training exercises with the Navy so they could get used to working with them. John Smale recalled:

> My particular troop was attached to the Polish Navy in Dartmouth, and it was always said with the Poles that they would go out in any weather at all. I've got some pictures of six or seven rather sickly-looking commandos sitting on the deck of a Polish ship in the middle of the Channel on a very rough night, and not being at all happy.

John Durnford-Slater himself suffered from seasickness. The remedy, according to one hardened sailor, was a couple of bottles of beer with some cheese and pickled onions, the dose to be taken at eleven every morning at sea. According to Durnford-Slater, the 'cure' worked.

On land, the training was like that for infantry – but infinitely tougher.

When we were with an infantry battalion, the training was dictated by certain training manuals: *Infantry Training Volume One* and *Infantry Training Volume Two*. Looking back on it, it was very restricted. When we got to the Commandos, it was a completely new world. We learned cliff climbing, we learned crossing wire obstacles, we learned street-fighting.

We also did schemes in the Highlands, both by day and by night. We had to be very careful because you could very easily come on a sudden drop or gully. In one case the leading man didn't realize the gully was there, and he just disappeared. Luckily, there was some sort of tree halfway down which he managed to hang on to; otherwise he would have gone on falling. Also, it so happened that we had a man from the Argentine with us, who brought his lasso with him. That came in handy for pulling the chap back. Of course, he took his lasso out because he hoped to lasso a deer, but I don't think he managed to.

The commandos trained fiercely, often for raids that were aborted at the last moment. Eric de la Torre recalled:

You had to prove yourself, and the only way you could do it until you went into action was being able to think that you could march further than ordinary infantry. You were put on long night marches, which might be anything – twenty or thirty miles – carrying all your equipment, and often in very bad conditions. You could be marching through rain most of the night. Once you'd completed, of course, you thought that maybe you were a cut above the others.

The South Africans had just created a world record for the longest march – and the commandos decided it was up to them to beat it. They covered sixty-five miles in twenty-four hours, as John Roderick recalled:

> We would have done better if the intelligence officer we had didn't make our last stop in a brickworks that was still functioning. The warmth of the brickworks... believe me, when you've got a whole crowd of chaps who'd flogged across the country, we couldn't rouse them towards the end of their resting stint.

Tiger Watson explained:

> Physically, they tested you to convince you that you could do a lot more than you believed you could do. In other words, when you were exhausted after being forcibly sent up mountains and then running down them, the day after you did that they would say: 'We'll do it all over again.' And they would then watch to see what your reaction was.

Buster Woodiwiss recalled one particular parade – designed to test how far they would go under orders – on Boxing Day:

> Most of the commandos were pie-eyed the night before, and they were marched up the road, down to the beach, into the sea and up to their necks before anybody called 'about turn'.

He also remembered another cruel trick played on novice commandos while training in the Scottish Highlands:

> Each day, the officer of the day went halfway up a mountain with a packet of raffle tickets of a certain colour. Every

recruit, if they wanted any breakfast, had to go up the mountain and get his coupon and come down the mountain and get his breakfast. Nobody missed breakfast.

Burt Shipton recalled:

> We were pulling garden rollers along first thing in the morning. They're pretty heavy. We had about six of these things, and we had to pull them for about 3- or 400 yards as fast as we could, and then once we had worked up a sweat they would form us up and we'd go for a swim off the jetty.

Herbert 'Algy' Forrester – in peacetime the *Daily Express*'s circulation manager in Cornwall – devised training exercises in scrambling up and abseiling down cliffs. Surprise was a key element in any Commando raid. Beaches were inevitably mined against attack, but not apparently inaccessible rock faces. The men had to be able to tackle these in full kit, complete with heavy packs and guns.

In the early days, the weapons shortage meant that arms were drawn from a central store only when needed for operations. However, as supplies improved, the commandos were allowed to keep their weapons and even take them home. Tiger Watson recalled:

> When I went home on leave with a Thompson sub-machine gun it caused a tremendous stir – it raised the morale of the local populace. I mean, here was a chap with an automatic weapon of his own – not a member of a machine-gun team, but a chap who actually had his own automatic weapon. It was extraordinary, the reaction.
>
> The reason why we were carrying them home on leave was because the German invasion was expected at the time. Churchill wanted to show that we still had some fight, and I think it did – it was quite a shrewd move. It was making

people feel, 'Well, by gosh, these chaps are going to go over the Channel there and really give them stick.'

The commandos lived in billets, not barracks; several met their future wives in this way. Des Chappell remembered his experiences in Dartmouth:

> We were given six shillings and eightpence a day additional pay, which was supposed to pay for our board and lodging. We normally found that people were only too willing to take us in, and the six and eight a day went in our pockets.
>
> I think in advance of our arriving there, they said: 'Oh, the commandos are coming. We'll have to be very careful with them – they're a tough crowd.' But we weren't a tough crowd at all, and once we got there and got settled down and they knew us, I think they were very sorry to see the back of us rather than the other way round.
>
> I met my wife in Dartmouth. I found myself a billet at 1 Old Castle Steps – that's on the end of Bayard's Cove, which is one of the older parts of Dartmouth. When I went in through the door, there was a girl down on her hands and knees scrubbing the floor. I don't know – we must have had eye contact – but she was mine from then on. That was obviously the woman for me. She must have felt the same way, because the next night she asked me to take her to Stoke Fleming, which is near Dartmouth, to gather some stuff off a friend of hers. We went out together, and from that minute on we were never apart. That was 11 November 1940, and we were married in March 1941.
>
> We were together for fifty-three years, so we must have done something right.

Des Chappell's wife, Frances, regularly used to strip his Bren gun and put it back together for him when he came back from night exercises. As he put it: 'My wife was part of the Commando, the same as the other boys' wives were. They all knew one another, and they were part of the force – it kept the unit together.'

The idea of placing the commandos in billets was to treat them as individuals, not numbers on a regimental roll, in the hope of encouraging initiative. However, John Smale recalled:

I think the War Office policy actually overdid it. They advised there should be no formal parades, men should keep their weapons with them and be responsible for keeping them clean and in working order. Now, this sounded all right, but it didn't work out. We found after a bit that weapons were not being cleaned. On one occasion there was a small street battle because people had got their rifles with them in their billets – that was in Plymouth. We found this independence business was overdone, so we had to withdraw the rifles and put them in troop armouries and have an arms storeman in the usual way.

After a while, because there were no parades, the older soldiers came up to us off duty, and said: 'Wouldn't it be a good idea if we could have a parade every now and again?' They missed that side of soldiering. So after a bit we had our normal formal parades in the morning, and the men's turnout was inspected in the usual way. I think everybody appreciated it, really.

Even so, the parades were hardly the same as in the regular Army:

When you saw them on parade you got a bit of a surprise, because in the early days we didn't have the green beret, and we wore our own headdress. With a few Scotsmen thrown in with their tam-o'-shanters, we really were a pretty mixed bunch.

Eric de la Torre, who came from Streatham and was originally in the Royal Army Ordnance Corps, recalled:

There wasn't so much 'them' and 'us' as there was in some of the other regiments. The officers were very free and easy with you and they didn't stand on ceremony. You paraded, but you didn't have to spend ages polishing your buttons and blacking your boots. It was a different atmosphere.

They moved, often at short notice, all across the country and were left to find their own billets. Eric de la Torre recalled arriving at the Isle of Arran on a Commando landing ship and being sent ashore to chat up potential landladies:

We were last off, and by then all the cottages along the seafront had been taken. There were some very nice houses uphill, and then we came to this bungalow. There were three of us, and we rang the bell. A very imposing lady came to the door and she said: 'What do you want?' So we said: 'We're off that ship in the bay, and we've been asked to look for billets.' 'Oh,' she said, 'I couldn't possibly take you. I've only got my old mother here and the servants have gone back to the mainland.' So we said, 'Oh, that's quite all right', and we turned and started to walk down the path. Then she called us back and said: 'Well, supposing I did take you in. Would you help with the housework?' We looked at one another. We said: 'Yes, all right.' So she took us in.

She was a very wealthy woman. Dundee was where her main home was, and her family were manufacturers of jute. Of course, in the First World War, so much jute was used in making sandbags. She used to have her food sent up from Fortnum & Mason – we ended up with a better billet than the officers had.

The other thing she said is: 'You must learn to play bridge. All my bridge partners have gone back to the mainland and I've got nobody to play bridge with.' We said: 'Well, we don't play bridge.' She said: 'I'll teach you to play – I'll show you.' Of course, the trouble was that after a hard day's training she'd get the cards out and it might be midnight or one o'clock in the morning before we got to bed. But we got up and we got the coal in and we swept the carpets and all that. It was a very interesting time.

Although there were group training exercises, many officers worked out their own ideas of what would be suitable for their particular troop. Michael Burn, who had worked as a foreign correspondent on *The Times* before the war, explained:

We went on really quite dangerous or difficult journeys without compasses, without maps, at night, without torches, not allowed to ask the civilian population where we were. People did get lost and turned up two days later from somewhere or other, that kind of thing. Of course, all that was great fun, really. It was partly a holiday, and this happened at a time when ordinary people in cities were being bombed and in much greater danger than us. We were having a good time on the whole, and also we were all in digs. But one moment I wrote to my mother that I thought that I should get out a printed card to send round to all the forty men in my troop, saying: 'Captain Burn at home, nine o'clock until five o'clock. Please bring your rifles.' That was more or less the situation. People did actually come on parade late, and their excuse was that their landlady had failed to call them.

We were left very much to ourselves, the troop commanders – anyhow in my Commando – to invent the kind of training we thought might help. Of course, there were the regular things: firing on the range, a certain amount of drill, schemes together with the whole Commando, but we could improvise.

I sent them all out one day as spies on missions to find out things that should have been secret, and they found them out. One of them – this was in the West Country – I sent out to find out the results of a German raid on a railway line along the coast of Devon. He dressed up as a Home Office inspector, he found out all kinds of details which the station office should never have told him, and all that was duly reported back to the War Office, and resulted in a rocket sent down to the stationmasters along the line. There was a one-day strike, as they said this was not the way that the Army should behave. But this was the way the Nazis were behaving, and very much appealed, I should imagine, to Churchill – it was the kind of thing he rather enjoyed.

Also, I sent another soldier out to find the state of public opinion. This was in Scotland, and he was a working-class Scot from Paisley. He was about twenty-one, and he, of course, had a few pints in pubs and he found out such a state of morale in that particular part of the country one felt that Churchill couldn't stay in power a moment longer.

If Michael Burn's version of training was political, John Roderick's was practical. He recalled:

When we were down in Weymouth, I did take my troops to the railway, and we learned how to destroy the best parts of an engine. I took them to the town's abattoir to see cattle and sheep and things being killed off. I thought it would be instructive for the chaps to see blood being spilled.

Corran Purdon, who had originally served with the Royal Ulster Rifles, felt this type of training was unnecessary. As he put it: 'We joined because we wanted to get stuck in to the Germans, so I don't think we needed any aggression training.'

Some people found the move to the Commandos brought quite a culture shock. Eric de la Torre, who was twenty-two when he volunteered for Commando service, recalled his initiation:

I was born at the end of the First World War, and I was always excited as a schoolboy about the great battles of the First World War. I had an uncle who'd been on the Western Front, and another one who was blown up counter-mining, so this is where I got my ideas from. Of course, at that age you think this is very exciting and you don't realize the enormous danger. So when I was called up I was hoping to get into an infantry regiment, and that's why I transferred to Commandos when they called for them.

We knew we would be assault troops, and we were told that we would be raiding parties, so that sounded really exciting. When I was sent to Number 3 Commando, I got in the orderly room and the sergeant major said: 'Name?' I gave him my name, and he turned to the corporal and said: 'Here's another bloody fool whose body will be washed up on the French coast.' So that was my introduction to the Commandos.

Tiger Watson, who had been serving with the Black Watch, recalled his interview with Colonel Charles Newman of Number 2 Commando:

I walked into the office where Colonel Charles was sitting, wreathed in tobacco smoke behind his desk, and I brought myself up to a magnificent salute, complete in my kilt and Sam Browne belt and everything: 'Mr Watson reporting for duty, sir.' He rather winced, and said: 'OK, sit down, please.' So I sat on the edge of my chair to attention, and he said, 'What's your name?', and I said, 'Watson, sir.' He said: 'No, no – what's your first name?' I said: 'Bill, sir.' 'Oh dear,' he said, 'we've got two Bills already. I can't call you that.'

He could see I wasn't going to relax, you know; it was very much the colonel and the young subaltern. So he said: 'Well, come on, let's go out to the pub.' He filled me up with beer and got me talking about myself. He was sizing me up, really. He was a shrewd operator, the colonel. His job in civil life had been to be the troubleshooter for a big building firm, going down when they were going to strike, so he was a great negotiator. So he let me talk and then he suddenly said: 'I've got it. You've got a grin just like Tiger

Tim [a character in a children's comic called *Tiger Tim's Weekly*].' He said: 'I'm going to call you Tiger – and see you live up to it.' So that's the origin of the name.

Buster Woodiwiss, whose father had lost four brothers in the First World War, remembered the efforts he made to get to where the action was:

> At first I was in a reserved occupation because I was making bricks, and they were considered quite important. So I organized a strike of the press operators in the brickmaking factory and was immediately discharged.
>
> I joined the Queen's Royal Regiment and found myself picking cherries, which I didn't think was much good really, so when they asked for volunteers for special service I immediately volunteered because my one ambition was to fight the Germans and get home.
>
> We weren't chosen; we volunteered. Every single person could leave the Commandos by just saying, 'I want to be returned to my unit' – and the only punishment for a commando was to be returned to unit.

Some found that life in the Commandos was not for them. Their face did not fit, or they simply did not have the physical stamina. In this case, there was no disgrace in leaving. However, for the dedicated commando, RTU (Returned to Unit) was the most dreaded sanction of all. As Buster put it:

> RTU made big men cry. We didn't serve the Commando for King and country and for the press – we were there because of our mates. We were David and Jonathan, we were brothers, we were volunteers – we were like Henry V's army at Agincourt. We were there because we wanted to be there. Not because we had to be there, or were told to be there – simply because we wanted to be there.

Buster and Dai Davies served together in the Commandos – and, more than sixty years on, are still best friends, despite the differences in their characters. As Buster put it: 'Dai would consider and make up his mind after logical thought, whereas I acted first and thought afterwards.'

Combined Operations 1940–42, a book published in 1943 by the Ministry of Information, included a somewhat idealized section on Commando comradeship under the heading 'Jack and John go out together'. The anonymous author described how:

> Jack always falls in beside John. If Jack is a Bren-gunner or an anti-tank rifleman, John is his number two and handles the magazines. When scouts are sent to front or flank, Jack and John go out together. Their teamwork is vital to the safety and success of the troop moving through enemy country. One of the assault courses over which recruits are sent when under training is called 'Me and My Pal'. It means just what it says. Its obstacles – and they are tough and numerous – have to be overcome together in anticipation of those which will be met and vanquished together on the field of battle. Friendship between two men engaged in the business of war is as old as war itself.

Such teamwork encouraged initiative and fostered a sense of equality. Buster Woodiwiss recalled:

> Officers carried exactly the same amount of equipment as anybody else. If they were muddy and their boots were dirty, they cleaned them. They had no servants – we had no servants. We were brothers. Nobody was ever put on a charge, because the ultimate punishment was to go back to your unit. If you didn't want to go back to your unit you did the most intelligent form of discipline, which was self-discipline. You were the discipline. You did what you thought was right when it was right – and if you found it was wrong, you listened to somebody else.

An idea central to the Commando ethos was that officers should lead from the front. To do this, they had to be at least as fit and tough as the men they led. Tiger Watson, who was not very tall, remembered the exhaustion of speed marches:

> Marching in step when you're a smaller man is much harder work than if you are six foot three. You were at a mechanical disadvantage, and one remembers being so miserably out of breath that one wondered whether one could carry on. I'm not now and never was an enthusiastic mountaineer – it's not my thing. The idea of running up a hill with full equipment on doesn't really appeal. But I had to set an example to the other chaps. If they thought, 'I wonder whether the little man can do it?', I had to do it.

Following the Guernsey fiasco, commandos were sent to a training school established on Lord Lovat's estate in the west Highlands of Scotland. Their base was Inverailort Castle, built on the shores of Loch Ailort. Here, they practised amphibious operations, supervised by a naval commander, and developed skills of stalking and shooting. Many of those whose activities appear later in this book passed through this training centre, including David Stirling, founder of the SAS.

Their instructors included Bill Stirling – David's older brother – and two ex-policemen, called Fairburn and Sykes, who taught unarmed combat. John Smale recalled:

> [It was] mostly very unpleasant, and the sort of things which you would never think of in ordinary life, such as poking your eyes out with a couple of fingers and kicking people in a very dangerous part of the body. It was all very ungentlemanly warfare, really.
>
> They'd served in Shanghai, where apparently there was a pretty mixed population, and the only thing I remember them saying they couldn't cope with was if your opponent should have a razor blade sewn into the peak of his cap. I

remember either Fairburn or Sykes saying: 'If you see a chap put his hand up to pull his cap off and swing it round like that to catch your face, there's only one thing to do, and that's to run.'

Fairburn and Sykes designed the FS fighting knife. It had a black blade, so it did not glint in the dark, and was designed for stabbing.

They taught us how to kill a sentry by creeping up behind him and putting an arm round his neck and jabbing the knife in. You just had to hope that he wasn't wearing a pack or a thick overcoat. They also recommended that you should have a second man handy who'd catch the man's rifle as soon as he fell down, so that it wouldn't fall down with a clatter.

But as far as this Commando knife was concerned, which got a lot of publicity, Durnford-Slater, our CO, would not allow them to be issued. He felt – and I think he was absolutely right – that if people had these knives, the next thing that would happen, there'd be a pub brawl and some-body would lose his life. The only time I ever saw a Commando knife in Number 3 Commando was being worn by the girlfriend of one of our officers. She was in some sort of women's organization which wore Sam Browne belts, and in her Sam Browne belt was a Commando knife which somehow she'd got hold of.

Members of Number 2 Commando were issued with the knives. Buster Woodiwiss remembered that they were most used for making toast. However, they were to discover that this was the weapon that the Germans most feared.

THE BAGPIPING MAJOR &
THE SARDINE FACTORY

'COMMANDO RAID AGAIN – IN YOUR CINEMA.' Excited headlines greeted the first film of a Commando raid, shown on cinema screens throughout Britain in 1942.

'Here is battle. The real thing – without crowd effects – straggling, scattered, stealthy,' wrote an anonymous *Daily Herald* reporter. 'Here is fighting on the beaches, in the streets, on the hills. You have to see it to know the meaning of a Commando raid.'

Newspapers seized on the story of 'Mad Jack' Churchill, the bagpiping major who led the boats in to the raid on the Norwegian island of Vaagso. 'THRILLING STORY'... 'COMMANDOS TREAT 'EM ROUGH'... 'BURNED-OUT HUNS SURRENDER'... 'ALGY THE DUDE BECAME KILLER'. The jingoistic headlines, the film and all the publicity that went with it ensured that whatever Churchill's raiders might do in the future, they would not do it unnoticed.

In fact, since the Guernsey fiasco, the Commandos had been having some success. There were the inevitable raids that were cancelled at the last minute, such as an attack on the island of Pantelleria, off the coast of Sicily. However, there were two assaults on the Lofoten Islands, 850 miles north of the Orkneys, during 1941. Commandos blew up enemy shipping and destroyed factories, including those that produced fish oil for use in explosives. They captured Germans and rooted out Norwegian quislings (named after the Nazi collaborator, Vidkun Quisling). They also brought back volunteers for the Norwegian forces. All this was done with only one British casualty – an officer who stuffed his revolver in his pocket and shot himself in the thigh.

John Smale, who took part in one of the Lofoten raids, in March 1941, recalled:

> One of our rather sillier officers went to the post office – a chap called Dick Wills. He wrote a telegram and got them to send it off to Germany: 'To Adolf Hitler from Second Lieutenant Wills. You said that no German territory would ever be invaded – well, we're here.'

He also recalled one dramatic piece of resistance encountered by British forces:

> There was one very small German vessel. This minute little ship with one gun on it opened up on the *King George V* [a fully armed British battleship, with fourteen-inch guns]. It was a very, very brave thing to do – and, of course, they had no option but to blow him out of the water. It was terrible to see.

However, in general, they encountered very little opposition. Bill Etches, who used his demolition training to blow up fish oil tanks, recalled a sense of disappointment that there had not been more action:

> There weren't many Germans there to surrender. Whether they were hiding or they were staying in bed, I don't know – but there wasn't a lot of enemy fire. I think by the British press it was regarded as a success. It was a bit of a flat effort by us. 'If that's all there is to Commando training, roll up the war' – you know. Nothing happened – no casualties, except people falling over on the ice.

John Smale recalled what was supposed to have been a morale-boosting visit from Admiral Keyes, who was in charge of Combined Operations:

> Keyes came and gave us a sort of pep talk, which I was very disappointed over. He struck me as very much the wrong man for the job, and of course from that point of view it was a jolly good job that Mountbatten eventually took over. I think they must have realized that he was unsuitable. He spent most of his time talking about the Zeebrugge raid that he did in the First World War. My reaction was, you know, silly old man.

The Lofoten raids were undoubtedly successful, particularly in the destruction of fish oil factories. These factories were vital to the German war economy. Glycerin obtained from fish oil is one of the basic ingredients of explosives – and fish oil is also a rich source of vitamins A and B. However, while the newspaper headlines were proclaiming Lofoten as a glorious success, the commandos themselves felt their hard-earned skills were not really being tested. Bill Etches recalled:

> Two or three of my friends in Number 3 Commando packed it in and went back to their units. They said it was pathetic. We were landing in force in a place where there was no opposition – so what were we doing? I felt much the same, but I was prepared to give it another go – and, sure enough, Vaagso came along about nine months later.

The commandos were to get all the action they wanted – and more – in the raid in December 1941, which made the headlines with which this chapter opened. Vaagso Island, midway between Bergen and Alesund on the west coast of Norway, was strategically important for the Germans. The fjords meant they could run convoys up and down the Norwegian coast almost without going out to sea – and Vaagso, at the entrance to the Nordfjord, was a convoy assembly point. Iron ore from Sweden and supplies for troops on the north Russian front passed through here.

The Commando targets included valuable oil installations at South Vaagso and a German garrison at Maaloy. They were also to sink any enemy ships they found, and – as with the Lofoten raids – bring back German prisoners and quislings.

This was a combined operation. Transport came courtesy of the Navy; the RAF provided fighters to fend off the *Luftwaffe* and bombers with smoke bombs to screen the landings. It had been planned for weeks, but bad weather caused a delay. Bill Etches, who was in charge of demolishing fish oil factories and harbour facilities in South Vaagso, recalled:

> We went from Scapa Flow to Shetland, then from Shetland to Vaagso. It was so rough in the Pentland Firth going to Shetland that we had to shelter there for twenty-four hours. The troops were all seasick. You could recover from that very quickly once you got ashore, but we didn't go ashore on Shetland at all for security reasons; we sheltered in some bay.

They travelled in converted Belgian and French cross-Channel steamers.

> We preferred them to landing craft, but they were top-heavy – they'd had their ordinary lifeboats taken away, and these steel landing craft put in the davits [shipboard cranes]. They were rolling like billyo and shipping a lot of water. I think they sustained a lot of damage in that crossing to Shetland.

In his autobiography, John Durnford-Slater noted that parts of the ship he travelled on were flooded to a depth of fourteen feet. He also noted that – despite their seasickness – some of the men were singing the Vera Lynn favourite, 'Yours', on the journey out.

They were left in no doubt about the dangers they were about to face, as Eric de la Torre, a wireless operator, recalled:

They gave you a big brown envelope each, and you had to put any valuables in it. You weren't allowed to take a camera ashore; you put your watch in it, if it was a good watch and you didn't want it stolen. The colonel was red hot on putting clean underwear on before a raid [to lessen the chance of infection if they were wounded]. Then he said: 'If you want to write a last letter home, put it in the envelope, seal it up, put your army number on and your name, and if anything happens to you, they'll know where to send your things.'

The cruiser HMS *Kenya* and a group of destroyers led the convoy up the fjord, and the troops landed at their various targets under cover of a bombardment. George Peel recalled:

It was complete darkness, and you could see little lights coming on on the mountainside, because they're early risers. It was the most beautiful sight. Then suddenly all hell was let loose. The *Kenya* opened up, and I thought, 'God – I thought this was supposed to be a secret bloody raid.' It was a hell of a din.

However, as he recalled, there was complete silence among the commandos as they got into the landing boats: 'Not a soul said a word. Each was obviously involved with his own particular thoughts.' Eric de la Torre recalled:

As we came up the fjord, we were looking through the port-holes. We could see one or two lights from cottages where the fishermen must have been just getting up, but that was the only sign of life that we saw until we came up on deck.

We got into our barge and we were lowered on to the water. The destroyers were going up and down. The *Kenya* was approaching Maaloy. Then at about eight o'clock the *Kenya* opened up with her six-inch guns. I think the bombardment went on for several minutes, and meantime we started to move towards the shore.

I had my wireless set on my back and a revolver in each trouser pocket. Up the front of the barge was Captain Johnny Giles with two Tommy guns and his wireless operator. He would be first off the barge, and he would run down the road and take the first house, which would be our headquarters there.

We were all crouched down on our heels, and I thought: 'Well – this is going to be the first time.' So we were chugging towards the shore, and the barges each had a little armoured turret with a slit in it. The sailor who was steering the barge, he was looking through the slit and he said: 'There's a lorry coming along the road. He's got a gun on the back. He's turning it on us – stand by.' Then a stream of tracer flew over the barge, but it must have been about five or six feet up, and it didn't look any more lethal than fireworks. Then it was flying through the air above us, and then all of a sudden we heard the sound of bagpipes floating across the water.

The colonel said: 'What bloody fool is playing those pipes?' And nobody answered. He knew who it was, and we all knew who it was. It was Mad Jack Churchill, the second-in-command, who was in a flight of barges approaching Maaloy. His batman told us after, he said Jack Churchill was standing up in front of the barge there, completely exposed, playing the pipes. As the barge touched down, he handed the pipes back to his batman, the batman handed him his claymore, and he rushed ashore waving his claymore. That's the sort of character he was.

The story of the bagpiping major was reported by the Reuters special correspondent who followed the raid, along with an Army film unit. Jack Churchill was exactly the kind of hero the newspapers loved – dashing (he had been a model for Brylcreem ads) and fearless. He had been known to fight with a bow and arrow, and had won an MC (Military Cross) in France.

Jack Churchill's group subdued the garrison on Maaloy relatively easily – but those who took part in the main landing at South Vaagso encountered stiff opposition. One of the bombers was hit by anti-aircraft fire, and a phosphorous smoke bomb dropped in a landing craft, destroying the craft and injuring most of the occupants. George Peel recalled:

> The screams of agony that came from the boat were unbelievable. The phosphorous was running all over their hands... the flesh was being burned right off their hands and faces. They were jumping out of the boat into the water to try and put it out, but it made no difference at all.

Eric de la Torre recalled:

> I saw a friend of mine rolling about in the snow with his battledress smouldering, but the colonel [Jack Durnford-Slater] shouted: 'Leave them! You know the orders. The medics will see to them.'
>
> All of a sudden two yellow-nosed ME-109s came over the top of the mountains. They came screaming down with all their cannon firing, and we found ourselves on the road up against the sheer wall. There was a hell of a racket, and then they got on to the tail of the Hampdens [bombers] which had laid the smoke screen. Once they were off us, we got to our feet and looked around. It was absolutely miraculous – nobody had been hit, nobody, with all the cannon shells bursting off the rocks and the road.
>
> We started to run down towards the town and heard a burst of automatic fire followed by two more bursts. Then Johnny Giles's wireless operator came running back, white-faced, and he reported to the colonel: 'Captain Giles is dead, sir.' Johnny Giles was a giant of a man; he played rugby for Herefordshire, and he boxed heavyweight for the Commando. The thought that Johnny was dead was a real shock.

George Peel saw the shooting at first hand:

There were Germans up in the trees, firing like mad – you could see the bullets dropping in the snow. Our CO, Captain Giles, stood up and said, 'Come on, Number 3', and then – bang – straight between the eyes. He dropped down just like that. We thought, 'My God, that's a fine start.'

Fortunately, his young brother was there, so he said: 'Come on, Number 3, down that road.' So we tore off. The snow was so slippery everyone was slipping and sliding – a lot of blokes got knocked off. But we kept on going, got to this house, jumped over this four-foot fence, straight into the back door – crashed in. There were about six of us, and the trouble was they were wooden houses, and the bullets were coming through one side and out the other. So we dived underneath the table and tried to calm ourselves down.

Bill Etches, who was in charge of a demolition party, recalled his landing:

It was quite a steep, rocky beach, covered in snow and ice, so it was very slippery. Getting ashore wasn't particularly easy anyway, because we were heavily laden. We shouldn't have had the smoke on the beach [from the phosphorous bombs]; it should have been a bit inland. Phosphorous smoke is not ordinary smoke; it's a very sick-making smell. People with a propensity for being sick were sick.

For many commandos – Bill Etches among them – this was their first taste of real action:

I'd been on a lot of field firing exercises – I knew exactly what it felt like to have bullets whistling around your head, but I hadn't ever experienced chaps actually shooting at me before. I woke up very quickly as I was hit in the elbow. It was like being stung by a bee, but I realized it was a bullet.

Some people were overawed by the opposition; some people were exhilarated, and some people – particularly the

ones who'd been in the landing craft which had been hit –
were in a pretty bad way.

He particularly recalled the reaction of one of the younger
members of his group:

> Four or five of us were carrying explosives ashore, and I left
> one chap to look after the trolley on the main road.
> Somebody else had blown up a factory or something, and the
> air was filled with debris. I shouted at him to clear the debris
> off the explosive, because I didn't know if some of it was
> burning, and he panicked and ran away.

John Durnford-Slater – himself in the thick of battle – took
note of incidents such as this. Any commando who did not
meet his exacting requirements would find himself returned to
his unit after Vaagso.

Battle headquarters was set up at a house near the landing
point, as Eric de la Torre recalled:

> We went into the house and it had obviously just been left,
> because the stove was still warm. We went upstairs and
> tried a bedroom door, which was locked. We thought of
> putting a bullet in there, but then we thought: 'Well, it's very
> unlikely there's Germans in there, and there might be the
> woman of the house, there might be children.' So we
> decided to do nothing. We came downstairs, and then we set
> to work reading messages from the ships and trying to get
> through to our forward troops. You could hear all the firing
> going on and explosions of grenades.

Tom Sherman still has a copy of the handwritten orders for his
landing group, under Captain Dick Hooper:

A   To capture enemy troops and equipment
B   To destroy industrial plant

C   To seize documents, codes and instruments
D   To arrest quislings
E   To withdraw volunteers.

Following these are notes on how these deceptively simple orders were to be carried out:

Watches synchronized. Constant vigilance against surprise and sniping. Maximum energy. Speed and dash... Demolitions only under supervision of an officer. Antifreeze mixture to weapons. Gloves. Water bottle slung. Grenades NOT primed. Completion of each task reported immediately. Careful conservation of ammo.

The final, even more deceptively simple instruction was written in capital letters: 'GET BACK.' Included with the orders was a list of forty-five Norwegian names – all suspected quislings, who were to be captured and taken back to Britain. Their occupations ranged from fish meal labourer to engineer, and their ages from seventeen to seventy-five. At the head of the list was Johann Gotteberg, the forty-year-old owner of a canning factory, which had been supplying food for Nazi troops on the Russian front.

A report in the *Daily Express* gave an eyewitness account of the demolition of a canning factory, although it does not specify whether this was the one owned by Johann Gotteberg. It described how the force of the explosion blew 'an enormous shower of sardine tin labels that went high in the air and then fluttered down among us like a pamphlet raid'.

The commandos had trained hard for the raid, and the opposition they encountered tested that training to the limit. As Tom Sherman recalled:

The initial intelligence was that these were second-class-grade troops, occupation troops rather than fighting troops, but in actual fact our intelligence was wrong. They were a crack unit; they'd been sent to Norway for a bit of a rest.

The concept was that we would go in on Boxing Day morning, when they were all nursing their Christmas hangovers and find them all in bed. But because we had to delay for twenty-four hours, they had recovered from their hangovers and they were all on parade, fully armed, going for a speed march to shake off their Christmas hangovers. All they had to do when we landed and the bombardment started was disperse among the buildings.

Street-fighting techniques, practised among bombed buildings in Plymouth, now came into their own as the commandos dashed from house to house in search of Germans. Reuters' correspondent Ralph Wallings reported in an eyewitness account:

Many Germans were roasted to death in homes they made strong points and from which they doggedly refused to emerge even when grenades or a fusillade of shots had set the rooms about them on fire.

In the house where they had taken refuge under the table, George Peel and his group of commandos had a sudden, unexpected reminder that this was supposed to be the season of goodwill. He recalled:

It took us completely by surprise – we had actually forgotten it was Christmas. The whole place was decorated beautifully. There was a Christmas tree in the corner. On the table was a bowl of fruit, and the Christmas cake was on the side table. We had been so ill on board with seasickness that we were all terribly hungry. For that one moment the war had ceased.

Just as they were getting stuck in to the food, he noticed a little silver casket on a sideboard:

On the front of it was a cross. I opened it up and inside were little tiny tissues of paper. I suddenly realized, even though it was in Norwegian, that it was extracts from the New Testament. I thought to myself: 'I need God right now to look after me – perhaps if I put this in my pocket He will.'

Then there was a God almighty scream from outside. We looked out, and at the back of the house was a small door that led out to a veranda, and outside was a young soldier screaming his head off in pain. He had been hit with a machine gun. We grabbed hold of his epaulettes and pulled him inside and cut off his trousers. The whole of his leg was shattered. He screamed: 'Please don't leave me, please don't leave me.' We said: 'All right, don't panic, we won't leave you.' We nicked a runner from one of the tables, and we used it for a tourniquet and then we had to get him out of the house.

We thought that the only thing to do was to knock down one of the doors to use as a stretcher. So we got the door down, and we said: 'Right, what do we do now?' There was a window just on the other side of the house, and we thought we'd bang the door halfway through, get the chap on it, and somebody would have to go outside and grab the other end.

It was a dicey business, so we tossed a coin and unfortunately I lost. So I got out and stood by the window and grabbed the door and waited for the people inside to push it out. My spine was tingling, I can remember to this day. Standing with that door I was an open target, and I was terrified that some German lad would pop me off. God – talk about panic. But nothing happened. They pushed like mad inside, I took the door towards me, and then a couple of other lads dashed out and we got this thing and pushed it down the slope into the road and got it to where the medics were. I thought: 'This little box has saved me.'

George Peel kept the casket as a good-luck charm throughout the war, and he is convinced that it saved his life. However, he always felt guilty about taking it – and during filming for the *Commando* series he was able to meet Mia Strand, the granddaughter of its rightful owner. Mia was happy for him to keep it.

While all this fighting was going on, the Norwegians were hiding wherever they could, or simply fleeing. Mia, who was only three at the time of the raid, remembered crouching in terror in the basement with her mother. She recalled:

> The noise was horrifying. There was an ammunition depot down here that blew up. I remember the grown-up people were crying, and some were shouting in pain. Of course, a small child when the grown-ups are crying... something is very, very wrong.

They eventually escaped and went back with the commandos to Scotland, where they spent the rest of the war.

George Peel recalled the sheer intensity of fire they encountered as they moved up the main street:

> They suddenly decided to hit us with mortar bombs, and it got a bit rough. At the same time as everything was mortar-bombed, they had a German howitzer on the other side of the fjord, bashing us with cannons. So we sent a radio message back to the ship, the *Kenya*, and said: 'For God's sake, can you do anything about this damned thing the other side of the fjord?' Well, in a matter of two minutes, tearing up the fjord came this destroyer – a beautiful sight. He came up and gave them one broadside and blew this flippin' gun right out of the cliff, turned very swiftly, and got the hell out of it. Oh, God, we cheered – thank God for the Navy.
>
> Of course, we were still being showered with these mortar bombs. That got a bit dicey then, because there is a technique of house-to-house hunting, and we lost quite a few of us in the process. The object of the exercise is to move forward and observe, see if the coast is clear, and wave the next man on. He goes forward, observes, waves you on, and you continue like this until you come against trouble. When suddenly you hit trouble – bang, bang, bang – you hope you're quicker than the other bloke is. This went on for some

considerable time as we got nearer and nearer to where the real schmozzle was going on.

The Germans were hiding all over the place – they were everywhere. Nobody knew what the hell was going on. All you were doing was killing, killing, killing as fast as you could, surviving as well as you could, running as well as you could. Your mind was in a turmoil and then eventually you think, 'Oh, God, I'm not going to survive this', but you do.

Then the order was given to retreat, and so we started retreating back along the road. I was doing the same house-to-house business, and I stood in this porchway. The door began to open, and I thought: 'It can't be a Norwegian – he wouldn't be that stupid. It's got to be a German.' So I put my boot up, kicked the door like mad, I brought my knife up and went straight into his middle. I let go and left it there and saw him collapse.

We had so much practice with fighting knives, yet having shoved it in I couldn't pull it out. It appalled me, what I had done. I didn't want anything to do with that knife any more. If I'd got it out I wouldn't have wanted it.

One commando, Denis O'Flaherty, showed conspicuous bravery in a series of assaults. He had originally been detailed to knock out a gun position – but, finding no trace of it, he and his group joined the fighting in Vaagso town. He shot one German whom he encountered in an alley by a fish factory, but had his nose broken by a grenade thrown by another. Shortly afterwards, his nose was hit again by a sniper's bullet. He finally fell after charging into a German-held warehouse. A bullet hit him in the eye, and came out through his throat. Despite this horrific wound, he staggered back on to his feet to try to alert the others to the hidden danger. In fact, he was eventually to recover – although he lost his eye. After two years in hospital and eight operations, he continued to serve as a commando.

The demolition parties had to operate with only revolvers to protect themselves, and in the ferocity of the fighting this made it difficult for them to reach all their targets. Bill Etches recalled:

> The far end of the town was never secured. The fighting was fairly intense the further into the town it got. Durnford-Slater sent for me to get up there and destroy a factory or something, but I hadn't got a fighting party with me. Six chaps pushing a trolley laden with high explosives were pretty bloody vulnerable.
>
> I destroyed all the targets I could find in the south end of the town, and in the centre. It's not a very big town: I suppose 6- or 800 yards from south to north. I went in about 5- or 600 yards, past the hotel where a tank was destroyed, and about 200 yards past the hotel was as far as I got. Then the opposition hadn't been suppressed, so I wasn't able to go much further. I then destroyed what I had missed: the harbour facilities behind me.

The drawbacks of the Commando ethos of leading from the front were demonstrated when the colonel, Jack Durnford-Slater, had a narrow escape after a grenade exploded in his path. He managed to take a dive for shelter around the edge of a building; his orderly, however, was badly wounded.

Two captains were killed in an attempt to capture the German headquarters at the Hotel Ulvesund. The Germans had barricaded themselves into a room. Algy Forrester had told his men to stand back while he threw a grenade. He was shot down by automatic fire and was killed after falling on his own grenade. Martin Linge, commanding officer of the Free Norwegians (who were fighting alongside the British), took control. He was struck down in his turn, his body falling across the hotel threshold. An actor in civilian life, Martin Linge became a Norwegian national hero. A sculpture of him now stands at the spot where he fell.

Each troop had its wireless operator – but the mountains surrounding Vaagso meant that the wireless sets failed to work.

The result of this was that the only way officers could find out what was happening was to go and see.

Frustrated by the communications difficulties, Eric de la Torre climbed up a hillside with his wireless to try to improve reception. He recalled:

> We were all netted in to one another. You'd spend ages calling Tango or Charlie or whatever it was, but you just couldn't get through. Finally, I said to Sergeant Simmonds, my sergeant: 'I'm going to go further up the mountain at the back of this house and see if I can get through up there.'
>
> I started to climb up, and something flew over my head. A split second later, I heard the crack of a rifle – there was a German up there. Fortunately, this place was littered with rocks, so I got behind this rock and lay there for a minute or so. Then I took my steel helmet off. It was a big rock, so I was well covered, although the aerial could be seen above the rock. I put my revolver inside the steel helmet and raised it up above the rock. Sure enough, another bullet flew over. I tried that once more and the same thing happened, so I knew quite definitely that up there was a sniper. He wasn't a good sniper, or else I wouldn't be here. In point of fact it was probably a silly thing to do, because if a bullet had hit the helmet, it could have ricocheted down on to me.
>
> I wriggled back down and reported to the sergeant. He said: 'I'll get one of the destroyers to plaster the hillside.' Unbeknown to us, further at the back of the town, the Germans did cause some casualties. They must have fled up the mountainside and got themselves behind rocks, and they were peppering our chaps.
>
> The sergeant said: 'There's nothing we can do. You'll just have to try every now and again to see if you can get through to a forward troop.' So we just contented ourselves with receiving messages from the ships, and then giving them to a runner who would take them through to the colonel. Vaagso was a washout as far as the radio was concerned.

The most important part of the job is to know what your forward troops are doing, and to be able to tell the colonel, because he wouldn't have needed to go forward to find out for himself. In the end that's what he did. He went into the town and got a grenade thrown at him. He was jolly brave, old Durnford-Slater.

When Durnford-Slater eventually made it back to headquarters, he had a task lined up for them – a chance to prove themselves under fire:

If he thought that somebody hadn't been in the fighting, then he would order them to attack a certain position. That's the only way you can find out what your men are going to be like under fire. He was always testing people, but he set a fine example himself, because he would always be up the front.

He came back to us, and we gave him any messages from the ships, and then he said to Harry Beasley, who was our sergeant major: 'Take Simmonds, Sutherland and de la Torre, collect a sack of grenades from the dump, and go and get those men out of that hotel [the Ulvesund, where Algy Forrester and Martin Linge were killed].

I thought: 'My God, this is going to be the end of us.' Old Harry looked at us and he said: 'OK.' We started to move down to the shore to get a sack of grenades each, and all of a sudden the recall rocket went up from the *Kenya*, because they'd got a message that the German bombers were on their way, and of course the Navy didn't want to get caught in a fjord. So the order came to retire, and the troops all started pouring back to the beach. That just saved Harry Beasley and the four of us.

Leaving much of Vaagso in flames, the commandos made their way back down the main street. Pieces of burning wood and lumps of debris were falling into the road – and they remained in constant danger from German snipers well entrenched in positions on the hillside. Tom Sherman recalled a narrow escape when a member of his troop tried to take a German helmet as a souvenir:

> On the withdrawal, we were covering each other, and a man called Fred Peachey, from Warrington – a very good shot – said to me: 'There's a body there, sarge. Can I go and get the helmet?' I said: 'Yes, but be careful. Watch out for snipers.' I shouted an order to cover Peachey and make sure that nobody fired at him. Fred went up and bent down to pick up the helmet, and as he got hold of the helmet the German turned round and looked up at him. Well, of course, there was a tremendous yell from Fred. We made him stand up and we had our prisoner. I think everybody had a souvenir off him – collar badges and things like that, which eventually we had to turn in.
>
> He was playing dead, you see, and thank God Peachey wanted the helmet, because we'd have left him there for dead, but anyway we brought him back.

John Durnford-Slater recalled an encounter with a dying German:

> I saw a handsome young German lying in the gutter, seriously wounded in the chest and obviously near death. He smiled at me. When he beckoned, I walked over and spoke to him. He could speak no English, but indicated that he wished to shake hands. We did. I think what he meant, and I agreed, was that it had been a good, clean battle.

Eric de la Torre explained:

> I think secretly the Commando admired the Germans for the resistance they put up. The hotel, I think, had been set on fire by mortars just before we left. I don't know what happened after that, but they were still in there, and nobody had been able to get them out. They made a real strong point of it.

The *Daily Express* reported what happened as the troops assembled at the rendezvous:

> The beach officer, a naval man dressed in battledress top and bell-bottomed trousers, ordered them to their craft by megaphone. Some of the troops mimicked him as they scrambled down the rocks. 'This way for the *Skylark*. Twice round the fjord for a tanner.' But they boarded quickly and in perfect order.

Many were still high on the adrenalin rush created by their first real raid. However, the journey back brought stark reminders of its human cost, as Eric de la Torre recalled:

> Sitting on my bunk was a young Norwegian girl with her daughter, a little girl of about nine or ten. They were both looking rather wide-eyed and didn't know what had happened. It may be that her husband was a member of the Free Norwegians; maybe she was going to join him. Anyway, I had a large bar of chocolate in my kitbag. I got that out and gave it to the little girl and that cheered her up – but just then a call came on the Tannoy. It said: 'Will everybody parade on deck for a burial at sea.' By now it was semi-dark, because darkness comes down quickly up there, and there were about five or six bodies lined up on the deck. A section of the railing had been taken away, and a chute had been put out. The captain said the words for the burial at sea, and then one by one they were put down the chute. I don't know who they were. I think two or three of them were German and I think a couple of ours. These were probably men who died on board of their wounds. I always remember that. We were standing around in the semi-darkness, and a lot of the chaps still had their bloodstained field dressings on. You know, listening to the prayers, and bodies going into the sea – it's something that sticks in your mind.

Altogether, seventeen commandos were killed and fifty-three wounded. Much of Vaagso was left in flames, and official reports claimed 15,650 tons of enemy shipping destroyed, together with munitions dumps, oil tanks, storehouses and a wireless station. Chief captives included the Nazi commanding officer of the Maaloy garrison (and those who survived the attack), the German naval captain of the port and nine suspected quislings.

Tom Sherman recalled:

> We were absolutely full of ourselves. This was probably the first time that we had structured press and film coverage of the operations. We had film cameras and correspondents. Almost within the week we saw ourselves on the newsreels, because there was no television. Of course, everybody else was envious of us, because we were the chosen few, and so we felt pretty good about it. I think we got a bit of leave afterwards – we were sent home to go and spread the word.

George Peel remembered having his photograph taken for the *Bristol Evening Post* and being recognized by complete strangers afterwards. As he put it: 'People were going, "Well done, well done – thank you very much", and I could feel myself going redder and redder.'

One lasting effect was to make Hitler nervous about the possibility of an Allied invasion of Norway. It forced him to build up garrisons there, diverting troops from the Russian front and elsewhere into defending Norway against an attack that never came.

In Britain, the Vaagso raid encouraged military planners to step up training for larger, bolder ventures. In February 1942 a new Commando training centre was opened at Achnacarry Castle. Its position in the Scottish Highlands made it ideal for the kind of toughening-up exercises that were to become routine. The stage was now set for the greatest raid of all.

PART TWO

The Silent Men of St-Nazaire

DEMOLITION!

Some aspects of Commando training had been a bit haphazard in the early days – particularly on the demolition side. This was amply demonstrated when John Durnford-Slater decided to show off Number 3 Commando's demolition skills to his land-lord, the Earl of Glasgow.

Durnford-Slater had been billeted at Kelburn Castle, just south of Largs. Standing near the castle was a Scots pine tree that was going rotten – and the earl asked Durnford-Slater whether some of his men would cut it down for him. Bill Etches recalled:

> He said: 'Oh, I can do better than that – I'll blow it down for you.' So he got some other chaps in the Commando who'd been trained in demolitions, and indeed a sapper sergeant, to blow this tree down.
>
> I went to see that they were doing it properly, and as far as I was concerned they were doing an excellent job. They'd cut a shelf on the other side of the tree from the castle, and they put the explosives on this shelf. I said, 'Perhaps you ought to open the windows of the castle', because I expected there'd be a fairly large bang with sixty or seventy pounds of explosive. It was a huge tree. So they opened the sash windows, and all the

maids had turned out on the lawn in front. They let the explosive off, there was a bloody great bang, and the tree came down and all the windows were out. All the glass showered over the maids and the servants who were settled on the front lawn. So John Durnford-Slater was not a very popular chap.

The problem was that the demolition officers had been unable to agree exactly how much explosive should be used. Since failure was unthinkable, an officer had slipped out during lunchtime to add a few extra sticks of gelignite. The final tally of smashed panes of glass came to 132 – no small matter in wartime. However, as commandos were expert scroungers, all were eventually replaced.

Desmond Chappell, who was in Number 1 Commando, recalled:

I was a demolitions expert, or supposed to be. I knew how to blow a house up, I knew how to blow railway lines up, telegraph poles down, and all sorts of other things. Had you put me among a group of Royal Engineers and asked me some formulas I wouldn't have known one from another, but I knew what to do with a packet of explosives.

For the next major raid after Vaagso – an attack on the dry dock at St-Nazaire, on the west coast of France – an expert knowledge of explosives was to be essential. For this, the commandos needed extra help. Bill Etches recalled:

We were trained by two sapper officers, Bob Montgomery and Bill Pritchard, who really knew their stuff. Some of the demolitions we'd been doing were distinctly ham and amateur really, even in Vaagso, compared with the demolitions that were necessary for St-Nazaire.

Bob Montgomery was just twenty-one at the time of the St-Nazaire raid. However, he was a Royal Engineer, and had always been interested in demolitions. He recalled how he and Bill Pritchard got involved:

Bill Pritchard was the son of the dockmaster of Cardiff. He knew how docks worked, and he went on holiday in the summer of 1941 down to Cardiff. The docks were raided, and they were only out of action for about twenty-four hours. He came back, and he said: 'You can't put a dock out of action by bombing.' That was, of course, in the days of conventional bombs – now, you can. But he said: 'We really ought to have some people trained in dock demolitions.' He was a man who could sell the proverbial refrigerators to Eskimos, and he went up to the transportation directorate of the Royal Engineers, and he sold this idea that we ought to be able to demolish our own docks if there was an invasion.

He had been in France – as I had – in 1940. I came out through Cherbourg; he came out through Dunkirk. He said: 'We didn't destroy the docks, and the Germans can use them now.' He sold this to transportation, and he was given the plans of a dock – actually, in fact, not of an English dock at all – and told to go away and think about it, and put up a plan for an assault demolition.

Bill and I worked for, I suppose, about a fortnight, three weeks. Every evening we'd go out to the pub and come back and sit down and thrash these things out. He put the thing up to transportation and they accepted it. We heard nothing more.

Meanwhile, plans were being laid for an assault on the dock at St-Nazaire, and the search was on for someone who would have the technical expertise for the job.

It [the idea] had been floating back and forth inside Combined Operations and the War Office and the Admiralty, and then obviously some file got into somebody else's hands, and it appeared that there were two chaps who knew something about dock demolitions. So we were pulled in to train the Commando demolition teams. They said there were two experts – well, we weren't really experts, because you can't be an expert until you've done something, I don't think, and we hadn't actually blown up a dock.

The dock at St-Nazaire was no ordinary dock. It lay six miles back from the open waters of the Bay of Biscay, at the mouth of the River Loire. The approaches were wide but shallow and full of dangerous mud banks. Anyone sailing up the estuary ran the risk of being caught like a rat in a trap. The area was ringed with guns and searchlights, because it contained U-boat submarine pens, as well as the normal dockyard facilities. Most important, it contained the commandos' main target – the largest dry dock in Europe.

This was the Normandie Dock, specially built for the construction of the massive French transatlantic liner, *Normandie*. It was capable of accommodating ships of 85,000 tons or more, and the Germans had made full use of it. The dreaded battleship *Bismarck* had been on her way there in May 1941 when she had been sunk in the Atlantic by British warships.

The German shipyards had just finished the *Tirpitz*, sister ship to the *Bismarck*. Merchant ships in the Atlantic were already suffering heavy losses from U-boat raids. If the *Tirpitz* got into the Atlantic, she could devastate ships bringing supplies to Britain.

St-Nazaire had the only dry dock on the Atlantic coastline capable of taking the *Tirpitz*; if the dock could be put out of action, Hitler would be unlikely to be willing to risk sending her out without a safe haven for repairs. However, it was a big 'if': destroying the dock would be a massive task.

Quite apart from the difficulties of reaching the target, there was the sheer size and weight of the structure. Each end of the dry dock had thirty-five-foot-thick sliding steel caissons, with internal compartments that could be filled with water. (A caisson is a lock gate that slides in and out rather than swings.)

These caissons needed powerful winding gear – and each one had its own winding hut.

To destroy these gates would demand enormous quantities of explosive – and so it was that the idea of an 'explosive ship' was born. The plan was that a ship, crammed with explosive on a delayed-action fuse, would ram the front caisson. Commandos and demolitions experts would scatter to lay explosives on the back caisson and winding huts, and generally create as much havoc as possible. Then they would beat a strategic retreat.

The military planners had one enormous advantage. As it happened, there were caissons of similar design and construction at the King George V Dock at Southampton. Rehearsals for the raid were carried out here, and at Cardiff Docks. Corran Purdon recalled:

> We trained on destroying every type of dock equipment you could think of: cranes, railway wagons, pumping stations, winding houses, caisson gates, lock gates. Anything that made a dock function, we were trained to destroy it. At that time, mind you, we had no idea we were going on a raid. Commandos were taught all sorts of things, like driving trains. I thought: 'Well, it's just another thing we're being taught, and when I go back no doubt I'll never do any demolitions at all.' How wrong I was.

Eric de la Torre recalled:

> We had a demolitions course within the Commando. You had written exams, you went up in the hills, and you used explosives. Explosives were quite readily available to us – I had plastic [explosives] in a shoebox under the bed. It's true that until you put a detonator in and a fuse it's all right, but there was no strict control on explosives like there was in the ordinary army. Today, it would be unthinkable for anybody to be able to take explosives back to their house.

We had a written exam at the end of this course, and I came out quite well in it. Some time later, the colonel called about seven or eight of us into his office and he said: 'Would you like to go on a demolition course? There's a chance of a bit of fun at the end of it.' That's the way he put it. All the Commando was split up into small teams. For the King George V Dock we were blindfolded, and then we had to feel our way down the stairs to these pumps and lay the charges, because they said that if you got to your target you may find there's no electric light and you've got to work in the darkness.

Then he timed each team and I suppose made a note of who was quickest, and they'd probably be allocated that particular job. Then we were put on a train to Cardiff and we went through all the same sort of thing again. Then we were told that the course was over, and we were going back to our units in Scotland. So we got on this train and were told that all the blinds had got to be drawn.

When they pulled up the blinds in the morning they found they were not in Scotland, but at Falmouth station. They marched off the train, straight on to waiting boats – and were told they were not to be allowed ashore again.

Corran Purdon remembered his excitement at being told that he was finally going to go on a raid after the frustration of numerous last-minute cancellations:

We used to get very cynical about it. I was determined I wasn't going to leave the commandos because I was sure we would get used, but a number of people left because they thought, Christ, we're never going to bloody well be used. We'd been sitting in landing craft in places like Dover harbour. We were going to raid Berck-sur-Mer, I remember, one night. We were all sitting there, and we were told to get out and go back. I remember feeling so deflated and hacked off, having to go back. It was a lovely summer's day, and I was driving through the English countryside – which was not nearly so built up as now – and thinking how lovely it all looked, but how much nicer it would have looked to me if I could have had Berck-sur-Mer under my belt, and a really good party ahead of me that night. We had a lot of cancellations – all Commandos did, not just mine.

Michael Burn, who had left the Commando for a job in London, rejoined when he heard there was the chance of some action. He recalled:

We were always going on raids that were cancelled, and for that reason I tried to get a job. I was for a week with General Gubbins in SOE [Special Operations Executive] – I'd moved from Scotland, from the Commando, to Gubbins's headquarters in Baker Street – and I was going along the Mall, and Charles Newman, my colonel, was walking along the Mall at the same time. I thought: 'That's rather odd. Why isn't he in Scotland?' And I stopped – I was in a taxi – and he said: 'You've got to come back. This is it.' And that's how I knew. I shouldn't have known, perhaps, but I went back. Gubbins, I think, was quite glad to get rid of me.

My own troop, I know from their letters and from what they told me, they were certain that my disappearance to London had meant that the raid had been organized. I knew absolutely nothing about it at all, but they knew that something was happening. It was also rather sad, because the Commando had to be split into two different groups: those who would stay behind, and those who obviously had been chosen for special purposes. It meant a breaking up of this kind of comradeship that we'd had, and it was a very short time of training. We knew very, very quickly that this was serious. We were always expecting that something might be cancelled at the last moment, but not this.

Of the people who were selected to go on the raid, they were divided into two groups: those who went to dockyards to practise street-fighting and blowing up installations connected with docks, and the other groups like mine who just went on training at Ayr, where we were stationed. But there was a clear distinction between the technicians, the people who would be responsible for blowing things up, and therefore would have to be probably very practical people, and people like myself who were less practical. I think it was right that I was not entrusted with blowing up a turbine, which I might have done by accident, but not by design.

Those selected for the raid were kept offshore at Falmouth, on a ship that had been a cross-Channel ferry: HMS *Princesse Joséphine Charlotte*. Only once safely aboard were they given a detailed briefing – and even then they were not told the exact location of their target. Michael Burn:

We were shown a diagram of a port, which we were told was a port in France which we were going to attack. Charles Newman [the colonel in charge] explained the operation, and he said to me: 'If you recognize it, please don't say what it is.' He knew I'd spent a lot of time in France. I didn't recognize it. One or two people did, especially some of the merchant seamen who'd been there. But all we were aware of was that it was something that was going to be very dangerous. We were not told the name until we were actually at sea on the way there.

We saw a model, a brilliant model. It was very, very clear. We were kept incommunicado on this ship; we weren't allowed ashore except with special leave. There were various intelligence dodges to explain our presence there so that any German agent would not have assumed that we were going to raid the French coast.

One member of the group who was given special permission to go ashore for supplies was Dr David Paton. He had qualified just the year before war broke out, and had been serving as the doctor to Number 2 Commando in Ayr. He recalled:

I was billeted on the minister of the parish of Ayr, a lovely old gentleman who was an MC from the First World War. I asked him how he got his MC and he said: 'Don't worry about that – they're all wrong.' I said: 'But you must have done something brilliant.' He said: 'No, no. The way it works is this. You send your regiment into battle and they all do splendidly, and they want to give them all a medal. After the battle, you get one medal. Now, who do you give it to? You give it to the padre, because all the other chaps will hate the chap who gets it.'

In the early days in Ayr, David Paton's services to the Commando had been relatively mundane:

They got a lot of skin trouble – they didn't get much in the way of other troubles. We went for a twenty-five-mile march one day, and I was disappointed in the officers because they didn't attend to their troops' feet. I examined every one of the soldiers' feet afterwards to look for blisters, and found them and did what I thought was appropriate. The officers went off to the pub with blisters on their own feet, which I thought was very silly – but that's the way commandos behaved. In fact, one of the commandos – I can't remember his name – had one of his blisters still there when he walked into Germany from St-Nazaire.

However, he was well aware that the commandos would need treatment for rather more than scabies and blisters on a real raid:

As a Commando, we had two huge hampers from the First World War. They contained all sorts of strange dressings and bandages: long bandages, short bandages, thick bandages, elastic bandages, thank God – I needed a lot of elastic bandages, because they provide pressure [to stop bleeding].

At that time, the idea of blood to a medical officer in the field just wasn't on. Even at the end of the war, with a field

ambulance with eight doctors, we couldn't do blood transfu-
sions. They needed all the blood for the bombed cities back
home anyway. I felt the thing to do was first aid only, and just
don't touch – keep your filthy hands out, and keep your filthy
breath out of the wounds. Leave the wounds open, because
inside the wounds are bits of uniform, bits of lead and bits of
apparatus, and all sorts of things, and don't touch that
wound until you get it to hospital.

The main problem was not necessarily the wound itself, but the
infection that set in afterwards.

David Paton was as much in the dark as everyone else about
exactly which French port was to be raided – but he knew that
any of them would be a very bumpy Channel-ride away from a
friendly hospital. He recalled:

Colonel Newman said to me: 'Is there anything special you
want?' Now, I'd just read in a medical magazine of the RAMC
[Royal Army Medical Corps] that these chaps in North Africa
were finding some success with these new things called
antibiotics. They poured this antibiotic powder into the
wounds and they were getting success, stopping inflamma-
tion and that sort of thing. I thought I'd better have some of
that. So I went ashore and I was told to go up to the naval
headquarters planning the raid where there was a red
phone. You picked up this red phone and you got the Cabinet
annexe [operational headquarters in London], would you
believe? A splendid chap on the other end said: 'Oh, you're
that Scots doctor, aren't you?' I said: 'Yes.' He said: 'What
is it you want?' I said: 'I want a pound of sulphonamide
powder.' He said: 'Can you spell it?' So I spelled it out for
him, and he said: 'It'll be on the next train.'

Having got this, I thought: 'How do I distribute this powder
among the troops on all these ships?' Then I had a brilliant
idea. I thought: 'I'll go and get sweetie bags from a confec-
tioner and put some in the sweetie bags.' Never mind about

the infection and all that – this was getting this magic powder. So I went into the sweet shop and said: 'I'd like to buy some of your sweetie bags.' She said: 'You can't have any sweeties, because you haven't got the coupons. I can sell you some bags, but I don't want any money for them. How many do you want?' I said: 'Fifty.' She said: 'Right. Here's fifty bags.' I got fifty bags, I filled up some of them and gave them to some of the chaps, but I don't think we ever poured any of it in [to wounds] – just as well, because people became allergic to the stuff.

Soldiers were also given individual supplies of morphine. This came in aseptic tubules, with a sharp needle at one end. The needle was tough enough so it could be injected through the uniform, if necessary, for emergency pain relief. However, once the needle was stuck in, it often proved impossible to get out without pricking your own finger.

Another practical problem came with Scottish commandos, who insisted on smuggling their kilts on board. (They were not officially allowed a change of uniform.) They were particularly attached to their kilts. They wanted to fight in them – and, if necessary, die in them. However, they provided nothing like the same level of protection as a regular uniform – and could be a serious liability. David Paton recalled:

They had trouble in the First World War with mustard gas. The kilties were the chaps who got the worst of it, because mustard gas attacks the moist areas of the body, and of course the kilts were dead exposed.

Tiger Watson, who had joined the Commando from the Black Watch, recalled:

The kilted troops in the First World War were called 'the ladies from hell' by the Germans. Donald Roy, who was a rabid Scot, one of the Liverpool Scottish and a troop commander, said: 'Why don't you wear your kilt, Tiger?'

I said: 'My kilt is a 1934 piper's kilt, which I'm very lucky to have got. I'm certainly not going to have it damaged in a battle.' He said, 'But all Scotsmen ought to wear kilts' – or words to that effect – to which I said: 'But I can't get all the things that I'm carrying – you know, fighting knife, automatic, grenades, all these things – into a kilt.'

Besides, a pre-war Highland kilt had an enormous amount more material in than a wartime one when cloth was short; therefore it would have been extremely heavy. If I'd got into the water I would have gone straight to the bottom before I could divest myself of it.

Understandably, having never swum in his kilt, he decided that now was not the time for experimenting.

While the commandos had been training and gathering supplies, there had been a certain amount of wrangling about what ships were to be used for this raid. The admirals were understandably reluctant to commit their best ships to such a high-risk operation. For the exploding ship, they eventually settled on HMS *Campbeltown*, a lend-lease American destroyer, formerly the USS *Buchanan*. This vessel, first launched in 1919, was to be disguised as a German ship and loaded with over four tons of explosive encased in concrete.

Lord Louis Mountbatten, who had now taken charge of Combined Operations, wanted the Navy to provide another destroyer to deliver and take off the men once they had completed their tasks. However, all the Navy could spare was a fleet of small motor launches. These were to be escorted by two destroyers – HMS *Atherstone* and HMS *Tynedale* – with a motor gunboat as headquarters for Charles Newman, in charge of the military force, and the naval commander, Bob Ryder.

From all accounts, Charles Newman – an ex-Territorial Army officer, and a civil engineer by trade – was a popular leader who never stood on rank. According to Michael Burn, Newman stamped his personality on the entire Commando. As he put it:

Colonel Newman was my ideal of a born leader, which included being not only very good at discipline, but a very free and easy manner and accepting everybody as he was, not demanding that they should conform to any pattern. He had such a light-hearted and affectionate manner, which was very well set off by his second-in-command, Bill Copeland, who was quite different, and knew what war was. Charles Newman was – I mean the word in the least derogatory way – a kind of slaphappy character, and he was fun. I preferred him to the kind of heroes I met later in Colditz.

David Paton recalled an incident during training exercises on the outer islands:

Colonel Newman said: 'But supposing I am hit. How would you get me back home, doc?' I said: 'Well, I'll get you back home, don't worry, provided I'm not hit.' And he said: 'No, show me how you'd get me home.' I said: 'All right. Stand up, sir. Now separate your legs a little.' And I threw him over my shoulder and lifted him up, and said: 'Now, where do you want to go, sir?' His pipe fell out, and a little denture fell out, and then Captain Roy [the kilted Scot] started to bump me like a schoolboy, and I said: 'You're not a schoolboy, for God's sake.' Then Colonel Newman – by this time he'd got his teeth back in – said: 'Look here, I needled the doc, and if I go to war this is the man I want beside me.'

Corran Purdon recalled:

He looked like a battered old elephant. He'd got cauliflower ears; he fought in the golden gloves. He was no pushover – he was a tough guy – but he was a wonderful leader. Everyone really loved him. We would have followed him everywhere, and I think we did.

As Tom Sherman put it:

He was a benign, super man – fit, friendly, disciplinarian, social. We'd have singsongs and even troop concerts on board the ship. He always played the piano, and his signature tune was 'When Day is Done'. He always had a friendly word, and was always smoking his pipe.

Bob 'Red' Ryder (the 'Red' was an acronym formed by his initials) had a considerable reputation to live up to. He had won a Polar Medal as commander of an Antarctic research yacht. He had also been in a boat that had been acting as bait for German submarines, with guns concealed beneath dummy deck cargo. The boat had been attacked and sunk 200 miles west of Ireland, and he had been left clinging to a piece of wood for four days without food or water.

Looking back at the St-Nazaire expedition – code-named Operation Chariot – Tom Sherman recalled:

The thing that always astonishes me in retrospect is how quickly we did things in those days. If you imagine that we'd come back from Vaagso at the beginning of January, and the raid was just three months [after that]. In that time, they'd commandeered the American destroyer, they'd altered the silhouette of it to make it look like a German destroyer, and they'd also built the steel shields so that the troops could lie down behind them as they went in. They'd mustered the flotilla of the motor launches, we'd done the rehearsal and they'd gathered all the demolition experts into their groups.

The men went on a trip to the Isles of Scilly so they could test the guns on deserted islands and get used to the motion of the motor launches. Most were very seasick. There was also a practice night attack on Devonport, which was not designed to inspire confidence. The idea was to test the port's defences – but, blinded and dazzled by searchlights, the motor launches landed their soldiers in the wrong places. Eric de la Torre recalled:

The MLs [motor launches] landed us, and we rushed ashore. I remember that the defending troops had coupled up fire-hoses to the hydrants, and the first thing to hit us was a jet of water – absolutely soaked us through. I think the general consensus was it was a bit of a shambles.

The exercise was called Operation Vivid, but as Tiger Watson put it: 'The only thing vivid about this muddle was the vulnerability of the illuminated motor launches and the language of the confused raiders.'

Corran Purdon recalled:

When the exercise was over we were all talking about it, and I remember people saying to me: 'Hope to God the Germans don't have searchlights like that, because we're not going to be able to see a bloody thing.'

Despite this, he never thought that this was an expedition from which he – or his friends – might not return. He had even made a date to meet his fiancée, Patricia (later his wife), at the Café Royal the following weekend.

Michael Burn recalled:

When we finally saw these little boats which we were to go in – most of us – we should have been appalled. But I don't remember being appalled: it didn't occur to me. Our whole training had been so very daredevil, it had been almost schoolboy – so when we saw these boats we thought: 'Oh, well, these are the boats we're going in and presumably it'll be all right.'

Mountbatten had issued orders that those with wives and families should be given the chance to back out if they wanted to, with no disgrace attached. No one did. As Corran Purdon put it:

We'd always been told this before every raid, you know: no one will think any less of you if you don't go. You knew bloody well if you said you weren't going – what a crow! You would have lost your name for ever. No one would have dreamed of backing out, but you were told: 'No one will think the worse of you.' I don't know who thought that expression up. Of course we would have thought the worst of them, certainly. We were volunteers. We'd joined to do these raids, not to back out of them when it seemed something was going to happen.

Eric de la Torre recalled:

You'd be a very brave man to say you're going to back out, so whatever anybody thought about the operation – and many of us thought this is sheer suicide – nobody dropped out.

I thought the suicidal bit was having to go about five or six miles up the Loire, especially for the little boats. I mean, the *Campbeltown* might make it, but I looked at our ML – it had just an Oerlikon [rapid-firing gun] fore and aft, and the boat was made of mahogany. I thought about all these coastal batteries they'd shown us on either bank of the Loire, and I thought: 'Well, if we get a shell hit us we're going to be finished.' So that looked pretty bad, let alone getting into the docks and actually reaching the target. I think the people on board the *Campbeltown* were happier, because they had steel plates bolted to the deck, and they were lying behind these steel plates, and she had a number of Oerlikons up on bandstands, and a six-pounder gun as well.

You know that on an exercise like that a lot of you aren't going to come back, but you don't talk about it, and you push it to the back of your mind. You've just got to concentrate hard on what you've got to do, and try to forget about what might happen to you. I did think: 'Well, if I do get a bullet, I hope it's a quick one.'

David Paton, who was also to travel on a motor launch, had similar reservations:

> I was a newly married man and didn't fancy it at all. I'd been married nine months before, during which I'd lived with my wife for six months, and I thought it was dicey – but I was part of the force. You can't walk off a ship and go home.

Tom Sherman was confident that, with an air raid to divert the Germans, and the vital element of surprise, they would be successful. He recalled:

> In my mind, I was quite confident it was going to be a bit of a cakewalk. I was oozing confidence to everybody and saying: 'Don't worry, you're all going to come back. I came back from Vaagso – we're going to come back from St-Nazaire.' This young man said to me his wife was pregnant, and he wondered whether he ought to take advantage of Mountbatten's offer, and I said: 'Don't worry. We'll be all right.' He wasn't on my ML and he was killed – I've thought about that all my life.

Des Chappell had become a father earlier that year; his young son was just two months old when he set off for St-Nazaire. He had seen him only once. However, as he put it:

> It never entered my head to withdraw. Not because I was brave, or not wanting to show myself up in front of the others – that didn't enter my head either. You just didn't do it. That was what I was a Commando soldier for.

Tiger Watson recalled:

> I thought it was so daring that we would get away with it. A lot of the more experienced and older, more sensible people did shake their heads. Two men came to me and said: 'We

want you to take these letters to our wives.' I said: 'But I'm going with you.' And they said: 'But you won't be killed.' They were and I wasn't – strange, this premonition people have.

Bob Hoyle remembered how his friend Arthur Blount, who was to be killed in action at St-Nazaire, whiled away his time at Falmouth playing solo whist:

You know, it might be thousands to one that it comes out – and it did. And he said: 'Oh, hell – that means I'm not coming back.' So he must have thought that the cards had told him he wasn't coming back.

The attack at St-Nazaire was the ultimate in suicide raids – a high-risk, dramatic piece of the most brazen daring it is possible to imagine. It was to be the most spectacularly successful of the Second World War Commando operations – but success came at a high price.

THE FLOATING BOMB

If it hadn't been for the satchels of explosives, you might have thought they were going to a party. Not wanting to give any hint that this was to be her last trip, HMS *Campbeltown* had been stuffed to the gunwales with food.

Pith helmets had also been taken on board, to fool any lurking German spies into thinking the ship was set for a trip to the tropics, instead of a destination much nearer home. However, at the last moment these were taken off under cover of darkness. The food was disposable – but nothing else could be carried which would add unnecessary weight.

From the outside, this floating bomb now looked like a German ship. Her four funnels had been reduced to two, changing her silhouette to that of a German Wolf-class destroyer. Closer inspection, however, would have revealed her real purpose. Her bridge and wheelhouse were reinforced, and there were low armour-plate fences on deck for the commandos to hide behind. The ship carried only enough fuel oil and boiler water for a one-way trip – and her bows were packed with four tons of explosive on a long-delay fuse.

Buster Woodiwiss recalled the party atmosphere as the

commandos set about consuming the enormous quantities of food that had been provided:

> There was a huge ham, which was hung up, and everybody could go down and use their fighting knife and slice off a large chunk. I personally grabbed thirty-six Mars bars and put them down my jumper, and I've never eaten a Mars bar since.

Corran Purdon recalled:

> Everyone was in tremendous form. We loved being with the Navy because they baked their own wonderful bread. People ate a lot of bully beef sandwiches and drank a lot of Navy cocoa, which is delicious. Then they started making sandwiches with Brylcreem in them and toothpaste, and offering them to unsuspecting friends.
>
> There was no boozing or drinking, or anything like that. I think I'm right in saying that on our last night we had one glass of sherry with Bill Copeland [the second-in-command] and the officers, and that was that. When you're going on an operation, the one thing you don't do is drink – but it was a tremendous feeling of light-heartedness and 'Thank God we're off at last.'

HMS *Campbeltown* travelled as light as possible, as there was the real danger that she might ground on the sandbanks at the mouth of the Loire. Just under a quarter of the men were packed into motor launches – small, vulnerable wooden craft – which were supplied with additional anti-aircraft defence. In order to explain this extra protection, it was put about that the flotilla's mission was to carry out anti-submarine sweeps in the Bay of Biscay. Falmouth, the port from which the expedition sailed, would have been a natural base for this.

After their seasick trip to the Isles of Scilly, those in the motor launches were somewhat uncertain about the sea voyage ahead. Luckily for them, it was a millpond journey.

Their destination had been kept secret until the last minute, but the significance of the mission was made clear from the outset. Michael Burn recalled:

> When Charles Newman was giving out his orders, he gave us a pretty clear idea about the importance of the dock as the only remaining refuge on the German-occupied Atlantic coast, and therefore something that had to be destroyed in order to assist our comrades.
>
> Every single one of us had it brought home that this was to safeguard our supplies, and we all knew that the total tonnage being sunk was appalling. Probably most of us had families who were in convoys. I had a brother in destroyers, and that made it particularly alive for us.
>
> This was one of the great advantages of our training. Right down to the least important soldier or sailor – and none were considered less important than any other – we knew what it was for. That was passed on from the colonel to the troop commanders, and the troop commanders to the soldiers.

Soldiers had been told to bath and to put on clean underwear before they left Falmouth. This would lessen the risk of infection if they were wounded. They were also encouraged to make a will – using a special form in the back of their pay book – and to write letters home in case they were killed. Michael Burn particularly remembered the letter written by Bill Gibson, a sergeant in his troop who came from Glasgow. He recalled:

> He was one of the few people who knew that he would be killed. He wrote to his father, and his father sent his letter to my father among his papers – I found it when I got home after the war. It was quite a long letter, and it was perfectly clear that he knew what the objective was. It's written in the idiom of the time, and he says as part of it: 'Peter [his mate, Peter Harkness, a corporal] and I will be together. Our task is very important and just a wee bit dangerous, but if we can

hold Jerry off it'll mean the saving of the lives of a lot of our pals [by which he meant people sailing in the convoys].

'It seems peculiar to be writing this. We've just finished tea and God's lovely sunshine is streaming through the port-holes. We've been on deck sunbathing all day. Peter's very red, as am I. It all seems so far removed from the job ahead of us. Spring is in the air and everything looks so beautiful. It's like being in a condemned cell.

'Well, Dad dearest, I'll close now. Don't be too unhappy. Remember what you always told me. Keep your chin up. I'll have done what chance has made my duty, and I can only hope that by laying down my life the generations to come might in some way remember us and benefit by what we've done.'

Michael Burn remembered Bill as being 'very humorous, inclined to be cynical' – not an exceptionally patriotic charac-ter. However, his bravery and determination were typical.

Preparations for the raid included measures designed to cut down on the dangers of friendly fire. The commandos had their uniform webbing scrubbed and whitened. (Webbing is the tough fabric used for straps and wound round the ankles.) Their faces were clean, not blacked, and they had blue pinpoint torches. Their password was to be 'War Weapons Week', with the countersign 'Weymouth'. The idea was that, even if the Germans got hold of the password, they would only be able to say: 'Var Veapons Veek' and 'Veymouth'. Their heavy boots would also give them away, as the commandos had new, silent rubber ones.

The fleet had a relatively uneventful passage across the Channel and into the Bay of Biscay. They had a skirmish with a German submarine; they also sank two French fishing trawlers, in case they were carrying wireless or German observers. They picked up the trawler crew, and when they learned that no Germans were aboard they let the rest of the fishing fleet go unharmed.

Strict precautions were taken to avoid arousing suspicion and to confuse observers. They followed a course that took them past St-Nazaire – as if they were going to the Mediterranean – then doubled back. The *Campbeltown* had a skeleton naval crew, but it was obviously important that the presence of the commandos went undetected. Frank Carr, who was on board the *Campbeltown*, recalled:

> We weren't allowed on deck a lot – only in limited numbers. A certain number of duffel coats had been issued so that we looked like naval gents if any submarine was having a little look at us, or aerial photographs – that was pretty strict. The same on the MLs. It was more uncomfortable for them, of course. It was a very uncomfortable form of passage on a motor launch, even with the correct crew, but with the addition of about eight or ten extra people it must have been exceedingly uncomfortable.

As they neared their destination, the escort destroyers left them, and Bob Ryder transferred to a smaller gunboat to act as guide to the fleet. With him was Charles Newman and a journalist named Gordon Holman. At the mouth of the Loire they had a prearranged rendezvous with a British submarine, HMS *Sturgeon*, to help them pinpoint their position. Corran Purdon recalled:

> This chap Bill Green, who was the navigating officer in the motor gunboat, was the most wonderful navigator. He brought us straight there from Falmouth doing a dog's leg course, and we got there absolutely on the button. I remember seeing HMS *Sturgeon* lying awash, and we could see the conning tower and the captain, a chap called Commander Wingfield. I remember him yelling out 'good luck', and us yelling out 'good luck' to him. It seemed so strange, that you could go across all this amount of sea and suddenly there was this British voice and this wonderful British submarine lying there. It gave you a feeling of confidence, and what a bloody marvellous Navy we had.

David Paton, who was one of three doctors on the raid, remembered his first sight of the submarine:

> Here he was in the water with a little blue light up right in the Bay of Biscay, about twenty miles from St-Nazaire. As we passed him he said, 'Good luck, doc', and I thought, 'That's funny. How does he know I'm doc?' But, of course, he knew the boat. He knew I was in Number 2, and I'd been at a party on his submarine the night before. I thought: 'Well, this is the real thing now. We're in.' I stood on the steps at the back of the ship beside the ammunition thing and watched what was happening, and there was no sign of the RAF at all.

It was now late at night on Friday 27 March 1942, and they entered the estuary in the darkness. Tiger Watson recalled:

> I remember the Loire estuary entrance, because I was so sure that we were going to get away with it that I'd had a jolly good sleep beforehand – which was not a bad idea, actually, as it turned out. I didn't get much sleep afterwards.
>
> I'd never been on the Continent – it wasn't so common in those days – and you suddenly were struck with the fact that you were now entering enemy territory and there was no going back. There was only one way, and that was forward. It was a very emotive moment. And, of course, there was the smell of the mud and the seaweed, and you realized that you were near land.

The port of St-Nazaire was further up the Loire estuary than it had seemed on the model, and there was some tension when HMS *Campbeltown* shuddered as she hit the mud flats. From his motor launch beside her, David Paton saw her grind to a halt twice: 'We could see the *Campbeltown* stuck, and we went past it, then it beat us again and we went past it again, then it got free again and came charging past us.' By now, as he recalled, the *Campbeltown* was flying the German colours:

It broke out an enormous swastika, just a black and white swastika, big as a ship. Huge thing. I thought: 'Oh, God, I'm going to be killed as a spy next. What a funny thing to do.' But apparently that's in accordance with the rules of war.

As Tiger Watson explained:

You're allowed to use these ruses as long as you're not opening fire. It's laughable to think there should be rules when you think of the horrible things that people do to each other, but the rule is that you must declare your own identity before you open fire.

The *Campbeltown* had another secret weapon – German identification codes, which had been captured in the Vaagso raid, as Tom Sherman recalled:

The most significant success factor of the Vaagso raid was the fact that we'd captured all the signal books and they didn't realize we had them. It was from those codes that we captured at Vaagso that we knew all the responses to the signals that were coming from the shore, and Ryder's signalman was responding with the right countersigns and confusing the enemy by doing that, and pleading that we were a friendly force just popping in for the night.

The signalman was wearing a petty officer's cap that – at a distance – might give him the look of a German officer. When the ship was challenged, he was able to buy time by using the correct recognition codes.

A diversionary bombing raid had been scheduled for 11.30 p.m. that night. However, this had the opposite effect to the intended one, as Michael Burn recalled:

We were told there would be an air raid, the purpose of which would be to distract the Germans' attention. In fact, the effect it had was to alert them, because the air force had political orders that they were not to bomb unless they could see their objectives, which were only to be military objectives. Those were orders that came direct from Churchill.

Consequently, as there was cloud, they bombed very little. Although it took the Germans a little time to realize that this was unusual, they did realize just in time for the German commander to give the order for all the guns to be trained on the sea rather than the air, and that a sea assault was to be expected.

In the early hours of Saturday morning, the Germans spotted the force advancing up the estuary. They pinned them with searchlights. At first they were fooled by the signalman with his captured German codes, but as the ships continued to advance their suspicions were aroused. A nervous gunner shot at the ship – and, with only a mile to go to the target, the *Campbeltown* ran down its German flag, raised the White Ensign, and started shooting back. The fight was on.

David Paton recalled the scene as the German gun batteries opened up on all sides, using coloured tracer shells to help them shoot accurately:

It suddenly became Guy Fawkes night, because the Germans not only had red or orangey-red tracer, but blue tracer and green tracer and yellow tracer and red tracer. I thought: 'These clever-dick Germans. They've got the best of us here. We've only got the one colour, and they've got four.' It was just like rain falling. You could have put your hand and got one in your hand, but that would be a silly thing to do. I remember once jumping in the air, letting it go underneath me. You could see it coming from a long way away, and what you don't realize, of course, is that there's only one tracer in four bullets or four shells, so what you're not seeing is two, three or four – you don't know they're there.

Frank Carr recalled:

There was a tremendous amount of shellfire going on of every conceivable colour, practically, and it even looked as though it was coming up out of the water. Of course, it's the reflection, but it was a weird experience. To give you some idea of the amount of firepower, I think there were something like seventy or eighty coastal guns dotted along both banks. They were dual-operation things – they could fire at aircraft or at surface vessels, and in addition to that there was heavier stuff behind. All this was firing and, fortunately for the MLs, in the earlier part it was directed at the destroyer.

The whole river became a garishly lit stage, as the commandos desperately tried to knock out the blinding German searchlights. David Paton recalled:

Most of them were firing, but really they didn't know what they were firing at. They were using up an awful lot of ammunition. One chap was banging away, and my skipper came down and said: 'Doc, could you stop this chap firing? We want some ammunition to go home with.' I tried, but he wouldn't stop.

As Buster Woodiwiss, who was on board the *Campbeltown*, explained:

The difficulty is that you can't aim at the light because it blinds you, so what you do, you half close your eyelids and you look at the light. Now, immediately the light goes out, you open your eyes and there's a glimmer showing in the centre of the light as the bulb gradually loses its heat. That's when you fire.

Everything we could fire was fired. We had rows of Bren guns with 100-round pans specially behind the screens, and they were firing at everything.

However, the searchlights had their uses. Bob Montgomery, the demolitions expert, who was on the bridge of the *Campbeltown*, recalled:

> Actually, the searchlights were for us in *Campbeltown*, and for Sam Beattie [the ship's commander] in particular, a good thing, because they lit up the lighthouse, and he saw he was going in the wrong direction, and was able to adjust.

The lighthouse, on the spot known as the Old Mole, was Beattie's marker for the passage to the dry-dock gate, and his target. In the darkness, he might well have missed it.

Bob Montgomery recalled the ferocity of the firepower that was focused on the *Campbeltown* in the last moments of her journey:

> Everything was concentrated on *Campbeltown*, which looked big, and was a bigger target. You could feel bumps, and there were bits coming off inside the bridge when something hit the outside. There were little bits of metal flying around – I didn't realize at the time, but I found I was full of them in my legs afterwards.
>
> Sam [Beattie] was right up the front, peering out through the slit. We were a bit behind him. The coxswain was hit – he was on the wheel, and he was killed. I think it was a leading signalman or something, he took the wheel and he was killed. I was just behind him, so I grabbed at the thing, and Nigel Tibbits [a naval lieutenant] luckily was standing beside me. He took it over before I was able to do any damage.

On the deck, behind shrapnel screens, and below, the teams were waiting for their orders. Two assault groups were to knock out gun positions and form a bridgehead for the troops to withdraw. Following them were to be two demolition groups, each with their own protection party. (The need to provide protection was a lesson that had been learned from Vaagso.)

One demolition group was to destroy the outer caisson if *Campbeltown* did not succeed, together with its winding hut and pumping station. Another, led by Gerard Brett – in civilian life, an assistant curator at the Victoria & Albert Museum – was to lay explosives on the inner caisson. Corran Purdon and his group were to attack the winding hut that went with this gate. He recalled:

> When we went to action stations, we went down to the ward-room and sat facing away from the dry-dock gate, so as to lessen the impact when we struck. I didn't see very much – what I did witness was the sound of shells of every calibre you can think of hitting *Campbeltown*. While we were sitting there, a shell shot through just above our heads – came in one side and went out the other. There was clang, clang, clang, bang, bang, bang, and, of course, there were flashes the whole time. One heard this cacophony of noise going on outside, and saw all the flashes, not just the searchlights, but the flashes of the explosives as they slammed into *Campbeltown*.

At the last moment, an incendiary bomb – possibly dropped in mistake by an RAF plane – landed in the *Campbeltown*'s bows and started a fire. Pinned by enemy searchlights and battered by gunfire, this ageing destroyer – crammed with her cargo of explosives and men – burst through a steel torpedo net and rammed into the massive steel gate. With a grinding sound and a shower of sparks and flame, her bows crumpled like a tin can as she rose some twenty feet into the air. Bullets and shells pinged off her armour plating, ricocheting around until they found a target – metal or human.

Buster Woodiwiss recalled:

> The assault Tommy-gunning group that I was in were the first people off, and the smoke from the fire that was on the bows was completely obscuring the scene. The decks were slippery with blood, because lots of people had been hit. The person

who was supposed to put the ladders down for us to climb down to get on to the dock had been killed, and the ladders had been shattered. One of my Tommy gunners was killed and the other one had been badly wounded and couldn't get off the boat. So that only left Nicky Finch [a fellow Tommy gunner] and myself to do the work that four of us had to do.

I crawled along to the nearest point where I could get down to the dock. I looked down and it was about nine or ten feet from the deck, but all the places where you could jump were all shattered with bits of timber that were sticking up all over the place. I lowered myself as far as I could under cover of the smoke and then dropped down on to the place that I thought I could land safely.

Once safely ashore, he took cover behind a large steel bollard:

It took fractions of a minute or seconds to get the smoke out of my eyes, and when I got out of the smoke I could see a hand grenade twirling through the air. As I had my prepared charge in one hand, and my Tommy gun in the other, the only thing I could do was kick the hand grenade, which circled back and fell among the people [Germans] who were throwing it.

I could clearly see the gun position and clearly see that they didn't know that I was ashore. So I lobbed two Mills grenades, having the firing pin out, counted four seconds, lobbed it high so that it detonated on impact. When you do this with a grenade they immediately think that it's mortar fire, and that they're being engaged from a far greater distance than they actually were, which gave me the opportunity of running as fast as I could to the gun position. Then I used two stun grenades; they were only recently invented for street-fighting. They were made of plastic and they contained a very high explosive charge but no shrapnel. They also had a blinding flash of magnesium. The advantage of them was that you weren't going to be hurt by the shrapnel from your own grenade, so that you could immediately follow in while they still had their eyes shut, and if they can't see you, they can't hit you.

Lobbing the grenades with such accuracy from such a tiny sheltering point used a skill he had learned in more peaceful times:

> I was a fast bowler in my village cricket team for years, and the correct action of bowling a bumper is to get the maximum height, and it drops down vertically. We used to practise for ages with a cricket stump at sixty yards and a three-foot circle round the cricket stump, and I could put four out of six in that circle. So it was more accurate than a mortar really.

He wrapped his explosive charges round the breech of the gun to immobilize it; altogether, there were four guns which his group – under the command of John Roderick – had to secure to help the commandos land safely. This meant killing the Germans who were manning them. For many commandos, this was the first time they had used weapons for anything other than target practice – and no amount of training could have prepared them for the harsh reality. John Roderick recalled:

> We hadn't faced that sort of thing before, but we'd thought about it umpteen times. I did have to kill two Germans outright – I think a number of us had to do things that went against the grain totally, but if it hadn't been them, one's own men would have been put down.

Some Germans simply ran away. According to Buster Woodiwiss, they were victims of their own propaganda:

> They thought they'd get their throats cut. We were portrayed in the British press as sort of psychopaths released from prison who had knives in their mouths and worked in abattoirs killing lambs and wallowing in their blood. This was picked up by the Germans, who used this propaganda all

over the world, and this was the thing that gave us a very, very bad name – which was exactly opposite to what happened. The Commando consisted mainly not of great big Amazons but of men who were not fit for the real army; who wanted to lead rather than be led; who wanted to use their brains rather than obsolete weapons that were outdated in the First World War; who could battle against stupid regimented military types in the German Army by using their intelligence and initiative.

The difference was that you had a group of men whose sole thing was not necessarily to destroy the Germans – we only destroyed the Germans if they prevented us from doing what we wanted to do, which was to destroy their capability to wage war.

Following the assault groups, the demolition men made their way off the *Campbeltown* as best they could, stepping over the bodies of the dead and wounded. Bill Etches, who was supposed to be in charge of the inner caisson demolition parties, had been lying on deck by a protective steel plate. However, this had offered distinctly limited protection, as he recalled:

I think I was lying on the wrong side of it. Had there been two steel plates, I'm bloody sure I'd have laid between them, but there was only one. Bill Copeland [the major in charge of the *Campbeltown* group] had told me that was my position. I thought at the time, 'That's bloody silly' – it was very exposed.

I had a sergeant with me, or a corporal – I can't remember – he actually saved my life. The first time we came under fire, I had splinters up my backside, and the immediate reaction was to get up. He held me down, and had I not been held down I would certainly have bought it, because there was a lot of metal flying around. I was hit in the leg, hit in the buttocks, hit in the lower leg, and hit in the arm by splinters from the shells bursting across the deck. They were forty-millimetre, thirty-millimetre anti-aircraft stuff, which were bursting across the deck. I was hit three times, and I was very frightened.

I was still lying there on the deck when it rammed. I heard the other parties getting ashore over the prow and I staggered up. I remember there was a bloody great hole in the foredeck, where a shell had hit it. I had some difficulty getting my way round that. I remember sliding down the scramble nets and on to the gate, and I remember seeing Bob Montgomery [the demolitions expert] and saying: 'I don't think I'm going to take much part in this operation at all, because I've been wounded.'

Bill Copeland had the job of marshalling the troops off the crippled *Campbeltown*, as Corran Purdon recalled:

I will never forget him. We seemed to have fire coming from every possible angle, and every coloured tracer you could think of, and a hell of a noise. There he stood, as calm as possible, yet with this tremendous grip. I can still see him standing there with his rifle slung over his shoulder and just saying: 'Right, Roderick off, Roy off, Purdon off...' You never thought of anything other than this man. He was the most important thing on the deck – to hell with all the fire that was coming. Bill Copeland made it all seem just as if it was in a way almost an exercise, except that people were being hit right, left and centre.

Johnny Johnson, who was one of my corporals, got hit. I got a little bit hit, but nothing much. Unfortunately, a thermite [incendiary] bomb had landed on the forecastle, and already the twelve-pounder gun had been knocked out, and the two three-inch mortar crews. Johnny Proctor [an officer in an assault group] was lying there with his leg almost off, but cheering us.

There was this hole in the deck with fire and smoke coming out of it, and poor old Bob Hoyle [a member of Purdon's demolition group] managed to trip and go down it.

Thank God, with his rucksack on his back, he couldn't disappear, and we hauled him up – but by then he'd had his trousers and his legs badly burned.

Bob Hoyle – a builder in peacetime – did not notice what had happened at first. He recalled:

We got to the ladder and there was one chap lying on the deck holding the top stays of the ladder to hold it firm, because obviously the side of the ship was all twisted, so the ladder wasn't firm. One by one we went down, and then somebody said to me: 'Your trousers are on fire.' There was smoke coming from the trousers, yet I didn't feel any burn at the time or anything.

Somebody said: 'You'd better take 'em off.' So I took the trousers off and just left them there, and we went off round the side of the dry dock heading for the winding house.

He carried on, trouserless. Meanwhile, their protection party was nowhere to be seen, and they had to go on without them. Corran Purdon recalled what happened next:

We just trotted up the side of the dock. There was a lot of firing, and every now and then we were lit up by searchlights. In hindsight, we were pretty visible from the top of the U-boat pens, but I didn't know that at the time. Anyway, we went up, and there was our winding house. Well, one thing I never had thought of was that the door would be locked, and I'd got no key to the door. So, having seen my cowboy films with everybody else, I thought: 'Well, I'll shoot the lock in – that's the thing to do in these circumstances.' So I put my Colt up against the lock, fired it, and Ron Cheung said to me: 'Look, I don't mind being murdered by Germans, but I don't want to be murdered by you.' The ricky [ricochet] just went past him, I think. So he produced a huge great sort of axe from his rucksack and slammed the lock in.

Then we went into the winding house. We knew exactly where to place everything, and we'd been trained to do it quickly and in the dark, so we laid our charges on all the vital parts of the winding house machinery, and we put a couple of ring mains out, joining them all up, and then we had more than one way of detonation as well, and that was done.

However, they could not set off the explosion until the party led by Gerard Brett – the Byzantine scholar from the V&A – had finished laying their charges on the inner caisson because their route back to the boats led past the winding house. This group had met considerable resistance, and had also encountered practical problems. Brett himself had been badly wounded, so Frank Carr, then only a sergeant, calmly took control. His bravery was to win him the Distinguished Conduct Medal, but his description of this incident is remarkably matter of fact:

The difference between the caissons, between our own in the dock at Southampton, and St-Nazaire, was that there was no entry above deck on the French ones. They'd all been decked over with twelve by twelve bolts of timber, which were laced together very tightly. On top of this, there'd been a Tarmacadam road. It was impossible to move it, so we couldn't get inside the caisson at all.

While we were started on the job, there were two ships – tankers or something – in the dry dock. They had skeleton crews aboard who were armed in the usual German way with lots of sub-machine guns – far better armed than we were. They kept their heads down wisely for a long time, but eventually some bolder souls came up on deck and started opening up at us. Since they were only twenty or thirty feet away, it was very uncomfortable, and all we had were pistols with which to reply to this.

We climbed underneath the decking to get some sort of cover and started firing back. We very quickly found that it wasn't a very sensible thing to do, because the bullets were ricocheting all around the metal part in there. It was rather uncomfortable, so we evacuated that, and I think it was Burtenshaw [Robert Burtenshaw, a tall, monocle-wearing lieutenant] said: 'We've got to silence that wretched boat.' He was quite a character. He was wearing a naval hat – I think it was Beattie's white-topped peaked hat – and most of the time he was humming a song: 'There'll Always Be An England', or some such thing. He was a real outgoing character, and we gathered along the side and opened up on this tanker with our pistols.

At the same time an attack came from the land side, with some Germans. We had to take care of ourselves, and quite a few people were wounded badly. Burtenshaw was killed – quite a number of others were killed on that operation there – and eventually we silenced the boat and got on with the job.

Frank Carr had to check the explosives inch by inch, to ensure that the ring main linking them had not been fractured, before setting them off:

There was a minute, or a minute and a half delay, and then there was the usual crump. I walked along the top of the caisson, and I could hear the water running through both ends, which I hadn't been able to hear before, so I knew that we had done something rather nasty to it.

Once they had finished, the group – including the walking wounded – set off back to the rendezvous. This involved crossing a lock gate covered in barbed wire – no easy task under fire, as Frank Carr recalled:

We had night vision by then – you get used to the dark, and you can see quite well after a while. There were fires everywhere, in any case, so they flung a certain amount of light about. But we had to cross over a lock gate, which was different from a caisson – the swinging things on hinges, you've probably seen them on the Kennett and Avon Canal – similar to that. They had a top about three feet wide, I suppose, but that was smothered in coils of barbed wire and we had to cross that. That was a bit tricky, walking through the barbed wire and not getting tangled in it.

Corran Purdon recalled the moment when he fired his charges:

I pulled my igniter pins and our winding house just seemed to jump five or ten feet in the air and then just collapsed like a pack of cards. It was my job to go back and satisfy myself that the demolition had actually been a success, so I started to go back – and the next thing I knew I was being held. My guys decided the searchlight was shining on it, and they wouldn't let me go until the searchlight had moved on. That's the way your guys look after you.

Once the light had passed, he did go back to make sure they had done the job. As he put it, 'we'd obliterated the bloody thing.' The winding house for the outer caisson had been similarly destroyed by a team led by Chris Smalley, whose fate will emerge in the next chapter. The debris from this explosion narrowly missed hitting Bob Ryder, who was standing nearby watching the *Campbeltown* sink. (Once everyone had been evacuated, the sea cocks were opened to scuttle the ship, leaving her firmly wedged at a forty-five-degree angle against the dock gate and impossible to move.)

Meanwhile, the pumping station – which it was essential to destroy if the dry dock was to be put out of action – had been successfully knocked out by another demolition team, led by Stuart Chant. Chant, who worked on the London Stock Exchange in peacetime, had been wounded in the knee even before he got off the *Campbeltown*. However, this did not stop him.

Like Corran Purdon, he found his first major problem was a locked door – but he blew it open with magnetic charges.

The pumping station had massive pumps forty feet below ground. One sergeant was too badly wounded to tackle the steps in the dark and had to be left to stand guard at the top. Chant was limping – but he and the rest of his team raced as fast as they could down into the gloom, with their rucksacks full of explosives. Their blindfold exercises at Southampton Docks meant they could do this almost from memory. They had just finished firing their charges, and were waiting outside for the explosion, when Bob Montgomery passed by to check up on them. He recalled:

> They all put down their rucksacks and were beginning to sit down underneath the wall of the pumping house and I pulled them out of there. I said, 'Back', which was just as well because a chunk of concrete came off the roof and hit one of the rucksacks and just went straight across it. They'd have been killed quite happily there. That went up beautifully, with 300 pounds of explosives – you know, forty feet under-ground, it was quite a confined space – bang!
>
> When we went into the pumping house again to demol-ish the electric motors, which were up on ground level, we found two of them had disappeared through the floor and the other two were looking a bit drunk, so that really wasn't necessary. The chap whose job it was to deal with all the dials and things with a fireman's axe and sledgehammer, he had a lovely time doing that. Sparks were flying in every direction – luckily, he had rubber boots on and rubber gloves. We cut the pipes on the transformers in the pumping house and tried to set the oil alight. We couldn't get it to light at all, but it wasn't really a major thing.

Within half an hour, almost everything the commandos had planned to demolish had been reduced to a pile of smoking rubble. However, as they made their way back to the rendezvous, they soon realized that not everything had exactly gone to plan. Corran Purdon recalled:

I reported to my colonel, who was standing by some railway trucks, and I said: 'Sir, we have blown up the northern winding house. I'm now ready to re-embark for England.' And he said to me: 'Take a look out over the river. I'm afraid our transport's let us down.'

ALL AT SEA

All that remained of most of the motor launches that had been supposed to take the commandos home was a sea of burning oil and driftwood. While HMS *Campbeltown* had successfully rammed the dock and off-loaded her cargo of men – albeit with many casualties – the motor launches had proved themselves totally unsuitable for the job. Of the sixteen that had set out from Falmouth, only two managed to land their men and escape relatively unscathed.

Although they were equipped with automatic guns, these frail craft were totally unable to stand up to enemy fire. Not only were they made of wood, but they had extra fuel tanks on deck for the long journey. The captains of each launch had been told to fill these with seawater once they neared St-Nazaire – but not everyone had obeyed the instruction. The result was that the ships were quickly turned into floating bonfires.

As HMS *Campbeltown* headed towards the dry dock, the motor launches had been formed into two columns on either side of her. Michael Burn, who was in a boat immediately behind *Campbeltown*, on the starboard side, recalled:

Because of the delay in the Germans recognizing that we were an invasion force, the people who were in greater danger and could take in the chaos of the river were the people further aft. I just remember searchlights and this tracer and then a jolt, or more than a jolt, and we were there. I never saw the appalling sight or the excitement of all the guns blazing on all the ships because I was already more or less ashore.

I wasn't aware that *Campbeltown* had hit the dock. I was aware of absolutely nothing except that we were still going ahead, and then Billy Stephens, who was commanding my boat, saying: 'Jump, now's your chance.' I thought, 'Why?' because we hadn't landed. I thought we would just come quietly alongside, I'd step graciously ashore and there we'd be. But it wasn't like that at all. I was forward of the bridge and I looked aft and the ship was on fire – so I jumped. I jumped into the sea, the drink, with all my grenades.

Arthur Young, who was a corporal in my troop, had already jumped. He was on some steps on the jetty, and he was able to pull me ashore. I remember I was sinking. I was so loaded that I would not have got ashore unless he'd given me a hand.

I had a Colt revolver, and there was a German on the jetty. I remember bashing him, and thinking: 'This is something I don't recognize in myself.'

He quickly realized that he had landed at least a mile away from his target. Arthur Young, who had helped him ashore, was wounded in the leg and could not carry on – so, with no sign of any of the others in his group, he decided to continue on his own. He recalled:

I knew that if they could land, they would land. They would possibly rejoin me, having rehearsed and remembered the route across the docks. But I was alone, so I just went on to the objective, where I could do absolutely nothing. I had no weapons except grenades, and I didn't have them left in the end.

I was hiding in a workshop, and a lot of German soldiers appeared outside – obviously a bit panicky – running towards the place where they assumed we had landed. I thought, 'Well, I'd better throw this grenade among them' – but then I thought better of it. So I didn't throw the grenade, and the Germans went on and disappeared. I went out and continued my course towards this bridge, and realized that I had a grenade in my hand with the pin out. The tension in my hand had helped the lever down, so I threw it in the drink. That was a very scary moment.

Then I just went on to the bridge, which I was supposed to defend against German reinforcements. I climbed up a gun tower I was supposed to set on fire, and I had nothing left to set it on fire with. I found a lot of the German sleeping quarters at the top, but there were no Germans in it – they were all obviously running towards the place where we had landed.

It was only on his way back to the rendezvous that he realized just how much fighting had been going on in the docks:

I remember the first time I saw a soldier terribly badly wounded, who was still alive. I gave him morphia – we had morphia, some of us – and I remember thinking, 'I do hope I've done it right', never having done a morphia injection before.

Then I was making for the Old Mole [an area with an easily recognizable lighthouse], which is where we were supposed to re-embark to go home. I was still in this mood of thinking, 'Well, we'll re-embark, some of us, and go home', and I found myself suddenly in the hands of three German soldiers. I'd been captured.

I heard one of them say [in German]: 'Shall we kill him?' Luckily, I knew German. I chatted them up and said: 'You really can't kill me. I shall be a very important prisoner.' I gradually drew them back to where I knew our soldiers were and let them take my compass. Then one of our soldiers challenged them, and they ran away.

All but five of the commandos in Michael Burn's launch were either shot or drowned; its commander, Billy Stephens, was captured, as were many of the sailors. One of them, a wireless telegraphist named Jim Laurie, recalled:

> About six or seven of us ran into these German soldiers who shouted: 'Hände hoch.' I don't know if I knew much German at that time, but it was quite clear what you had to do – put your hands up in the air. A couple started firing revolvers in the air. I don't know why – wasting ammunition, I think. We went into the courtyard of a house. There were searchlights all over the place, a terrific noise everywhere. They got us into a line. There was a wall behind us and this may sound a little dramatic, but it's true enough. Those of us with steel helmets and lifejackets, these were taken from us, and the guards there who had rifles actually started fixing bayonets. We thought that they were going to bayonet us. They were also fumbling around with boxes that may have been ammunition boxes. The point was, they were probably more frightened than we were. We knew why we were there, but they didn't.

In the end, they were not bayoneted but simply taken off for interrogation.

Eric de la Torre was in the second launch in the starboard column, under the command of Mark Woodcock. He recalled:

> You couldn't see anything. The portholes were blacked out and nobody was allowed on deck; you all had to stay below. Mr Woodcock occasionally came down the stairs and said: 'We're nearly there.' Otherwise, all you heard were the guns when they were first challenged.
>
> You thought, 'This is the start of it', but only one or two shells were fired, and then *Campbeltown* managed to bluff

and went on. But then, of course, as she got near to the lock gates all hell broke loose. The noise was tremendous. Then Mr Woodcock came down the stairs carrying a big stone jar of rum. We all had a tot except 'Nosher' Brown, which was extraordinary, because 'Nosher' Brown was the prime drunkard in our lot – he was always drunk, but this night he refused to have a drink. I just couldn't understand it, but on the other hand maybe he thought you think clearer if you haven't had a drink, and looking back I think possibly he might have been right.

Loaded with a rucksack full of explosives, as well as a crowbar that had been thrust into his hand at the last minute, Eric de la Torre landed with his demolition group and their protection party. Their target was a couple of lock gates and a swing bridge. He recalled:

I shouldn't think we ran more than about ten yards towards a wooden fence with an open gate in it, but as we ran towards it a stream of tracer went past my legs, and then he [the German gunner] must have swung his gun to the right and hit Hempstead, who was running alongside me. Hempstead was the protection party sergeant, and he fell to the ground – he didn't make any noise, but I just had the impression of him falling.

I think possibly one of the Oerlikons [rapid-firing guns on the motor launch] managed to stop the gun from firing, because no more tracer came along. But then, as we went through this gate and ran towards our target, suddenly somebody shouted: 'Get down!' We flung ourselves on the ground and there was a tremendous explosion and I was buried under rubble. Bricks and all sorts of stuff came down.

They had landed a little later than planned, because their launch had overshot the mark and had to turn round to find the right landing place. Meanwhile, the demolition party led by Chris Smalley had laid their charges on the southern wind-ing house – and it was the rubble from this that now blocked their way. Eric de la Torre recalled:

I had to take the rucksack off, because I couldn't move. Sergeant Churchill then struggled out, we looked around, and there was nobody else there. He said: 'Where have they all gone?' I think what must have happened was that Mr Woodcock realized that the way was now blocked by all this masonry so he'd gone back to the boat and was going to cross to the other side and try and approach it that way round. Anyway, Churchill said to me: 'You run down and call the boat back, and I'll bring Hempstead [the protection party sergeant, who had been shot in the stomach].'

So I did a rugby dive through this gate, I got up and ran down to the quayside, and shouted across to Burt [the naval lieutenant in charge of the launch] that we had a wounded man, and would he bring the boat back. George [Churchill] came through the gateway with his arms under Hempstead, I got hold of his feet, and we got him over the rail. Then, just as we started to pull away, Private Wilcox from another group came running along – he'd been hit in the arm, and he jumped aboard – and then another officer with a big mous-tache, whom I didn't know, came running along. That was Captain Smalley, I found out afterwards.

When I first got on board, Woodcock said to me: 'Get down below, because you'd only get in the way of the sailors if you were wandering about on the deck.' So I went down the three or four stairs to the mess deck. There were two or three men lying across the table; I don't know whether they were dead or just wounded, but they were slumped across the table, and there was another one on the floor. Shells were coming through the wall and out the other side, and I thought: 'My God, I'm not stopping down here.' I was safer on deck. So I went up on deck and crouched down by the stairs leading up on to the bridge.

Then Smalley came along, and he said to me: 'Come on, we'll get this forward Oerlikon going.' The gun crew were dead, and the coxswain shouted out: 'You can't get it going – it's out of action, it's had a hit.' So, anyway, Smalley runs down to the gun with me following slowly behind, because I thought: 'You've been told it's out of action – there's no point in trying to get it going.' He strapped himself into the Oerlikon, which has two fitting shoulders, and then I don't know whether he got hit by a shell splinter, or whether the gun recoiled on him, but all I could see was a headless figure standing in this frame.

Robbie Roberts, who was the second officer on the ML, said to me: 'I shall never forget Smalley's head rolling across the deck.' I never saw any flash of shellfire, so I think it was the gun that did it. All I can remember is the headless body hanging in the gun.

Shortly afterwards, with the motor launch on fire, the order came to abandon ship. Eric de la Torre found himself hanging on to the rope handle of a Carley rescue float, drifting down the Loire with the tide. He recalled:

Corporal 'Nosher' Brown, the one who didn't take the rum, came swimming up, and he said: 'Can I hang on to you? I've been hit in the foot.' It was a desperate scene, because there were small lakes of burning fuel floating on the surface of the water, and you had to steer your raft past these lakes, and shells and small arms fire were still hitting the water and sending spurts up. It was all confusion – men shouting, men drowning, I suppose. But a most strange thing – suddenly, in the middle of all this confusion, I heard a voice singing one line of 'Oh, God, Our Help in Ages Past'. Then he started the second line, and it went dead – so presumably he'd got shot, he was killed. I think it must have been one of the sailors. Commandos generally weren't a religious lot. I think it was more likely to have been one of the naval chaps, who have a much greater sense of God.

We went on drifting down. One or two dropped off who'd been wounded, and couldn't hang on any longer. Eventually, we managed, by each kicking out, to get towards the shore-line. As we got nearer, we saw a group of figures and we thought: 'Oh, this is great. The French will hide us, and maybe we'll escape.' But as we got nearer we saw the Germans' steel helmets, and, when we got very near, a young German officer sent his men into the water and they dragged the raft ashore. Then he said, in very good English: 'What do you all need?'

They must have been tracking us coming down the Loire, because every now and again a searchlight would come on you. I suppose they'd followed the road down, and they had a lorry waiting there. They took the stretchers off the back of the lorry and moved the wounded on. Then he looked at me, and he saw the pistol sticking out of my trouser pocket, so he signalled to one of his men, and said: 'Take those pistols.' Anyway, I handed them over and this chap took a ring off his finger, which was a cheap ring with the coat of arms of St-Nazaire on it, and he gave it to me. It was a souvenir ring that he'd bought in the town, I suppose, and I'd probably still be wearing it if it hadn't been taken in the wash house, because one day in prisoner-of-war camp I went in to wash, put it on the side and lost it.

They were very good to us, they really were, the way they sorted the wounded out. One or two of them were patting us on the back. I suppose they probably thought: 'How on earth could they ever expect to get up the Loire and destroy the docks? They must be mad.' I suppose as far as the motor launches are concerned, it was a mad conception. They had no chance against the German batteries – the only people who really got a decent landing were the men on the *Campbeltown*.

The third and fourth motor launches on the starboard side of HMS *Campbeltown* burst into a mass of flaming petrol after coming under heavy fire from the shore. Of the eighteen commandos on board these boats, only five survived; the rest either drowned or were burned to death.

The fifth in line, commanded by Leslie Fenton, a film actor in civilian life, was disabled by a direct hit. Tom Sherman, who was on the bridge at the time, still has the twisted remains of the handle of his commando knife – buckled by the heat of the blast – as a reminder of the ferocity of the fire they came under. He recalled:

We came into the searchlights, and the troops were lying on the deck with their machine guns. I was bellowing: 'Aim for the searchlights.' We were returning fire, but then we were hit and we all went down. The bridge was a shambles, the wheelhouse was knocked out, and, of course, the steering gear went, so we were helpless.

Everybody picked themselves up, apart from Dickie Hooper, who'd been hit in the hips, and the captain [Leslie Fenton]. I managed to pick myself up – I just had a few shrapnel wounds, or scratches if you like – and I was rather concerned, because I had a bag of grenades slung from my belt, and I was rather concerned that the explosion and the fact that I'd been hit could have triggered off some of the fuses. I said to Dickie Hooper, 'I'm throwing this overboard, this lot', and unhitched it and threw it overboard.

Then we had to get Dickie Hooper looked at, and there was this big Welshman called Taffy Lloyd. He heaved Dickie Hooper down off the shambles from the bridge and took him down to the wardroom.

Both engines were out of action, and we were veering away and losing any momentum at all. The Navy produced this emergency tiller, and I had to detail one or two of my lads to go and help them erect this emergency tiller. In the meantime, all I could hear in the background is a starter motor going. In those days every little car had a starting handle, and I'm thinking: 'Oh, God, why doesn't he start cranking it?' I went down into the little engine room, and one engine was absolutely knocked off its mountings and covered in foam. There was this engine room artificer, to whom we owe our lives, working on this other motor. I said, 'What are the chances?', and he said, 'Oh, a good chance here. Might just get it going.'

I then went and had a look at Dickie Hooper. There was Dickie lying there, and they were slapping field dressings on him. There was blood everywhere, and blood coming out of the welts of his boots, and I said: 'I think you're ready for some morphine, sir.' Well, I won't repeat what he told me to do, but he said: 'I don't want any morphine. The next thing is you'll be cutting my leg off.' Expletives deleted.

Anyway, he got on his feet and they got the engine going and the emergency tiller. By this time Leslie Fenton, who'd been knocked unconscious, came round, and they had a little conference. Whether there was any communication with other landing craft I don't know, but I think somebody said they'd seen the withdrawal light signals, and we decided to withdraw.

They had been lucky in managing to escape the attention of the gunners on shore after the initial hit; under cover of the general chaos, they managed to retreat back down the Loire estuary and out into the Bay of Biscay. On the way they saw the ferocious battle between one of the launches and a German destroyer which will be described later in this chapter. They steered well clear of this, and arrived at the rendezvous with HMS *Atherstone* at the same time as Bob Ryder, the naval commander. Tom Sherman recalled his feelings once safely on board the destroyer:

We were frustrated that we weren't able to land, but rather relieved that we were getting out. I said to Gordon Holman, who was the press man, 'I'm sorry we didn't do our job,' and he said, 'But you did,' so I said, 'Well – tell me.' I can't remember the exact conversation, but he said: 'I saw the

Campbeltown in the lock gates and I've come out with Commander Ryder, and the whole thing is a wonderful operation and a wonderful story.' I probably just said: 'Thank God.' Then I decided to go and have my few wounds attended to. When I got to the room that was the medical room, which was the wardroom converted, and I saw Johnny Proctor [who had been wounded on the *Campbeltown*] with his leg off, I just turned round and came away. I thought: 'Well, I don't need any attention. Let them look after these chaps.'

Tom Sherman's group had had orders to destroy two gun positions north of the lighthouse at the Old Mole. This was the place where, under the original plans, the men were supposed to be taken off to safety after they had completed their tasks. But because the motor launch was unable to land her men, these guns were able to continue to wreak havoc – a pattern that was to be repeated elsewhere.

In retrospect, Tom Sherman feels that the crucial problem was that they had lost the element of surprise:

Once the surprise had gone, with the *Campbeltown* going into the lock gates, the MLs then became vulnerable – and they were even more vulnerable because the forces like my lot didn't get ashore. If we'd got ashore, then we'd have subdued those gunners, which would have allowed the landing craft to go to the Old Mole to be withdrawn.

However, despite the chaos, the last launch in the starboard column somehow managed to land its commandos safely. Having done so, the launch took off some thirty of the crew of the *Campbeltown*. Some others embarked on the motor torpedo boat, which brought up the rear; this also fired two delayed-action torpedoes into lock gates leading into the main basin by the submarine pens.

The motor launches in the port column had orders to land at the Old Mole. This was a stone projection, marked by a lighthouse, some twenty-five feet above water level. It had a ramp on one side, but landing was a suicidal task not only because of the gun positions but because of the danger of grenades being tossed into the boats from up above.

Several launches tried to land their men but were beaten back. David Paton, the doctor, was on one of these:

When we got near, I saw what was to be my medical inspection room, the pillbox, and there was an anti-aircraft gun on top. One little German had the courage to get a clip of four shells and carry it up the stairs all by himself to his gun, shove it into his gun and prepare to fire it. He was following me, and I said: 'Why's he following me?' Then I realized I'd got the white badge with the red cross on it – I was the only obvious thing on the ship. So I took it off and stuffed it in my blouse.

Then he didn't follow me any more. He elevated the gun a bit and started to fire. There was a corporal beside me on the deck busy firing at something he could see on the land, so I said: 'Oi, there's a chap going to kill us over there.' He said: 'I've got plenty of time here, doc.' Then this chap fired his four shells. One landed about ten yards from his gun, so he elevated it a bit. The next one landed about twenty yards from his gun. The third one disappeared into my ship, and the fourth one went past me. I only found out on the way back that the one that went into the ship had hit a stanchion below deck where the engineer was sitting making his calculations – and he was still sitting there. It hadn't gone off, because it was an anti-aircraft shell and it would only go off at 22,000 feet!

The stuff was raining on us, like stair-rod rain. I heard it said that our skipper counted an area of a foot with eighty bullet marks in it. That was an area of these big cork rafts they have. Carley floats they call them. It's marvellous we floated.

We got lost – we overshot and had to come back – and we got into the Old Mole on the town side. We crunched against something as we got there; it was probably another motor launch. We put up ladders, and all these ladders were immediately pushed into the sea from above; the Germans just pushed, so we couldn't climb up the ladders. A chap in the Enniskillen Fusiliers, Dragoons or something – he's dead now – he climbed up on to a soldier's shoulders and used his Bren gun. Up above him – I saw this happen – a German tin hat appeared, and then more of the tin hat and then the chap's eyes. Then he fired his Bren gun. He said: 'I think I blew his head off.' As the gun kicked, he fell off the shoulders and finished up on the deck. I went down beside him, and he said: 'I think I killed that chap.' I said: 'Will you go back up there to see?' But he couldn't get back up.

While the commandos were fighting to get the landing ladders in place, they also faced a barrage of what David Paton at first took to be stones:

Things about the size of your wrist were rolling off, and the chaps on board were kicking these things as they fell. I said to a sailor: 'What's all this, these stones?' He said: 'Them's not stones, sir, them's bombs.' So I started kicking them too! None of them went off. I think they were British bombs, because the Germans used a stick bomb. I think these were probably Mills bombs left behind by the British Army when they left St-Nazaire after the Dunkirk episode. We probably left millions of Mills bombs there, and that's what they were throwing at us – but either they didn't go off because they were British, or they didn't go off because they hadn't got time.

Having failed to land the soldiers in one place, the skipper pulled out and tried another. David Paton recalled:

The boat that was going to give us protection when we landed was on fire, burning happily – it looked like an American sort of gaming boat. It was all on fire inside, and burning very fiercely. In the water was a chap shouting: 'ML, ML.' He had his hand up, so I got him by the arm and pulled him right in like a fish. He started panting like a little puppy. I said: 'This is a fine time to get an attack of asthma.' He said: 'It's not asthma, doc.' I said: 'What is it?' He said: 'This thing's too tight.' Remember, we had these Mae Wests [military slang for inflatable lifejackets, named after the film actress]. It was just half a tyre. You put it on, then you brought this half-tyre around with a very long linen thing, and you tied it in front. He had tied it tight, and going into the water it had shrunk, and he couldn't breathe. I used my dagger to try and free him, but of course the dagger wouldn't cut it. I had a big pair of scissors in a pocket, so I took them out and cut it, and he got a big breath and was delighted.

There was another shout of 'ML, ML', another hand in the water. This time it was David Birney [a commando from the launch in front of them]. I could see him, because there was so much glow from searchlights. I got my hand round his wrist, and he got his hand round mine, and we pulled. At that moment the skipper put on full speed reverse and towed the launch out into the clear water. Our hands parted, and he was found the following morning dead half a mile down the river.

David Birney had been supposed to lead an assault party to knock out the guns on the Old Mole. Because they were unable even to land, let alone deal with the guns, the commandos who followed were heading into the jaws of death.

In all the chaos, the skipper of David Paton's launch realized it would be impossible to land his men anywhere on the Old Mole, so had decided to withdraw. Even before this happened, pulling men out of the water was not exactly an easy task, as David Paton explained:

The flames were licking all over the water. It's a strange expression, but that's what they do. When you put your hand into them, you don't feel burned but the hairs become fish-hooks: they all burn at the ends.

As the motor launch retreated down the estuary, David Paton was busy dealing with the injured. However, he also had an unexpected call on his medical supplies – from the engineer:

> He said: 'Have you got any sticky tape left?' I said: 'I've got bags of it.' He said: 'Well, all the tubes are busy leaking everywhere, and I've run out of sticky tape.' I had lots and lots of Elastoplast, so he used that to keep his ship afloat.

Des Chappell, who was in the last boat in the port column behind *Campbeltown*, recalled the sense of helplessness they felt when they, too, were forced to retreat:

> When we got to the Old Mole, we found that the launches in front of us, a lot of them had been set on fire, and we couldn't possibly get in there. The sea was burning. One of the worst memories I have is seeing people – I don't know whether they were soldiers or sailors – swimming in the burning water and shouting, 'Pick me up, pick me up,' and we were saying, 'We'll pick you up on the way back,' knowing damned well we couldn't do it.

The only launch in this column to land its men successfully contained Bill Pritchard, the demolitions expert. Dick Bradley remembered his reassuring presence just before they landed:

> Captain Pritchard came round and offered each one a drop of brandy from the bottle. Well, I took a little drop – it wouldn't have mattered if he hadn't come with it – but it was very nice. Everybody got ready to land, and we had an Australian seaman who got off and he tied us on. To me it looked perfect.

Tiger Watson recalled the bravery of the launch skipper:

> The commander of my ML was quite a well-known yachtsman called Tom Collier. He would be in his mid-twenties. We

got on so well, the soldiers and the sailors there. He said: 'Well, if things get sticky for you on shore, I'll be waiting to take you off. I won't leave you.' I often wonder whether if he'd made smoke he'd have got out, but he did wait for us and, of course, they got him.

There was a lot of self-sacrifice that went on unrecorded in the darkness and the whole confusion that we'll never really know about, among those naval people. I've got a great deal of admiration for them. They hadn't volunteered to go to St-Nazaire; they had volunteered for the Navy, and the Navy just sent them. That's rather different.

The scene as they landed was chaotic, as Tiger Watson recalled:

Coming up to the Old Mole I was conscious of some horrible screaming from a motor launch that was on fire. There was another motor launch coming out full speed astern, and I thought: 'Good, they've landed their troops.' We also saw as we approached on the skyline some Germans running away with their hands up. I could easily have mowed them down, but I don't shoot at people with their hands up normally, so I thought they must be surrendering to our own chaps. In fact, they were just using that as a ruse to get away.

My orders were that at all costs we must hold the Old Mole. That was our disembarkation point, and even if I got no further I should stay put and hold off the enemy.

His first thought was to deal with the pillbox, which had been sheltering Germans as they shot at the motor launches.

There was a ladder against it – it was newly made, still smelled of wet concrete. As I climbed up, the captain, Bill Pritchard, who was in charge of the whole demolition operation, said: 'What the hell do you think you're doing, Tiger? For God's sake, get on.'

They assumed that the Germans they had seen with their hands up had abandoned the pillbox and would be prevented from returning by the British soldiers in front of them. In fact, as we have seen, there were no troops in front of them. The launch they had seen going full astern was only doing so because her engine had been jammed into reverse; she was unable to land her men. The Germans were to return to the pillbox and wreak further devastation. Had Tiger disobeyed the order to leave the pillbox alone, many lives would have been saved.

Tiger Watson was in charge of the protection party for a demolition group. However, they came under disastrously heavy fire, as Dick Bradley recalled:

Our party started going towards our object, which was to put all our demolition packets on different parts of the bridge going across the entry for the U-boats. We were walking towards them very slowly. It would have been better if we'd have gone fast, but we couldn't because these rucksacks were so heavy – all our demolition packets were in ruck-sacks ready made. As we walked along, all of a sudden I thought somebody had given me a heavy push, and then I could feel blood running down my back and front, and I just sank down and that was the end of me. Tiger Watson gave me a morphine injection – don't know where he found the time from, but he did, and they left me there.

A bullet had hit my chest, gone through the lung and come out the back. Having had this morphine injection, I gradually lost consciousness, and while I was losing consciousness I was thinking of my mother more than anybody else, you know, and maybe said a prayer, thinking that might be the end of Dickie.

I kept coming to. Two of our men ran past me, and one shouted to the other: 'Oh, he's a goner.' I well remember that. The next thing I knew when I was half-conscious again there were two German soldiers standing there, and one said to his friend [in German]: 'I'm going to put a bullet through him in case he plays a trick on us.' The other one said: '*Nein*. Leave him alone. He's dead.' Of course, I kept more still than ever.

Despite his semi-conscious state, Dick Bradley had no problems understanding the Germans' conversation, as his family had originally come from Germany. (He had changed his name from Goebbels to Bradley just before the war.) He was taken to an air-raid shelter, where his wounds were dressed by some French women, but eventually he was captured.

Careful precautions had been taken against friendly fire, but there were still occasions when the commandos ended up shooting their own side by mistake. Tiger Watson recalled:

We were playing cowboys and Indians round some railway carriages, and the Germans were very close. Suddenly, this shadow leaped out with his hand raised, and instinctively I fired, and probably others did too. When he fell, to our horror we saw that he'd got scrubbed gaiters on, and therefore he was one of our people. I said to the others, 'Hold your fire,' went out, confirmed this and gave him some morphia, but I think he was a goner. He was still shuddering, but I think he was dying. We didn't know who he was. Of course, you can't hesitate when you're at very close quarters – it's the chap who fires first who lives.

One of our demolition party got shot in the shoulder by one of our own people, and Micky [Michael Burn] says that he saw a man that he thought he should take a beat at with his pistol, and as he turned his head it was me. I'm not sure whether he might have mistaken somebody else for me, but anyway he didn't shoot, thank goodness.

Burt Shipton, who was in Bill Pritchard's demolition control party, recalled Pritchard's enthusiasm for using his skills at every possible opportunity. The group's main targets were a lock gate and a swing bridge – but that did not stop Pritchard from laying charges on two tugs in the dock on the way:

> It didn't make a very loud bang – it was more like a thump than a bang – but the hissing afterwards [from the ships' boiler rooms] was quite something. You could hardly hear yourself talk.

Apparently unmoved by the danger from the soldiers all around, Pritchard then went on to check on progress elsewhere. He was killed by a German on the way. Some accounts suggest that he was bayoneted. Philip Walton, a schoolteacher, was also killed in a single-handed attempt to lay charges on the swing bridge. In fact, the commandos' failure to blow up this bridge – known in the battle plan as Bridge D – was something they were later able to turn to their advantage.

Burt Shipton recalled what happened to him and two of his fellow commandos after Pritchard left them by the exploding tugs:

> When we started to move off, the whole place became like a stage – it was light. So we feigned death, just fell on the floor and stayed there. I saw some railway wagons, so I thought the best thing for us three to do was get near the railway wagons, because we were absolutely out in the open. When we got there, I saw these two great colanders – they're cable drums really; they have an inside where they put all the cables. The three of us got inside: there was Jimmy Deans, myself and Chetwynd. Unfortunately, the damned thing was facing towards the top of the submarine pens, and somebody let us have a burst. I didn't get a thing, but Jimmy just sank, Chetwynd just sank. I got down to them, they gave a gurgle each, and that was it. They were dead.
>
> I knew Jimmy Deans well; he'd only been married six weeks. I didn't know Chetwynd at all, but he did tell me that

his wife had just had a baby, and he hadn't seen it. I was lucky, there's no doubt about that.

Extricating himself from the cable drum, he set off towards Bridge D (this was before Philip Walton was killed there):

I looked around, couldn't find anything anywhere, so I went under the bridge and I saw this pivot, and I thought, 'My God, it'd take a hundred blokes to blow that.' It was a really big bridge – a miniature sort of Tower Bridge – it lifted up and swung round.

Anyway, I clambered out underneath that, and when I got on to the road I could see there was a sort of armoured car, and the Germans were starting to come towards the bridge. I ran into the old town, cautiously, very cautiously, and I met all sorts of German groups there. They were shouting and giving commands and searching. So I obviously went the opposite way to which they were coming, but I got back on to the alleyway that brought me out towards the Old Mole, where I bumped into Tiger Watson and his crowd.

People were gradually coming in twos and threes to re-embark again to go home. Of course, I knew very well they weren't going to get home, because I'd seen all the ships just burning by the jetty. Tiger said that you fight your way over the bridge, and that it was every man for himself. Well, I'd been up that bridge, and I knew what it was like, so I wasn't going to go again. So I thought I would look for a spot where I could hide away somewhere, and perhaps nip aboard a fishing fleet and get taken out to sea – perhaps they might even take me home if I bribed them well enough.

Unfortunately, as I was mooching along between these two warehouses I came across Dai Davies, who had been very badly wounded in the ankle on the *Campbeltown*, and he was hobbling, he was in dead trouble. So I decided I would stay with him, and I thought the best thing to do was to find a place. We went into the side of this warehouse, and there were loads of corrugated paper and flat boxes, so I pulled a few of these away and made a little entrance. It was very small, but at least inside there was a little cubbyhole we could get into.

As daylight came, however, they were discovered and taken prisoner by the Germans.

TROUBLE AT
THE OLD MOLE

Meanwhile, the other survivors and walking wounded were assembling at the Old Mole, where they realized that their troubles were only just beginning, as Tiger Watson explained:

> We were appalled once we saw the river again to see just flaming hulks burned down to the very water's edge, and no whole ships at all. Although there was a lot of shooting going on, everything went absolutely silent for a moment or two. We suddenly realized that the alternative plan would have to be used.
>
> The colonel called the officers and said, 'Well, chaps, we've missed the boat home,' or words to that effect. 'We'll have to walk.' Now, we had been briefed that if you were left behind and you got out of the town you should make for Spain, but you mustn't declare yourself to Franco's police, who were pro-fascist. You should get to Gibraltar, and if you were captured you were to say, '*Prisionero de guerra escapado*', because if you were an escaped prisoner, according to the Geneva Convention you should be repatriated. If you were escaping from a battle you would be interned.
>
> I remember saying to the colonel: 'So it's *prisionero de guerra escapado*, is it, sir?' And he said: 'That's right, Tiger.

We're going to have to shoot our way out. Tommy gunners to the front.' Well, I was a Tommy gunner, so I went in the front. One of my demolition chaps, Corporal Wheeler, who escaped to Spain [he was one of only five to do so], said: 'Why don't you come with us? We're going to make a break that way.' I said: 'I can't do that, because I'm part of the assault force in front.' So I lost my opportunity of escaping, but I'd probably have got bumped off somewhere else.

Tiger Watson recalled the moment when he tried to shoot at a sniper, but found that his Tommy gun's magazine was empty:

We came to a corner where there was a German who kept on popping out and taking a shot at us. Donald Roy [the kilted Scot] was walking up the centre of the road, flinging grenades right, left and centre. I was being more orthodox, and was running up the wall on the side – but, of course, it's a difficult angle to shoot at. You've got to lean out from the wall, and you have to expose yourself in order to shoot right-handed. I must have wasted a few bullets, anyway.

Then I thought: 'Right, I must now come out, and before he reappears I must get there first.' He reappeared, and I squeezed the trigger of my Thompson sub-machine gun. Of course, the magazine was empty. I just ran on with no clear idea of what I was going to do, but that I must stop him, because he was going to damage us if I didn't. Then the rifle was swung round, and I thought: 'This is it. I deserve this after making such a mess of everything.' I was lucky, because the bullet was so close – it was about ten yards away, I think – that it went straight through. It broke my humerus, my upper arm bone, and it went straight out. If it had been a few inches that way, I wouldn't be here, and if it had been a few inches the other way, maybe I'd have been able to beat him. I don't know what I'd have done – kicked him in the goolies, I expect. I don't know – something very ungentlemanly!

As he fell to the ground, other members of the party picked up the Tommy gun and his pistol, leaving him with just his Commando knife.

> Shortly after they'd gone, two Germans cautiously came round the road with their rifles presented. I said: 'It's all right. You don't have to be frightened. I can't hurt you.' I think my voice reassured them in a way, because they did shoot one or two of our people on the ground. Scared men with rifles are dangerous men. They saw that I was wounded and got me to my feet. Then they found my fighting knife and started screaming at me.
>
> It was then that Gerard Brett came round and said: 'Well, what's the difference between a fighting knife and those bayonets that you've got?' Then they calmed down. Besides, it was going to be a jolly good souvenir – wasn't it, a fighting knife? – and I was an *Offizier* anyway.
>
> I think they were particularly frightened of the fact that we could move silently, because we had rubber-soled boots, and you could hear them in their boots crashing along all the time. We were the silent men of St-Nazaire, they said.
>
> When I was lying wounded, men came up to me and looked at my boots and said: 'Ah, *fallschirmjaeger*,' which means 'parachutist'. They said: 'You couldn't have come up the river – you would have to be very foolish or very brave.'

By one of those strange coincidences of history, the Commander-in-Chief of the German submarine forces had been visiting St-Nazaire at about the same time that the commandos set sail from Falmouth. He had asked the commander of the submarine flotilla, Herbert Sohler, what he would do if the British attacked St-Nazaire. Sohler replied that there were emergency plans, but such an attack was highly improbable.

Many accounts of the raid suggest that the Germans guarding St-Nazaire were not exactly crack troops – although reinforcements arrived later. Bob Montgomery explained:

They were not trained as infantrymen and in street-fighting. They were sailors, most of them; they were naval ack-ack brigade, and not the main chaps who were down along the coast. The chaps in St-Nazaire probably a lot of them were the cooks and bottle-washers. I should think they probably were very frightened. We were – but we knew what we were up to.

As Burt Shipton put it: 'I don't know how frightened they were – I've no idea, because I didn't bump into them. I made sure I didn't. My name's not James Bond!'

The original battle plan had called for the demolition of all the bridges surrounding the dock area. This would have created a relatively safe island for the commandos to re-embark on the motor launches. However, since the motor launches had either retreated or turned into floating bonfires, it was just as well they had not succeeded in destroying all the bridges. As they broke out of the dock, Bridge D – the bridge that Philip Walton had died trying to blow up – was a vital escape route. Without this, they would have been caught like prisoners in an exercise yard.

A protection party led by Donald Roy had knocked out a gun emplacement that covered the bridge. However, with snipers all around, the journey across was uncomfortably like Russian roulette. Frank Carr recalled:

The bridge was something like a large empty metal box, just a girder box, and the bullets were flying all around this thing, pinging from one to the other. We ran from one stanchion to the next and hid behind them. We were all pouncing down in time until we got to the other side, then we nipped down the road out of the range of the snipers.

By this time, those who had originally been in demolition parties were no longer encumbered with rucksacks full of explosives. However – unless they had been able to take a weapon from a dead German – they were armed only with pistols. Corran Purdon recalled:

The Germans by then were beginning to get a grip of the situation, and they were bringing in reinforcements. I remember seeing an armoured car coming along spitting fire. It sealed off one way that we thought we were going to go, and it was after that we did what we call the St-Nazaire obstacle race, where we went through people's houses and got over their garden fences into the next lot of terraced houses and so on.

Frank Carr recalled:

The Germans had lots of guns on the crossroads, and road-blocks. We were OK, because we were rather silent with our rubber-soled boots, but you could hear the Germans dashing along and yelling to each other, so we couldn't stick to the roads. We had to take short cuts across blocks of buildings and over back gardens – even through houses. I remember one house we went through, the table was set for breakfast next day, and we all tramped through this. I think one of the lads said they ended up in a chicken coop.

If anyone got too close to us or threatened us, we fired, but if they didn't we just let them walk on by. Someone was telling us that two German groups were actually shooting at each other because they heard someone at the other end walking. They hadn't realized that they were not going to hear us anyway. They heard these feet clamping on the road and they thought, 'Ah, Englanders,' and started shooting each other up, to the great delight of us.

But we ran out of steam eventually. Colonel Newman said: 'We'll have to look for a place to hide.' We saw a big house, which was open-fronted, and went inside and had a look. There was a nice cellar down below, a rather deep one, and we thought: 'Well, it's worth a try. We'll hole up here and see if we can wait until nightfall tomorrow, and then carry on and get through the town and vanish.'

We were rather unlucky, because it transpired that the German headquarters was directly opposite. They conducted a house-to-house search, and, of course, they came across us quite easily. They never showed themselves, but they had these potato masher grenades ready to drop down, and there wasn't a thing we could do about it. It would only have taken one of those and it would have cleaned us right out in the cellar, so Colonel Newman thought: 'Well, let's call it a day.' He just went up. I didn't hear what he said exactly, but he said to us: 'Righto, chaps, come on up.' We went up and there was a whole line of Germans solid across to the headquarters on the other side. We had a big grin when we saw where we were.

Bob Montgomery, who was also in the cellar, recalled:

Tony Terry, who spoke fluent German, was put at the door. We started stuffing morphine into people who were badly wounded, and taking bits out [from the wounds]. Somebody took a bit out of my behind. We were fairly quiet down there. They were obviously searching all the houses, and we thought we'd got away with it because they were just about to go out when there was a shout from up above, saying: 'Have you looked in the cellar?' And at that stage they started coming down to the cellar and Charles told Tony to say that we surrendered. Why they didn't just chuck a couple of grenades into the cellar I do not know. I think if I'd been them I would have. But they didn't, and so I'm alive to tell the tale.

By now it was getting light, and the unspoken question in all the commandos' minds was: when was the *Campbeltown* going to go up? Bill Etches, who was too severely wounded to move out of the cellar without help, remembered lying on a table in a morphine haze as he watched the others being taken away:

Charles Newman came across to me and gripped my hand. I knew what he meant: 'Don't tell 'em about the bloody explosives [on board the *Campbeltown*].' I wasn't about to tell them anything.

Those who could move were marched out of the cellar and searched, as Frank Carr recalled:

They took any weapons we had, and they looked for documents – which, of course, we weren't carrying – lots of watches were purloined, and even razors were taken away. They overlooked the fact that we carried a knife [in a pocket of their combat trousers]. We didn't think about it, because in fact we wouldn't have given it up voluntarily, anyway. I think one chap must idly have shown it somehow or other, I don't know how. The officer in command there, who was a bit of a desk wallah, I expect, he flew into an enormous rage, had everybody stripped and searched. Oh, he was going frantic. 'You're hiding weapons, you haven't surrendered all your weapons.' Germans don't like knives at all, any more than we do, really. I think the whole idea of them is unsoldierly, not the thing to do.

But they subjected Colonel Newman to rather embarrassing searches. Of course, being the man he was, he just took it and shrugged it off. There was a little office place, a spare room, and they lined up everybody with no clothes on. The door opened, and a proper soldier walked in, an officer, and he said, 'Stop this nonsense now,' in German, and said, 'Everybody get dressed.'

I think this chap was not used to fighting at all, and faced with us he was extremely worried. He must have been, when he saw the knife. I expect he thought he was going to be attacked, but they already had half a dozen or so people in there with sub-machine guns, so there wasn't much we could do in the attacking line with the toothpicks that we had.

Some commandos became separated from the group and were captured individually. One of these was Bob Hoyle, who had decided to try crossing Bridge D underneath, rather than dodging bullets on the top:

> I just crawled under the bridge a bit. I thought: 'Well, I'm out of sight here, and I can think about what I might do.' But then I gradually realized that my options weren't very great, because having seen all the mayhem on the river I couldn't see myself dropping into the river and trying to make my way out that way. The only option that seemed to me was to wait until there was perhaps a lot of people rushing about and there might be some French people. If I could just get hold of one, he might help me. But that didn't materialize, because after a while there were so many Germans there it was unbelievable. Eventually, they came and they rooted under the bridge, and I just had to come out and hold my hands up.

He was still trouserless, having had to abandon them after they were set on fire when he fell down a hole in the deck on *Campbeltown*. This was to lead to a misunderstanding, as he explained:

> Later that day, when they marched us through the town, the French people there thought I was Scottish. I had a big long scarf that I was wearing, and they thought: 'Oh, a kilt. It's the Scottish who go to war with a kilt and no trousers on.'

As the commandos were rounded up, they were kept captive in a variety of places. Some of those who had been on motor launches ended up in a building in the dock area. Among these was Eric de la Torre, who recalled:

> When I walked in there were about twenty or thirty men in there, and I immediately thought we were the sole survivors. They brought a seaman in who had been fished out of the

water. He was unconscious, and we tried to bring him round, but he died on the table in the room.

On the way over I was reading *White Maa's Saga* by Eric Linklater. White Maa is a type of gull, and this was a story of a medical student in Scotland. Before we landed I tucked this book inside my battledress. I said to myself, I'm going to finish this book, so I was the only person who had a book among all those who were captured. Of course, it was soaking wet, but I finished it, and then it went round other prisoners.

Other captured commandos were held in a café in nearby La Baule. Here, they started a panic after they picked up some abandoned cues and began playing a game of billiards. Burt Shipton explained:

Some German joker rushed in and said: '*Nicht, nicht, nicht* – don't you understand?' He wanted to take all the cues off us because he thought we were going to use them as truncheons of some sort.

Buster Woodiwiss, who was also playing billiards, remembered that the officer hit the guard and smashed the cues in his agitation.

Michael Burn recalled his capture:

After I was captured, I walked past the *Campbeltown*, embedded in the dry dock. It was already well past the time when she was due to explode. I met Sam Beattie [the *Campbeltown* commander], who'd been captured in the river during the night. We both tried not to look too curious about the *Campbeltown*, but we were uncomfortably close to her at one point. Both of us must have been thinking – I certainly was – 'Why hasn't she gone up already, an hour ago, and is she going up any moment now, in which case I shall go with her?' A number of us were in that state.

I remember also being photographed. I saw a film team,

and I thought, 'This is for propaganda,' so I put my hands up in the V-sign, and that got home. A photograph of me went through the British Embassy in Stockholm, which was neutral, of course, and it got home to Combined Operations headquarters, and ultimately to my parents.

Meanwhile, out at sea, the battle was by no means over. The last boat in the port column behind *Campbeltown*, which had been unable to land, hit trouble when they reached the Bay of Biscay. They were just reloading their Bren guns when they found themselves surrounded by German ships, as Des Chappell recalled:

> One detached himself from the rest and came towards us. He put on his searchlight, which fell directly on us. At the same time, he opened fire and came at us like a bloody great carving knife. He raked along our side, and he gave us a pasting then with some small arms stuff. I found myself shot in my left leg and my right thigh. I slid forward on the deck and was hanging over the side, with my legs dangling down towards the water. I wasn't in the water, but somebody came and pulled me back.
>
> This fellow went around and gave us another pasting and shouted out in English: 'Have you had enough?' We just fired back at him. We thought we'd had it in any case.

Several men had fallen overboard after the German destroyer's first attempt at ramming the launch. One lost his toes in the propeller; others drowned. The naval captain died after his leg was blown off. Des Chappell ended up unconscious, with shrapnel in his brain. Ralf Batteson, a naval gunner on the boat, recalled: 'The size of the guns and the amount of guns – there's no comparison. We were just like using peashooters against a blooming tank.'

The most conspicuous piece of resistance came from Tom Durrant, who was wounded but carried on shooting until the end. Ralf Batteson recalled:

He'd got his own machine gun, and when our gunner on the twin Lewis gun got knocked down, he went and got on that, because it fired bigger bullets than the gun he had. He asked for people to supply him with rounds of ammunition. He fired one burst at the German destroyer and broke the glass in the wheelhouse and came very close to hitting the skipper on the bridge. He kept firing – he was riddled with bullets. You'd wonder how he could actually survive with that many holes in him.

Ralf Batteson recalled what happened when he went to try to pick him up after they had eventually surrendered:

He was a lot heavier than me, and with him being covered in blood I couldn't really get a grip on him. I said: 'Come on – we'll get you on to the destroyer.' Well, I just couldn't – so he said: 'Leave me. Go and help somebody else. I'm finished.' He was a very brave man.

Corran Purdon, who was later to have the unpleasant task of identifying the dead commandos, counted twenty-seven bullets in his body. Tom Durrant was posthumously awarded the Victoria Cross on the recommendation of the German skipper who had seen his bravery at such close quarters.

As daylight came, and survivors on land were being flushed out of their various hiding places by German troops, the one question in everyone's minds was: why hadn't the *Campbeltown* blown up – and was she going to? They all knew that the explosives in the bows had been set on a long-delay fuse – but the ship had been supposed to explode a couple of hours after they landed.

By mid-morning the ship was crowded with German sightseers and souvenir-hunters, completely unaware that they were aboard a floating bomb. The survivors of the bloody sea battle with the German destroyer had anchored nearby and were being taken ashore under guard. They had grandstand views of what happened next, as Ralph Batteson recalled:

> The Germans were lined up alongside their boat looking out at the damage that had been done in St-Nazaire, and one of them shouted down: 'There's a boat you won't use again in this war.' I looked over to where he was pointing, and there was the *Campbeltown* stuck half-in and half-out of the dock gates. He'd hardly got the words out of his mouth when she went up. There was such a bang – you've never heard anything like it. It blew the ship to pieces, and as that went up and blew the lock gates to bits, the suction dragged the *Campbeltown* back into the water. But first of all there was a wave coming out of the dock, and it rocked the boat that we were on – we were going up and down like being in a rough sea. There was dust and debris coming down – the ship's sides and wood, bits of arms and legs and bodies... there were about a hundred killed, if not more than that.

Michael Burn recalled:

> We were all trying to hide our curiosity about what happened to the *Campbeltown*. Then suddenly, Sam Beattie was being interrogated, and rather scoffed at by a German interrogator, who said: 'How can you British be so stupid as to think you can put out of order a dry dock with such a flimsy destroyer? We'll have her towed away by this afternoon.' At that moment, she went up, and all the windows were blown in in the room where he was being interrogated. We cheered, of course – it was a great release. If she had not gone up, it would have been too awful. It would have meant that we would have succeeded brilliantly in ramming the dock, but something had gone wrong with the demolitions. Nobody quite knows why the explosion was delayed, but it was complete and total.

Corran Purdon recalled:

It was a thunderous explosion, and there was no doubt about it – that was *Campbeltown* going up. Everyone gave an enormous cheer, and the Germans got a bit agitated then.

All those on board HMS *Campbeltown* – most of them on the upper deck – were killed, as were large numbers of bystanders. German estimates of the numbers of dead put the figure at around 100; French sources suggested it was nearer 380.

However, after the euphoria of realizing that they had succeeded in their aim, the captured and wounded were left to face the reality of their individual futures. Many propaganda pictures were taken of the bandaged and bleeding casualties as they were loaded on to lorries to face the painful, jolting journey to hospital. They were taken to the incongruously grand setting of a fashionable luxury hotel just a few miles away at La Baule. Bill Etches recalled:

> The casino was turned into an emergency hospital, and we were laid out on the floor of the casino. I could see there must have been sixty people there, some very seriously wounded, some less wounded. I suppose I was lucky – I was one of the less seriously wounded. The German naval doctors were doing their best, but they hadn't got any anaesthetics – no anaesthetic to spare for me, anyway – and they tried to remove the splinters from my leg without it, by putting probes in. I let them know that that was not my favourite occupation.

Corran Purdon recalled:

> We were made to lie on the carpet – I've an idea there were palliasses on it – and we were made to put on the most bloody awful sort of white smock things. In spite of the fact that everyone was obviously pretty wounded, the Germans walked about, threatening us with Tommy guns. There was bugger all we could do. I mean, we hadn't got any weapons

or anything. I think probably then I had the lowest morale I've
ever had in my life, quite honestly. I know Stuart Chant said
to me: 'I think they'll come and rescue us, you know, they'll
come in on the beach and they'll take us away.' What a hope.

The dry dock was put out of action for seven years, freeing the
Atlantic from the threat of the *Tirpitz*. The mission had been a
success – but at a terrible price. Of the 611 men who took part
in the operation, fewer than half made it home. A total of
169 were killed, and 215 taken prisoner.

In their prison camps afterwards, the survivors endlessly
reran the events of that night in their head. Would fewer British
men have been killed if the RAF had been less scrupulous about
where they put their bombs? What if the Navy had been able to
provide destroyers instead of tiny motor launches?

Those who managed to escape encountered only the
dimmest understanding from many at home of what they had
been through. David Paton recalled the moment when his
motor launch finally reached Falmouth:

The ships in the harbour all blew their hooters. There was a
brigadier dressed up in his riding boots who welcomed us
home. He pointed to me and he said: 'You. Where are your
prisoners?' I said: 'I'm the doctor. I've got no prisoners.'

Some of the commandos felt that the RAF had let them down,
and they booed at the RAF ambulances that came to pick up
the wounded. David Paton recalled:

I went up and spoke to the ambulance drivers and said:
'Forget it. It's not you they're booing; it's just something that
happened out there. They don't hold anything against you.'

The story of Churchill's political orders to the RAF, which was
the reason for the limited bombing raid, was made public only
after the war. It was only then, too, as the commandos and sailors

returned from their prison camps, that the individual stories of bravery became known. Altogether, five Victoria Crosses were won at St-Nazaire, and six of the survivors whose accounts appear in this book won the Military Cross. The two command-ers – Charles Newman and Bob Ryder – were awarded VCs. Newman was taken prisoner, but Ryder managed to return to England in a motor launch after a series of ferocious gun battles. One of his gunners, Bill Savage, was awarded a posthumous VC. The fifth VC went to Sam Beattie, in command of HMS *Campbeltown*. The medal citation noted that this was awarded 'in recognition not only of his own valour but also of that of the unnamed officers and men of a very gallant ship's company'.

Looking back, some commandos have their doubts about the raid. As Burt Shipton put it:

> All the heroes are in the cemetery. There was too much death. Your own mates were being killed, parents were losing their sons, wives were losing their husbands, children were losing their fathers. Sometimes I wonder whether it was worth it.

Michael Burn, however, disagreed:

> I think that it could have been less dangerously organized, but I think it was worth it not so much for what it achieved tactically or strategically or politically, but for the effect it had on morale in Britain and in France. From then on, the French realized that the rest of the free world was not stand-ing by apathetically.

The French Prime Minister, M. Ramadier, summed up this feel-ing as he awarded the *Croix de Guerre* to Newman and Ryder in 1947. He said simply: 'You were the first to give us hope.'

PART THREE

Pirates of the Sand Seas

DESERT SCORPIONS

Working behind enemy lines in the North African desert added whole new dimensions of danger. The constant risk of discovery and destruction was compounded by all the natural hazards of a hostile environment. Here, in this waterless wilderness, soldiers had to survive carrying all they needed in their vehicles. They had to be independent – or die.

By a strange paradox, members of the Long Range Desert Group (LRDG), one of the most effective special forces units of the Second World War, came from two of the greenest, coolest countries you could think of: Britain and New Zealand. Operating in the bewildering extremes of glaring heat and freezing cold that make up the desert climate, they penetrated up to 1,000 miles into enemy territory. They worked in small, independent columns, and their first and most important role was reconnaissance. But as the war progressed, their brief widened. They kept road watches and harried enemy soldiers, emerging suddenly and unexpectedly to raid key bases and attack lines of communication. The Italians called them *Pattuglia Fantasma* (Ghost Patrol), and they chose as their insignia the scorpion: small, deadly and hard to spot until you feel its sting.

The battles of the North Africa campaigns of 1940–43 were fought mainly along the narrow coastal strip bordering the

Mediterranean. Inland was the Libyan Desert, an arid waste-land the size of India, and vast, apparently impenetrable tracts of sand. Navigating across these featureless sand seas, with their hidden depths and dangers, posed the same problems as navigating at sea. This was the area the Long Range Desert Group made their home. They established a chain of supply dumps for refuelling so they could travel ever greater distances, feeding a steady stream of intelligence back to HQ. The information they provided was crucial in the series of events that led to the Axis surrender in May 1943.

The origins of the Long Range Desert Group go back to the period between the wars and the enthusiasm of a group of friends led by one man: Major Ralph Bagnold of the Royal Signals. Major Bagnold had served as a sapper officer in France in the First World War, and had then been posted to Egypt. Here, he devoted every spare moment to exploring the desert.

One road hugged the coast from Cairo to Tunis, and a few branches led off it, but Bagnold's favourite territory was the wide, sandy expanses of deepest desert, uncharted and unexplored. Driving nothing more sophisticated than a Model T Ford, he would plunge off the road, navigating by a simple sun compass by day and the stars at night. Sometimes he would find himself following narrow wheel-tracks made by the Light Car Patrols of the First World War. Sometimes he would reach landmarks named by those earlier drivers – 'Williams Pass', 'Owston's Dump' – but more often than not he might as well have been driving on the moon.

As the expeditions developed, he moved on from the Model T to the Model A pick-up truck, and turned his practical mind to a variety of modifications to make the vehicles more desert-worthy. Rupert Harding-Newman, who joined Bagnold's trips in the 1930s, recalled some of them:

Spare springs were tied on to the vehicle in various places, but very little was allowed to be inside the body which couldn't be fitted in and secure. We took off mudguards and bonnets. We took off the bonnet altogether, and of course in those days the radiator was held by two steel tie rods, and you took those off because they were rigid, and we put on a wooden slat from the centre of the body to the centre of the radiator, which would allow it to move about. It wouldn't fall out because you had screws or metal to hold it in place, but it allowed the radiator and the body to move when you were going over really bad rough country, otherwise you would have torn your radiator to pieces. And of course we cut off the overflow pipe and put in a half-inch copper pipe, soldered into the radiator cap. That was then led with a big rubber tube down to a two-gallon tin on the running board which acted as a condenser, and if the car got hot the water would go into that and condense, and then it would be sucked out of the car and the radiator cooled off. One of the first jobs you had to do the first one or two nights was to listen at the radiator to see whether it was sucking air in round the radiator cap and therefore not drawing the water back from the tin.

By the time Harding-Newman joined Bagnold's hand-picked crew of enthusiasts, Bagnold himself had been posted to India. This did not stop his desert exploits, however. He simply drove overland from India to Cairo. One expedition in 1932 involved a round trip of over 6,000 miles of African desert – with considerable cost in rubber, as Harding-Newman explained:

In the old days, with the high-pressure tyre, if we had a lot of soft going you let the pressure down, so you got a bigger expanse of the tyre on the desert. But of course there the tendency was, you tore out the valve of the inner tube. That happened in '32, because Bagnold didn't want to go the normal way he had done before, he wanted to do a new way... the ground there was white limestone rocks, sharp edges, and in between, soft sand, and you wanted the tyres low down for the sand. I forget how many tubes and tyres we wrote off on that trip.

Luckily for them, the RAF stepped into the breach and flew out a supply of new tyres. Within a few years, wider nine-inch tyres were available which were considerably more practical. But it was all extra expense. There was some support from the Royal Geographical Society (the 1932 group included an Oxford geologist and an archaeologist), but generally money for the trips came from the members' own pockets. Rupert Harding-Newman, then only a subaltern, remembered taking out an overdraft to pay for his share. For this small group of dedicated explorers, the desert had become an addiction, as Harding-Newman noted:

> We knew we were going places where no one had been for a good many thousand years. Coming in in the evening, five o'clock time, you could really feel the silence, complete and utter silence. Very little sunset, of course. You didn't get a brilliant sunset as you do in England – the sun went down very quickly. But it was the most fascinating air.

Bagnold's explorations might simply have remained words on the pages of geographical journals had it not been for one of those lucky accidents which happen in wartime. He was on a troopship heading for a posting in Kenya when his ship had an accident in the Mediterranean, and had to put into Port Said for repairs. His presence was reported in a gossip column of the *Egyptian Gazette* as evidence that, at last, the War Office was making some efforts to put the right people in the right places. In fact, it was simply chance.

Italy had yet to enter the war, and there was little sense of urgency when Bagnold first put forward proposals for small, specially equipped patrols to carry out reconnaissance missions in the deepest desert. No doubt his superior officers were suspicious of his unconventional approach and unwilling to risk scarce resources on an experiment they felt was doomed to failure. But all that changed after Italy declared war on Britain in June 1940.

Suddenly, there was a desperate need to find out about the enemy's intentions in North Africa. The Italians had occupying forces in their colony of Libya, which stretched right up to the border of Egypt. The British had a strong military presence in Egypt, an ex-colony that had theoretically gained its independence but with which Britain had a defence agreement. If Italy could seize Egypt from the British, they would control the Suez Canal and access to British colonies in Asia and the Far East. Loss of Egypt would also cut off British access to the vital oilfields of the Middle East. General Sir Archibald Wavell, Commander-in-Chief of the new Middle East Command, needed to know if the Italians were ready for an immediate fight – or if he had time to await reinforcements for battle.

One way of finding this out was by sending patrols way behind enemy lines to check on numbers of men and equipment. Third time lucky, Bagnold sent a note to General Wavell. Within half an hour he found himself sitting in an armchair, explaining his plans. Rupert Harding-Newman recalled:

> Wavell said, 'Yes, this is the thing', and he gave him a chit, to all departments in the Army: 'Give this man, Major Bagnold, anything he wants at once' – and that was how it all started up.

Much to his disappointment, Harding-Newman was unable to join the newly formed group, as he was destined for a staff course in Haifa. But he was able to help them gather equipment and was later to have a role co-ordinating their operations. Bill Kennedy Shaw, an archaeologist, was one of the original Bagnold crew. He had been censoring newspapers with the Colonial Office in Palestine, but he jumped at the chance of joining what was initially named the Long Range Patrol Unit. As he put it in his account of the group:

> Here was the Army proposing to pay me to do what I had spent a lot of time and money doing for myself before the

war. In two weeks I was out of the Colonial Service and into the Army.

He was to remain as an intelligence officer throughout the desert campaign.

Edward Mitford, who had explored independently as far as Kufra, joined the group from the Royal Tank Regiment. He recalled his first meeting with Bagnold:

> I had read his books and that sort of thing, and I read a lot of books about the desert, but suddenly I had a telephone message from Major Bagnold saying, 'Come and see me', and I thought, 'This is going to be rather fun.' So I went and saw him, and he said: 'Will you come in to Long Range Patrols?' And I said: 'Yes, I'd love to.'
>
> I had no idea what was going on. But he then explained what was going to happen, that we were going to have New Zealand soldiers and we were going to have a series of patrols, and I would command one, going in to the desert, which I thought was the greatest fun. I had to get permission from the division I was in, Armoured Division, to leave them and go in to this extraordinary thing, you know, a sort of private army, and I was given permission to go, and that was grand.

The involvement of the New Zealanders was partly the result of a wartime accident very similar to the one that had led to Bagnold's presence in Egypt. The New Zealand Expeditionary Force had arrived in the Middle East without much of their arms and equipment, which had been lost at sea. This left them temporarily unable to take their place in the Western Desert. Bagnold went to see their commander, General 'Tiny' Freyberg, to ask if he would release some of his men. The request left Freyberg in something of a quandary, as David Lloyd Owen recalled in his history of the LRDG:

Freyberg appreciated that here was a great opportunity to get his men doing something really well worth while, but it also meant that his commanding officers might lose some of their best men, for Bagnold obviously wanted nothing less. He wondered also as to how the men would react to being under the command of those whom they were pleased to call 'Pommie bastards'. He must have been struck, nevertheless, as Wavell had been, by the sincerity of the tough, wiry little major who had come to ask for his help.

Freyberg recommended that they could go, and the men chosen as the first two New Zealand officers were given the task of sifting through 1,000 applications for the mystery mission.

Bagnold opted for the New Zealanders, in his own words, because he wanted 'responsible volunteers who knew how to look after things and maintain things, rather than the British tommy who is apt to be wasteful'. Many of them were farmers, used to maintaining vehicles and unfazed by the idea of long stretches in remote terrain. Bill Kennedy Shaw noted that they had a maturity and independence not found in British people of similar age:

Physically their own fine country had made them on average fitter than us, and they had that inherent superiority which in most of a man's qualities the countryman will always have over the townsman. Many were owner-drivers at home and therefore naturally disposed to take care of their cars, regarding them as a thing to be preserved rather than, as was sometimes the British attitude, as the property of an abstract entity, 'the government', whose loss or destruction was small concern of theirs.

In six weeks, the new desert group had gathered together the men – all volunteers – and the equipment it needed. It was decided that thirty hundredweight trucks would be best to carry the extra firepower needed for war. The Army had nothing suitable in Egypt, but Bagnold found fourteen with the Chevrolet Company in Alexandria, and nineteen more were begged second-hand from the Egyptian Army. Doors, cabs and windscreens were stripped off, extra leaves were added to the springs, and the trucks were modified to carry wireless sets, a sun-compass, condensers, machine guns, spare wheels and sand channels (heavy sheets of steel which could be put under the wheels to 'unstick' a car bogged down in sand). Each truck was as self-sufficient as possible, carrying enough water and food for the men to last three weeks, and enough petrol for a journey of over 1,000 miles. After intensive training in navigation and desert driving, and a couple of practice runs, the patrols were ready for action by the end of August 1940.

Bill Kennedy Shaw, in his history of the Long Range Desert Group, recalled the bewilderment of staff at GHQ in Cairo at some of their requests:

> We asked, for example, for sandals while everyone else wore boots; for an Egyptian shopkeeper's whole stock of trouser-clips, because there was nothing else to be had for holding maps to map-boards; for nautical almanacs, yet we were not sailors; for ten-ton diesel lorries, but we were not RASC [Royal Army Service Corps]; for a 4.5 howitzer, usually given only to Gunners; for Arab headdresses; for an apparently scandalous quantity of tyres (most army vehicles ran on roads or passable tracks); for two aircraft; for a paraffin-worked refrigerator to preserve the MO's [Medical Officer's] vaccines in the heat at Kufra.

Rupert Harding-Newman is convinced that without Bagnold's determination there would have been no Long Range Desert Group.

> There was no one else with the knowledge and the drive and the vision. All the people he had with him, none of them had

that sort of capacity – I think he led everything. There was no question about it that it was one of the best and most efficient private armies in the whole of the war, and it achieved far, far more than many others.

Part of the secret of Bagnold's success was that he was a perfectionist. Edward Mitford remembered:

He was absolutely keen on getting everything right. But he was a Royal Engineer, and they're all like that – mad, married or Methodist, he used to say.

Soldiers would find his meticulousness infuriating – all the more so since they knew he was right. An example Edward Mitford gave was his attitude towards the tedious chore of pumping tyres:

In that part of the world, if you were in soft sand you let your tyres down so they were flatter, and then of course you had to pump them up afterwards. Our soldiers didn't like doing that – they were fed up of pumping tyres. And one chap had said to himself obviously, 'Well, I've pumped it enough', and Bagnold came along and pointed to the tyre and said, 'Look – that's not done enough', and he said, 'Yes, it is', and Bagnold said, 'No, it isn't – do it.' And when Bagnold said 'do it', you had to do it, you see. And he marched off and the chap said, 'The trouble with that bugger, he's always right.' So there it was.

Information that the Long Range Desert Group could provide was needed urgently in the summer of 1940. In particular, Wavell needed to know if the Italians were building up troops at the oasis in Kufra. This was 700 miles across the dunes and waterless desert. Some officers were sceptical about the desert patrols' chances of success. They predicted that they would get lost or bogged down, or die of thirst – doom-mongering that largely arose through a deep-seated fear and ignorance of the desert. Wavell, however, came personally to wish Bagnold's patrols luck as they set out for their first active task. It was a sign of his confidence in the man to whom he had given carte blanche.

They were indeed venturing into the unknown, as Edward Mitford recalled:

> We started with no maps at all. We had bits of paper, ordinary bits of white paper with lines on – longitude and latitude lines which we then filled in – and by the time the thing was over we had filled in all the information that they wanted.

One patrol discovered the existence of the Kalansho Sand Sea the hard way – by running into it. They watched supply routes and observed bases. On occasions, the glaring sun was so unbearable that there was nothing to do at midday but crouch under tarpaulins stretched between the cars for shade.

Bill Kennedy Shaw described the debilitating effects of the Libyan *qibli* – a hot summer wind:

> Many countries have their hot winds: the *khamsin* of Egypt, the *sherqiya* of Palestine, the *harmattan* of West Africa. Add all these together and blow them, with sand to taste, northwards out of the gates of hell and you may begin to know what the *qibli* is like at Kufra in the summer.
>
> You don't merely feel hot, you don't merely feel tired, you feel as if every bit of energy had left you, as if your brain was thrusting its way through the top of your head and you want to lie in a stupor until the accursed sun has gone down.

After their first successful raid, during which they had captured a bag of official mail, they were able to tell Cairo that the Italians were not ready to start their invasion. Graziani, the Italian general in charge of the enemy offensive in Egypt, was short of transport. Wavell therefore gave Bagnold's crew a free hand to stir up as much trouble as possible to provide a diversion.

Communications were by army number 11 radio sets. These had been designed to work over a range of only thirty miles, but the Long Range Desert Group signallers using Morse communicated over ranges of more than 1,000 miles. By simultaneously popping up hundreds of miles apart in the desert for raids, they succeeded in exaggerating their own numbers and keeping the Italians busy. The Italians had assumed the natural barrier of the sand seas was their best defence, but they were being proved wrong. Soon, they were forced to withdraw forces from the front to protect convoys and airfields in the remotest spots of the desert.

Wavell, meanwhile, was able to buy time to call in armoured reinforcements, and in December 1940 he led 30,000 British troops to defeat 250,000 Italians. In the history of special forces, no other group started with such great success and proof of their value.

The Long Range Desert Group was never short of recruits, and many dropped rank so they could join. As the group expanded, the recruitment net was spread wider. Many had very little idea of what they were letting themselves in for. Arthur Arger, who was with the Yorkshire Hussars, a Territorial Army regiment, recalled the story of his war:

We had gone to France with horses and swords, and the Germans had tanks, so we thought, well, that's not a level playing field. So we went to Palestine and relieved some of the infantry, or whoever else was there, to come back to England. We were there in Palestine, and Dunkirk came and went, and Italy came in the war, and we never moved. And I thought, well, this isn't right, and I applied for various things like air gunner for the RAF. I applied to go and join the RAOC [Royal Army Ordnance Corps]. I went on a training test, passed it, and they still wouldn't let me go. I applied to go to war with Lord

Wingate's Commando, which was going down through the Sudan to attack the Italians in Ethiopia, but that didn't work. And then in about November 1940 this officer came round for personnel for the Long Range Desert Group. Not knowing anything about it, I applied. Desert – I think the desert part attracted me. So I applied for that, and I had this interview with him. There were quite a few lads on the same thing, and one of the things he asked me was: 'What are your hobbies?' Well, I wasn't a boxer or anything like that. I said I used to breed budgerigars. 'Oh,' he said, 'you'll do for me' – and that was it. I thought, I'm going to be in charge of a pigeon loft.

As things turned out, though, he felt he was as well qualified as the next man.

When Bagnold said, 'Right – I'm looking for people who can live together under adverse conditions in close proximity over long periods of time,' well, he wasn't looking for bruisers or thugs or anything like that. He was looking for people who were ordinary people who could do this sort of thing. He was right, because we were – all the yeomanry patrol – we were all Saturday-night soldiers. We weren't regulars or anything like that. We had enjoyed our Territorial Army days and now we were paying the bill.

Arthur Arger vividly remembered making friends with the rest of the group and being introduced to the trucks that were to be their home for weeks on end. Each team of men gave their truck a name; his was called 'Who Cares?'.

Then we went training how to negotiate trucks in the desert. Well, you haven't got to go far out of Cairo but there's a road – they used to call it the Military Road. It used to run from Cairo to Alexandria – not along the Nile; it cut across the desert. You could go past the pyramids and then you could go on to the desert and there were the sand dunes which you could try your luck on. And that's where the fun and games came in – how to negotiate sand dunes – which gave me the impression that the desert was all sand dunes.

However, it was not long before he found there was rather more to it.

You could go hundreds of miles on flat, hard ground, and then the next thing you can hit sand dunes that run to 2- or 300 feet high, and how the dickens do you get across that lot? Well, you go like a bat out of hell up to the top and take your foot off the accelerator when you're at the top, and then you tip over it. You can do it quite well after a bit of practice. But one lad misjudged it, and the truck went – they measured it up afterwards – ninety-six feet from where the truck left the top of the sand dune to where it landed at the other side. It shook them up a bit, that. I think there were a couple of broken ribs and a broken arm, but that was just unfortunate.

These were by no means the only injuries caused by the sand dunes; one soldier broke his back when his truck rolled over on top of him.

Driver Archie Gibson, who joined the LRDG from the Scots Guards, remembered how they learned to 'read' the textures of the sand:

Sometimes it would be sort of browny with a few pebbles and you would just sink in that, and a powdery dust would come up. Then other times, when you got the same conditions in another part of the desert, maybe Tunisia or something, it was beautifully hard. When you found hard going that was great. On the long straight plains when you could bat along at thirty-five, forty miles an hour, you could steer with your knee and we had competitions to see how you could roll cigarettes with one hand like the cowboys.

Alf Saunders, who was only nineteen when he arrived in Egypt from New Zealand, recalled the sheer boredom of long stretches of empty desert:

> Sometimes we'd sit back and steer with our feet... but we had to have a stick to push the throttle down. Oh, all sorts of bloody stupid things. In between the Egyptian Sand Sea and the Kalansho Sand Sea was 150 miles of absolute flat plain, and it's got little pebbles on about the size of a fingernail. That's where I taught our navigator to drive. And while he was driving, to stop the boredom, I got him to drive alongside another truck. You know what we used to do? I bet you won't believe it. Each of the drivers would get their bayonet, hang on to the side of the truck, and one of them would have a bloody bayonet fight while they're going at sixty miles an hour – now you know where all the bad drivers of today come from – just to break the monotony, you know.

Occasionally, they would take a pot shot at a gazelle, to supplement their rations, which were, in fact, considerably better than in many other parts of the Army, and meticulously calculated. A soldier's daily allowance included 3/28ths of an ounce of Marmite, an ounce of rum, and a sixteenth of a bottle of lime juice. However, despite this, desert sores were a constant problem. In many of the pictures of the LRDG patrols, at least one soldier has a telltale bandage on a limb.

Food became all-important in an atmosphere where long stretches of boredom were punctuated by moments of sheer terror. New Zealander Buster Gibb had the unenviable task of controlling the rations for his patrol:

> Our doctor, when he made up the diet, included a meal or two of herrings in tomato sauce. Now I never eat fish anyway, but these herrings in tomato sauce, when they canned them, they canned them with the roes in, and of course the roes got all hard and woody, and the blokes

wouldn't eat them – they said they weren't going to eat pregnant herrings. They kept coming to me and saying, 'Well, can I have something out of tomorrow's?' I said, 'If you're not going to eat the pregnant herrings – finish. I'm not going to break in to tomorrow's rations.' So I wouldn't. Some of them liked them – they just discarded the roes, and the herrings themselves weren't too bad, they said. So anyway, I finished up the trip with God knows how many tins of pregnant herrings they never ate.

When we got into an oasis, we used to barter tea. We used to save the tealeaves after we'd used them, we'd dry them, and then when we got into the oasis, we would barter the tea for eggs. Now a family would come along and they might have a dozen eggs and there might be a dozen in the family, and they would all come along with one egg and expect a good dollop of tea.

Many soldiers can remember details of what they ate right down to the brand names. As Arthur Arger recalled:

I would say we lived very well in a rough sort of way. It was all out of tins because you couldn't take anything else. So in place of bread you had biscuits. The biscuits were very good; they were made by Peek Freans, and they were in packets in a big tin. We had corned beef, Spam, tinned fish, of course, tinned cheese... There were sometimes dried peas, but then we used to get tinned potatoes, little new potatoes in tins – I thought, 'This is great.' Of course, when you had these things the water in the tins supplemented your own water ration, so you were saving in one way. We always used to take with us a couple of sacks of dried dates, and there was tinned fruit – Yacht Club peaches. We used to take – I always remember it – Olé margarine.

Porridge was usually on the menu, although no one wanted to clean out the pan after it was cooked. Cleaning was usually done with sand – water was too precious to waste on such niceties. In the extreme heat, the individual water ration was six pints a day: one in tea at breakfast, two in tea in the evening, one in lime juice at lunch, and two in the water bottle to be drunk when needed. Bill Kennedy Shaw, in his history, recalled how soldiers divided into 'sippers' and 'gulpers':

> One would put his water out on a tin plate in the shade and accept loss by evaporation in exchange for the resulting coolness; another would save up for a drink of Eno's [indigestion powder] and water in the evening, and a third would spare a few drops to wet a handkerchief to put against the back of his neck. A more elaborate plan was to have a Thermos which, left open to cool its contents by night, gave a cold drink the following day.

Arthur Arger recalled:

> It's surprising how many people could go all day and never even touch their water bottle. It became a thing you got used to. You got used to your tea, if at all possible three times a day, and there was your water bottle, so the treat at night-time, as far as I was concerned... [was] to take rum with [it] for medicinal purposes. People don't believe it, but it kept the malaria down. It used to be two-gallon stone jars, two in a box, Wood's rum. You can see it in the shops today in bottles, but this was army issue, and we always used to make sure that we took medicine with us. And what I used to do, after I had finished my evening meal, at night-time I used to pour out the water in my bottle on to a tin plate and add a touch of rum to it and some lime juice. We used to sometimes have lime in bottles, sometimes we had lime in powder form, and then just let the breeze blow over it, and it would cool off after about an hour and then you could sit and have your rum and lime for medicinal purposes, keeping the malaria down.

You didn't wash, you cleaned your teeth out of your tea. The only time you did wash was if you came across wells in the desert. There are wells all over the place, but if you had to keep clear of everything, you were going A to B and you hadn't got to be noticed, then – water – the truck had first go at it and your meals had second and your water bottle came third. Washing went by the board. So imagine a patrol coming back after about a month in the desert, unwashed – even the Arabs wouldn't go anywhere near us. In fact, it was, you know, the relief of coming back and getting water to wash and a shave. You finished up with a white face with two brown eyes for a couple of days, because I used to shave as soon as I came back in. I hated beards.

Alf Saunders remembered one spell when he went for eleven weeks without a wash:

Some of the fancy jokers cleaned their teeth – I never bothered. But the moment we got back into our base oasis, we did just jump off the trucks and went straight and dived into one of these big holes with water in it, and stayed there for an hour and sucked all the water back into your body and it was great. And we never got diseases. The only thing I ever got was a bloody great big gumboil.

Boils, scurvy and desert sores were all related to vitamin deficiency, and they usually cleared up after a diet of fresh vegetables and beer back at base. However, they could be very painful while they lasted – especially desert sores, which occurred where the skin was broken and exposed to the sun. In severe cases, ulcers could go through to the bone. Another problem, recalled by Alf Saunders, was *cafard*, or desert madness – bouts of irrational anger first identified among members of the French Foreign Legion when they spent long periods in the desert.

I had a good cobber, Clarkey Wakeford, and I was sitting across a table having lunch. I was lighting a smoke and I said, 'Throw us your matches over, Clarkey', and he said, 'I can't be bothered.' The next thing I had him by the throat... the boys pulled me off, and I calmed down after five minutes. I didn't know I had done it.

The excitement of seeing some action drew many recruits in the LRDG. Archie Gibson recalled his initiation:

I was a dispatch rider with the Scots Guards, which was the best job in the regiment, really – no one knew where you were. And I came back one day and found three empty beds where my friends had been, and someone said, 'Yes, an officer from some new outfit arrived and they all volunteered, packed up and went, all in the space of an afternoon.' I was really pissed off with that because I had heard a little bit about what they were going to do. So I went up to the citadel [Army headquarters] and saw them off, and really it was like your sweetheart going away, that awful feeling of loneliness.

Then the Germans got my truck and there was a lot of ammunition in it. I was driving just with a pair of shorts and bare feet, and they got the truck. An armoured car, which had been shooting at the Germans, picked me up, and when I got back there was a corporal there. I said to him, 'I'm sorry, but I've lost my truck.' He said, 'Oh, that's good.' I said, 'Why is it good?' He said, 'Because I've got an application for a driver-mechanic from the Long Range Desert Group', and I was in a truck that night off to Cairo. We got bombed going down to Cairo, and I met up with all my friends and we chatted about this and that.

Then at one o'clock in the morning, when we got our heads down, there was a hell of a noise, and the Germans dropped four bombs and killed three or four taxi drivers who were parked outside. It blew the wall in, and Jock and his blankets flew through the air. There was actually no one hurt, but there was lots of flying masonry and stuff; you know, it was a big bang. So that was my welcome to the Long Range Desert Group, but it was great, it was what I was meant to do. You get that feeling. I always enjoyed driving, and I had been driving in the desert for years, so that's how I came to be there, and I enjoyed it all, I loved the desert. There were hairy times, uncomfortable times, but there were also very beautiful times.

Archie recalled the photographer Cecil Beaton's reaction to their wild and woolly appearance:

Cecil Beaton came, and he did photographs of us just back from a raid, and he said we were like things from outer space: hair clustered with sand and standing up, and blood-shot eyes.

Many new recruits to the LRDG were attracted by its informality; the lack of drills and parades, as Edward Mitford recalled:

There were no parades of any sort in the desert. You were in your vehicle and you went off and did whatever you had to do, and that's all there was to it. When we were in Cairo, Anthony Eden said he wanted to come and see the Long Range Desert Group, so we thought, 'God Almighty, we've got to do something about this.' So the soldiers were put in to three straight lines, you know, and we looked very smart. But generally speaking we had nothing of that sort.

Uniform was a fairly haphazard affair, comfort being the prime consideration. Each soldier had whatever had been supplied by his original unit, with army boots replaced by Arab-style leather sandals. In the early days, they had official desert-issue pith helmets, but these usually ended up being abandoned and crushed in the bottom of the truck.

The LRDG badge was designed by Corporal C.O. (Bluey) Grimsey; the scorpion that features in the middle was said to have been modelled on a green one that had stung Grimsey three times. He survived, but the scorpion died and was kept in a pickle jar. After 1941, there were also special shoulder badges, and a *keffiyeh*, or Arab headdress. This was thought to be more practical than standard army berets or hats, as it was warm in winter, cool in summer, and ideal for keeping out sandstorms. Edward Mitford recalled the origin of its distinctive colour:

> Well, I went to the bazaar and I bought a certain number of headdresses, a lot of them in fact. I thought, these are white and glarey; I must do something about it. So we brewed up a whole lot of tea, you know, very strong tea in an enormous great thing, and dipped them all in that, and then hung them up to dry, and they came out a very nice sort of tan colour, which worked very well indeed.
>
> I do remember driving the patrol back to Cairo all wearing our headdresses, and there were some soldiers who were driving past. We caught them up and passed them, and they looked at us and thought what an extraordinary sight, you know, these people in headdresses. Who are they? And so we drove on and we didn't tell them who we were or anything like that. But it was a great sight really, I suppose.

While the popular image of soldiers in the desert might be of bare-chested men in shorts, they quickly learned to muffle up like natives when required, as Alf Saunders remembered:

> In a sandstorm, we took a tip from the Arabs. We would get our battledress on and the sheepskin coat and a hat, and a balaclava if you had one, and you would drive in this heat wave in that. If all your spare parts were covered, you sweated a bit, but you didn't lose your valuable moisture,

A commando training in Scotland, knife at the ready. Faces were usually blacked for night-time raids, although at St-Nazaire they were kept clean so they did not shoot each other by mistake.

Vaagso blazes: a view from high ground on Maaloy Island. The huts had been set on fire by a naval bombardment; the black smoke rising above the commando's head is from a hotel that the Germans had made into a stronghold.

Sailors and commandos show off a Nazi ensign captured in the combined operation at Vaagso.

This photograph, taken after the St-Nazaire raid, was used as German propaganda and captioned: 'A picture of a British commando.' Commando Tom McCormack, pictured still wearing his fighting kilt, was to die of his wounds in hospital two weeks later.

A German photograph of a commando amid an oily sea of wreckage, taken the day after the St-Nazaire raid.

A German propaganda film unit recorded the capture of the 'silent men of St-Nazaire'. Michael Burn (far left) made the V for Victory sign as he held his hands up in surrender so that any British viewers would know that their mission had been successful.

Those who died at St-Nazaire were buried with full military honours in a field at Escoublac, later to become a permanent cemetery. Here, captured British soldiers lower a coffin covered with a Union Jack while a German pastor-soldier gives the last salute.

HMS *Campbeltown*, scuttled after she rammed the dry dock at St-Nazaire. Neither the sightseers in her bows, or the German photographer, had any idea that she was to explode shortly after this picture was taken.

Rupert Harding-Newman poses by a car loaded up for an early trip through the desert. Notice that everything possible is strapped down.

David Stirling wearing his cap with the distinctive SAS badge.

A study of men of the Long Range Desert Group at Siwa Oasis
by Cecil Beaton, an official war photographer.

Members of the Long Range Desert Group ready for action.
Note the (dented) condensor by the radiator, which prevented overheating.

Marble Arch, Mussolini's triumphal monument; the Long Range Desert Group
spent many weary but rewarding hours on road watch near here.

Y Patrol of the Long Range Desert Group training
in Egypt, 1941. (Photograph from Harry Chard)

Parachute training using trapezes.

These parachute packers were hardly likely to forget how important their job was.
Olive 'Snowy' Quayle is third from the left.

Members of X Troop pose on the Tatton Park drop zone
in a break from training for Operation Colossus.

Abandoned parachutes litter the drop zone after the Arnhem landings in September 1944.

because that's what the Arabs did. They dressed up to the nines. They had their eyes showing and their cloaks were long and loose, and the sun can't suck the water off your body. It caused a draught inside and you sort of absorbed it back again. That's the story in the hot desert.

Merv Curtis – like Alf Saunders, a New Zealander – also remembered practical tips for everyday survival in all conditions:

You didn't speak much during the day when you were driving because you lost too much moisture from your mouth. Oh, yes, that's the thing you've got to do – keep that mouth shut. You could tell a fellow, whether he would survive in the desert or not – like you see a lot of people who walk around with their mouth half-open. They wouldn't survive – they're breathing out too much moisture and losing too much moisture from their body through their mouth.

The soldiers soon learned to spot the signs of approaching dust storms or sandstorms, which each brought their own distinctive problems. Merv Curtis recalled:

When a dust storm springs up in the desert you stop where you are, full stop. You stayed where you were until the storm abated, whether it took a day or two days. The sun vanished, and the whole place became an orange glow. You got your tea, your food in a dixie, you would have to cover it, put the cover over your head, hold the spoon through the cloth and eat like that. You couldn't see, you wouldn't know where you were – absolutely impossible.

Of course, a sandstorm – that's abrasive, and even travelling over it, the underneath of those vehicles would be shiny to the metal with the sand being chucked up, little bits of sand being chucked up, and the draught underneath – you would think they had been sandblasted.

Sandstorms also generated static electricity. Buster Gibb recalled one radio operator being knocked unconscious when he got an electric shock from touching the truck. However, while a sandstorm was in progress, it was possible to escape its effects, as Buster Gibb explained:

> We were thankful for the *keffiyehs* when we got them because you could wrap them around your face. If you allowed the sand to hit your face it was like a gunshot or a powder blast; it brought up blood spots all over your face. But often you could stand up on top of the vehicle, which was six, seven feet high, and be from the waist up out of the sandstorm.

Dramatic extremes of temperature also caused problems.

> The man who said 'Until the sands of the deserts grow cold' never had a clue. I've seen ice in the desert in the wintertime. In the summertime it was so hot that you daren't touch a vehicle because it burned you. We had rubber mats on the seats; we would flip them over before we got in, and we'd sit with the arms tucked in until you started moving. In the wintertime it was so cold you had all your woollies on; you had your battledress and you had your greatcoat. Some of the blokes wore balaclavas, and then after a while they issued us with sheepskin coats. They had evidently just taken them off the sheep, sheared them, and they stunk like hell. Some of the blokes wore them, but I used mine for a mattress. It was so cold because the vehicles were open, and because it was cold when you were standing still, it was that much colder when you travelled. It was like an icy blast in a freezer.
>
> But I came to almost enjoy the desert. I never really had any problems. I didn't have any of the desert sores. I didn't have any sunstroke. We had one bloke who had sunstroke on the first trip, and of course naturally the thing to cure that is

something cold – icepacks, or whatever. We had no icepacks. Strangely enough, you could get a bit of cool water or semi-cold water by putting it on a plate and putting it in the shade. You could even sit it on the hot sand and yet it would cool – the quick evaporation would cool it – but you never got enough to swab anybody down with. We had a medical orderly – he was a Scotsman who came from London – and I said to him, 'Look, we've got methylated spirits here; let's try that.' So we swabbed old Rex with methylated spirits, and it worked. The quick evaporation of the meths had the effect that we desired, you see, and so he recovered from it fairly quickly.

Despite the hardships, the desert had its own, unique attractions, as Alf Saunders recalled:

Gee, I'd go back tomorrow, I would. Right in the middle of the sand sea – beautiful. You have never seen stars in all your life until you have laid down by a truck in the middle of the sand sea. The atmosphere is so clear that the stars shoot in all directions, and all different colours – yellow and blue, white, not this fiery thing that we see, a shooting star, oh, no. It's a beautiful place – you've got no idea.

His army nickname – Tufawi – came from his enthusiasm for one particular place where his patrol camped overnight.

I woke up in the morning and I saw all this beautiful sand, and I really thought they were little diamonds, you know – they sparkled. I got a handful and I said, 'Well, you jokers, when the war is over I'm going to come back here and buy a million acres.' They said, 'What the hell for?' They just took the mickey out of me. I said, 'See all that beautiful shiny sand?', and they said, 'Yes', and I said, 'Well, I'm going to come over here, and I'm going to put up a cement factory, and I'll make the prettiest cement the world has ever seen.' That's where I got the word Tufawi from.

Those who have never been in the deepest desert imagine it to be a very quiet place – but Buster Gibb recalled: 'You seemed to have a roaring in the ear; it seemed to be noisy, and yet it was dead quiet.' On one occasion, when his patrol was sitting having their daily rum ration, this noisy silence caused a major panic:

> I had the rum jar sitting on the tail of the trunk and the cork out. There was no wind blowing, and yet we suddenly heard this broom, broom, broom, like a motor convoy. I heard it, and I said, 'Hey, listen to this,' and we heard this broom, broom, and, 'Cor, Jesus – a convoy, a convoy. It's somebody coming!' The thing that annoyed me most was that the blokes kicked over the bucket with the water in; they kicked it over, rather than put a lid on it or something. I grabbed the cork from the rum jar, and I poked it in, because it was about a quarter full, and I wasn't going to lose that. I said, 'Hey – listen. Not a sound.' I took the cork out: broom, broom. It was the air blowing over the top of the jar. I said, 'Panic is over,' but it really annoyed me that they panicked when they heard that noise, because I couldn't see any sense in it.

Alf Saunders remembered some very convincing mirages, caused by the reflection of light:

> I saw two positive ones, and then several hazy ones. The first one I saw was an oasis with the palm trees growing upside down. The next one, we were about 300 miles from the coast, I suppose, and this was a steamboat going along the Mediterranean, and it was upside down, the funnel. It was steaming along, black smoke. We didn't take any notice of them after a while; we just had a good laugh. One joker said: 'My God, the captain is going to get crook when he wakes up and finds his boat travelling along upside down.'

Merv Curtis recalled:

The most compelling mirage I saw, we were travelling behind some trucks and all of a sudden the dust that they were throwing up became water, as if they were travelling through water and the water was actually splashing out the sides. We were heading towards what was undoubtedly a lake fringed with palm trees – that was there, everyone could see it – but then it just vanished into the heat haze and it was gone.

The heat haze in the deepest desert was one of the reasons why the LRDG was used for reconnaissance instead of aircraft.

In the daylight, if a plane flew over a hundred feet up in the air it couldn't see the ground, the heat haze was that terrific. All they could see was like a layer of snow over the whole area, so that aerial reconnaissance was useless. Not that they had any planes that could get in there.

Travelling in such remote areas, for such long stretches of time, the LRDG patrols had to be totally self-sufficient. This was partly why they had rum in their rations: they might as well have been at sea, like the Navy. Patrols had medical orderlies, but they could carry only very basic supplies. Alf Saunders recalled:

I didn't think about getting wounded or getting hurt in the truck – it was getting appendicitis, that was my one dread, 1,200 to 2,000 miles away from the nearest hospital, because in those days if you got peritonitis and it busted, you were dead within 24 hours. We were 800 miles behind enemy lines, and you couldn't go up and ask the enemy: 'Could I go to your hospital?'

Another effect of the isolation was that any personality clashes became magnified. The New Zealanders in W Patrol eventually developed a great respect for their English commander,

Edward (then Captain) Mitford, but cultural differences caused problems in the early days. Buster Gibb recalled:

> As a matter of fact, all the boys were talking about doing him in, because of his whole attitude. He lost sight of the fact that the New Zealanders weren't the ragtag of a local population; they were educated men, they had diplomas, they were farmers, they were accountants. They were all bright enough people. I suppose you could say that I was the least educated of the lot, because I left school when I was fifteen.
>
> Every night we used to park two trucks together, and we had a great tarpaulin that we laid on the ground and ran two back wheels over the edge, then pulled it up over the trucks and had a bivvy inside. We used to use one of the metal sand trays that we carried for getting us out of the soft stuff. We would prop this up in the centre and have our Primuses and all that under cover. All the blokes used to sit in there drinking their rum. They would tell these lies, all the stories about their dogs on the farm, and how the dog would go up on the top of the hill and shade his eyes from the sun and look over the territory, and all these sorts of things.
>
> Mitford used to sit way out; he wouldn't come near. So one night I went over and I said: 'Why are you sitting out here? Why don't you come in and listen to these clowns telling their lies? You might learn something.' He didn't move then, but the next night he came and he sat against the front wheel of the truck, and all the blokes were inside. Things changed a little bit then, but he wasn't in the popularity stakes at that stage.

Matters came to a head after the successful capture of the Italian convoy. Bill Kennedy Shaw took a truck to return the prisoners to Cairo, leaving Edward Mitford as the sole Englishman. Buster Gibb remembered the events of that day:

My birthday coincided with the day we captured the truck-ees, and I asked him if I could issue extra rum. 'What for?' I said: 'Well, it's my birthday, and we've made our first capture.' 'Oh, OK.' So I said: 'Righto, you jokers, you can have extra rum tonight.' One bloke said: 'I don't want mine; you can have mine.' So I quaffed this gill measure off, and another bloke said: 'Oh, I don't want mine; you can have it.' I had about nine of these, and we went on from there. We also had six bottles of Italian Chianti, you know, in the big wicker-covered bottles, and I remember sitting on the running board of the truck with one of these bottles in one hand and the gallon jar [of rum] in the other hand. I would take a swig out of this gallon jar and then I'd take a chaser out of this Chianti bottle. Somebody said to me, 'Come on, give us those', and they grabbed them and said, 'You're not going to hog the lot.' Well, the moment they took them they upset my balance because the whole world tipped upside down and I flaked out.

Buster Gibb was threatened with a court martial for the events of that evening – although by the time they got back to base the idea was forgotten. This was probably just as well for long-term relations between the English and New Zealanders.

Alf Saunders – like Buster Gibb, an early member of W Patrol – put the initial problems down to culture shock:

It's the way they were brought up. You know, in New Zealand it doesn't matter who you meet – the Governor-General, anybody – if you can't remember his surname you call him by his Christian name. Nobody thinks anything about it. But that's different in English society – it's been ingrained there for centuries and centuries.

But Edward Mitford was a good bloke after that. He actually cried when he left the patrol, and we didn't want him to go either.

LIBYAN TAXIS LTD

The Long Range Desert Group's early outings amply demonstrated its skill at reaching parts no one else could reach, and patiently watching when it got there. It was not meant as a raiding force – and some thought its ventures into this territory exposed the men to unnecessary risk.

The group's first raid had been the capture of two Italian lorries on the track to Kufra on 20 September 1940. Bill Kennedy Shaw recalled:

> One burst of Lewis gunfire over their heads ended that great battle, and we had our first prisoners – two Italians, five Arabs and a goat and our first booty: 2,500 gallons of petrol, a nice line in cheap haberdashery and, best of all, the bag of official mail.

However, Merv Curtis, who had thought the men were simply on road watch, was not so positive about this encounter. He recalled:

> The major sent me about a mile or so south to hide behind a dune in case we were attacked from that direction. The rest of the patrol were behind the big dune, observing the track

from the top. We could see the cloud of dust – it transpired they were two big Italian diesel trucks, and they were carrying supplies to Kufra. They were civilian trucks; they had about half a dozen Arabs – traders – a couple of goats, and they were laden with trade goods.

I could see this coming, and I thought that we were just observing what went up the track. You can just imagine how I felt when all of a sudden these cowboys, this patrol, came out and they charged there and captured these two trucks and brought them back behind the dune, and I got a recall signal. When I came there I was almost speechless with rage. At one stroke we had captured two trucks that were completely bloody useless to us, about seven prisoners who were even more bloody useless, some drums of... I think it was aviation fuel – it was synthetic sort of stuff – and worst of all we had destroyed our greatest weapon, which was secrecy.

The first patrols had been instructed to take Italian newspapers to use instead of toilet paper, so meticulous were the efforts to cover their tracks. Merv found it hard to reconcile this with what the group was doing now. What he did not realize at the time was the strategic value of the bag of mail that was on the trucks. But it was certainly true that by surfacing like this, they were inviting attack. The intelligence they gathered was too important to be risked.

In the closing months of 1940, the desert patrols were involved in an increasing number of minor skirmishes. Apart from reconnaissance trips, their first direct action role was to lay mines on the roads used by Italian convoys. Enemy aircraft were a constant threat. In late November 1940, Edward Mitford's W Patrol was bombed for over an hour at Uweinat, but although more than 300 small bombs were dropped, skilful driving enabled them to escape unscathed. In his history of the unit, Bill Kennedy Shaw recalled:

Air attack was the one danger to LRDG; this was the first time we had experienced it and Mitford was fortunate, for in the next three years we came to learn how destructive and unpleasant it could be.

There is little cover in the desert, where there is no vegetation and where the sand-charged wind rounds off all the natural features into smooth shapes which give no shadow. Moving cars, throwing up dust, are easy to spot, but if you could hear or see the aircraft first and stop, you would probably escape notice for stationary trucks are hard to pick up. Taking it all round we were amazingly lucky. Again and again I have heard men tell how aircraft passed over them unseeing when they had heard them first and halted or when they themselves had stopped for a moment for some trivial reason.

Uweinat was an Italian outpost at the base of a 6,000-foot mountain, and it consisted of two areas: Ain Zwaya on the west, and Ain Dua on the south. Each had water and a landing ground. The LRDG attacked Ain Dua, but did not have either the manpower or the firepower to take the garrison. However, the men killed at least six of the enemy and inflicted as many casualties. Two New Zealanders were awarded medals – the MM (Military Medal) and the MC – the first of many such decorations to be earned by the Kiwis in the desert.

Meanwhile, a different patrol successfully captured a small Italian fort at Aujila, 600 miles to the north. It was an ideal ploy to exaggerate their numbers and to keep the enemy guessing.

In December 1940 the group officially became known as the LRDG. Some New Zealanders had to go back to their original units, to be replaced by officers and soldiers from the Coldstream and Scots Guards. W Patrol was disbanded, and its vehicles and equipment went to G Patrol. The navigator was Bill Kennedy Shaw, who, according to the patrol captain, 'had done as much desert travelling by camel and car as anyone alive'.

Two patrols – a total of seventy-six men and twenty-three vehicles – set out from Cairo on Boxing Day 1941 for a 1,500-mile trip through the desert. Avoiding the routes leading to wells and oases, they did everything they could to keep their intentions secret. Their objective was, with the Free French, to attack the Italian garrisons of the Fezzan in south-west Libya.

The town of Murzuk, with its airfield, machine-gun posts and stone fort, was their major target. On the road they met the local postman – and captured him to act as their guide. One part of the force headed for the fort, the other for the airfield.

Initially, they had surprise on their side, but the Italians returned heavy fire. One New Zealander, Sergeant Cyril Hewson, was killed, as was Lieutenant-Colonel d'Ornano of the Free French, who was shot with a bullet through the throat. Another French officer was hit in the leg, but calmly he cauterized the wound with the lighted end of his cigarette and carried on fighting.

At the fort, the patrols set the tower alight and burned the flag and flagstaff. Here, there were some unfortunate extra casualties, as Bill Kennedy Shaw remembered:

> In the middle of the attack, a touring car drove up to the gate. In it was the Italian commander, who had probably been out to lunch, and also, as some said afterwards, a woman and child. One shell from the guards' Bofors put an end to them; it was unfortunate about the woman and child, but people should arrange their lunch parties more carefully.

On the airfield, the hangar was burned, together with three fully loaded bombers, and rifles and ammunition were seized. Some twenty-five prisoners were taken, but all except the postman and a senior air force officer were released due to limited rations and transport space.

The patrols withdrew the way they had come, the Italians being prevented from pursuing by a thick dust storm. Bill Kennedy Shaw picked up the postman's bicycle, which had been left on the road, and hitched it to the back of the truck, planning to use it back in Cairo. (This never happened, as the bicycle was destroyed, along with the truck, in a skirmish near Kufra three weeks later.)

On the following day, they returned, captured two *carabinieri* on camels and surrounded Murzuk. One of the *carabinieri* was sent in to the fort with a message that its defenders should surrender or be shelled. Just as they were getting ready to start attacking, strange noises came from the edge of the village, as Bill Kennedy Shaw recalled:

> Was this a garrison of unexpected size massing for a sortie? Then a small crowd left the western gate. Gradually, it came nearer across the open ground, an extraordinary procession. With banners flying and drums beating, the *mudir* and his elders were coming out to surrender the village in traditional Fezzan manner. Trailing behind the crowd were a few sheepish-looking *carabinieri*.

The next major operation was a planned attack on Kufra Oasis, where two LRDG patrols were to act as advance guard under the command of the Free French. This went badly wrong when the attackers' trucks were spotted by the Italians, and one patrol came under Italian fire at Gebel Sherif, sixty miles south of Kufra. It was a combined ground and air attack, and it was not long before three trucks were burning and one New Zealander and two prisoners were killed (one of them the unfortunate postman from Murzuk).

The truck carrying Pat Clayton, the patrol commander, had two tyres punctured by machine-gun fire, and a leaking radiator and petrol tank. The crew changed the tyres and refilled the radiator but ran out of fuel. Eventually, Clayton was wounded in the arm and taken prisoner, along with two other men.

When the survivors met up with the other patrol at an agreed rendezvous, it was found that four soldiers were unaccounted for. It was assumed that they, too, had been captured.

In fact, they escaped, going on to make an epic journey through the desert with only a partly filled two-gallon can of water and a pot of plum jam.

Trooper Ron Moore led the group, his foot – which had a shell splinter in it – bandaged with a handkerchief. Guardsman John Easton had a piece of metal lodged in his throat; fitter Alf Tighe and Guardsman A. Winchester were uninjured. All were dressed only in shorts and shirts, all footwear and headgear having been destroyed with their truck. At night, near-freezing temperatures made it difficult to get any sleep; they had to dig a hole in the sand and put their arms round each other for warmth.

After five days, Alf Tighe, who was suffering from an old internal injury, could not keep up, and he was left with his share of what water they had. Eventually, he made his way to a mud hut at Sarra – 135 miles from their starting point – and was found by a group of French soldiers with a British liaison officer.

Of the three others, Moore and Winchester had continued to walk, and had survived. Easton was lying in the sand, still alive when he was picked up, but hardly able to swallow because of his injured throat. He died the same evening. David Lloyd Owen recalled:

> The British liaison officer told a wonderful story of Easton's courage and sense of humour right up to his end. He was suffering terribly from his wounds, and his body was almost withered. Yet when the French made him some tea, weak and sweet, he drank it and smiled, saying, 'I like my tea without sugar.'

After the debacle on the track to Kufra, the LRDG were released from their obligations towards the French, although one New Zealand truck crew remained to help with navigation. Eventually, after a ten-day siege, the Italians surrendered Kufra on 1 March 1941. This was a key strategic garrison, but the French did not have enough troops to defend it. That task fell to the LRDG, who were left in some frustration at their position. There was no question of leaving it undefended, as Rommel's advance party had arrived in North Africa in February, bringing a new threat from the Germans. But the LRDG was not supposed to be garrison troops. What was more, Kufra was an ideal base from which to launch raids – yet the group did not have enough petrol for anything other than essential journeys.

Eventually, a new system of convoys brought more reliable petrol supplies. By the summer of 1941 the Sudan Defence Force – which was made up of regular Sudanese soldiers – was able to take over the task of defending Kufra. Meanwhile, the LRDG had been reorganized into two groups, one – with additional soldiers from Rhodesia – based at Kufra, the other at Siwa.

One important function for the LRDG was transporting agents behind enemy lines. It was this role that led to the nickname 'Libyan Taxis Ltd'. One of their 'clients' was Vladimir Peniakoff ('Popski'), a Russian Belgian who had obtained the trust of the Arabs to become a very effective secret agent. The members of the group also transported British spies, as Alf Saunders recalled:

We took a couple of Arabs out one time. They sat by themselves and ate by themselves, and wouldn't speak English or anything like that. You can just imagine the language we used against them, and they didn't turn a bloody hair. We thought, 'Oh, well, they can't speak English.' Then we took them out and picked them up about ten days or a fortnight later, and they marched in and they were footsore and weary because they had army boots on. We reckoned they had pinched the army boots from dead soldiers, you know, and saying this in front of them... I've never been so embarrassed in all my life in another couple of hours' time.

Don Steele was the patrol leader. He went up and spoke to them, and I said, 'How the hell can he speak to them? They bloody don't talk English.' But he brought them over and lined us up, and he said, 'I'd like to introduce you to two personnel of the British Intelligence Corps. He said Major so-and-so, Colonel so-and-so... and the things we'd been saying. I thought, Jesus, we're all going to be shot; we'll all be in the bloody military prison, you know, the glasshouse for the rest of our war career. Bloody hell, we were frightened, and those jokers started laughing. One said, 'We've been repaid for all the insults you gave us, the expression on you jokers' faces when you knew... We're pleased because you lived with us for over a week in your company and you never twigged that we weren't Arabs, so we thought we were doing a good job.'

On their journeys, the desert patrols also often rescued downed pilots, or those who for a variety of reasons had simply become lost. As Bill Kennedy Shaw put it:

A good many men in the 8th Army must owe their lives to LRDG, but for every lost man found by us how many are still in the desert, now only a skeleton with a few rags of clothing round it and an empty water bottle beside, and, maybe, with its teeth fastened in the dry stem of some desert shrub?

Julian Thompson, an ex-Royal Marine Commando, sums up the strengths of the LRDG in his *War Behind Enemy Lines*:

The LRDG needed adventurous spirits, but never tolerated 'cowboys'. They were utterly reliable. If they said that they would arrive at an exact spot in the desert 1,000 miles away at a certain time, they almost invariably did. They made their radios work over long distances. They got the messages through. This demanded high standards of driving, maintenance and navigation. This was the legacy of Bagnold and the early members of the LRDG: a capacity for taking pains; of thinking the problem through; an intellectual rather than what we would now call a 'gung-ho' approach.

The gung-ho approach was found in vast amounts among the men who were to form the Special Air Service (SAS) – and the partnership that developed between the two groups made the most of the strengths of each.

At the beginning of 1941, a force of Commandos had been sent on the long sea journey to North Africa. They were known as Layforce, after their leader, Brigadier Robert Laycock. Carol Mather, who had volunteered for Commando service after Dunkirk, recalled:

Before we left Scotland – we were then anchored off the island of Arran, where we'd been doing some training – Admiral Keyes came up. He was then in charge of combined operations. He addressed us and said we were off for a big adventure, but he didn't tell us where or what it was going to be. So that was quite exciting. Then we set sail off into the blue.

Our first port of call was Sierra Leone, and then it became clear that we were going round via the Cape, and up towards the Middle East. It was quite a long journey. I suppose it took us three weeks to a month, going round the Cape, and then up and finishing up at Suez.

As far as the men were concerned, they were sleeping in hammocks, and their sleeping quarters was also the mess deck. So it took them about two hours to stow their hammocks and swab the mess deck, then put up the tables for their lunch. And the same process in the evening meant this occupied most of the day. Otherwise we did what train-ing we could, which was weapon training, and keeping everything in good order, and as much exercise as one could around the deck. But apart from that, there wasn't much to do. The officers were playing cards, doing a bit of gambling. It was a fairly boring voyage, really.

There was a war diary being written at that stage on the boat, and the first person to be put in charge of the war diary was Randolph Churchill, who was Winston's son. Then the job was taken over by Evelyn Waugh, the novelist, who was also with us. But looking at the archives later, there were almost no entries at all, except the crews joining us or leaving us at a certain point.

They survived the long and tedious sea journey to arrive safely in North Africa. However, after all the build-up they never managed to match the success of the Commandos in raids on German-occupied Northern Europe. This was partly because the Navy, which was meant to have taken them on raiding operations, was otherwise occupied – partly because the large size of the unit tempted generals to use them as infantry. They were worn down fighting desperate rearguard actions.

In July 1941 Layforce was disbanded – much to the frustration of the commandos themselves. As Carol Mather put it: 'We had some really marvellous men, and we were very highly trained in the work we were going to do, and so it seemed to us an awful waste that we should just be thrown on the scrapheap.' The general feeling of disgruntlement was expressed rather more bluntly by a piece of graffiti on a troop deck in HMS *Glengyle*: 'Never in the whole history of human endeavour have so few been buggered about by so many.'

Some commandos were saved for a last, ill-starred mission. General Erwin Rommel and his Afrika Korps were doing much to reverse losses suffered by the weakened Italians. Rommel himself had acquired almost mythical status, becoming known as the Desert Fox. If he could be tracked down to his lair and killed, this would be a tremendous propaganda coup. The operation was timed for mid-November, aiming to cause maximum disruption on the eve of the long-awaited Allied offensive, Operation Crusader.

In pouring rain, the commandos landed in rubber dinghies from submarines near the village of Beda Littoria. On the moonless night of 17–18 November, a party of about thirty soldiers reached the supposed headquarters and found it full of Germans ready for a fight. Their intelligence had been completely wrong. The house they raided was not Rommel's headquarters – and at the time of the attack he was not even in the country. He was at a birthday party in Rome.

Two survivors escaped and spent the next forty-one days walking back to the 8th Army lines, which they reached on Christmas Day 1941. The rest of the Commando party were either killed or taken prisoner.

The amateurish nature of this operation was matched by a parachute raid on the same night by the newly formed SAS, most of whose members had originally been part of Layforce. This, too, was a fiasco – but it had a more positive outcome. For it was this raid that brought the founder of the SAS, David Stirling, into contact with the LRDG.

David Stirling, who died in 1990, was one of those characters who did not fit particularly well into conventional regimental life. His outspokenness made him enemies (including, at one stage, General Montgomery) – but his determination and charisma made him a natural, if somewhat maverick, leader.

Carol Mather recalled his first impressions of him:

I met David Stirling a little earlier on in 1940, when we both joined this ski battalion, Scots Guard Ski Battalion. The idea was we were going off to help the Finns. And we went off to France, training – Chamonix. So I knew him then, not very well. Then we, together, joined this Commando. We were in the same troop, so I got to know him much better, almost too well.

There were three officers from this particular troop sharing this cabin, which was built for two. It was extremely uncomfortable. David Stirling didn't think much of this, and he spent most of his time fast asleep. We had a nickname for him in those days; he was known as the great sloth. He was to emerge occasionally for food, and otherwise he spent the whole morning sleeping.

I think by the powers that be, he was known as rather an idle officer – but he was a man of great charm, actually.

He was a very amusing companion. He had big ideas about various things. Just before the war he was training himself in the Rockies in Canada, to climb Everest, because he was a very keen mountaineer. Almost impossible to explain what type of man he was really like, unless you actually met him.

After we landed, and things seemed to be going wrong, he had various ideas, you know – what he might do next. And he eventually came up with this idea that he should form a very light raiding force for the desert, not nearly so big as a Commando, but obviously highly trained, and ready to do really very daring operations. This was his great thing, that no one – let alone the Germans – expected the raids that actually took place. This was the secret of their success, really. I mean, apart from being very daring they were also highly dangerous to us.

Driver Archie Gibson recalled:

I associated David Stirling with sleep. The first time I met him, the Scots Guards were on manoeuvres at Popham, and I was detailed to go to the station and pick up a Guards officer. Well ... no one came off that train, no one came off the next train, and I thought, I'll wait for the third train. And he came, he arrived, tall, sort of stooping and dressed in the wrong order. He had the Guards' chequered hat on, service dress, sand-brown, everything was wrong for manoeuvres – typical David. So he got in the truck and I said, 'I'll take you to where the manoeuvres were the last time I saw them,' and there was nobody there. So by this time David was asleep. He had this ability just to sleep in the passenger seat. So I thought, well, I'll let him sleep for a bit. Just before he went to sleep he'd said, 'Wake me up if anything exciting happens.' Well, nothing... I looked around for a bit, parked under a tree, and he slept for two hours, that was his manoeuvre. I think it's just as well because some higher-up officers would have b****cked him for turning up in the wrong gear.

But the man I met in the desert was a very different guy: he knew what he was doing. And the first time I saw him in the desert, he just came straight to the truck because the name intrigued him because his motto was 'Who Dares Wins', and that was it. I drove him from then on.

I was very fond of David because he didn't look at all or sound like a great warrior, but he was a man of steel. He was a very interesting man and certainly didn't look like a guy who could do things and influence the people that he did. Gifted. Every generation brings forth a few gifted people like that.

In wartime Cairo, David Stirling and his brother Bill were legendary for their maverick behaviour. In *To War with Whitaker*, the wartime diaries of the Countess of Ranfurly, there are stories of how their Sudanese servant would have to drop to the floor in the middle of laying the dinner table as the bullets from their shooting practice came through the wall from the next-door room. On one occasion, having lost all their money at cards, they rode home on a 'borrowed' donkey. This then took up residence in their third-floor flat, liberally manuring the drawing-room carpet.

David Stirling originally thought up the idea for the SAS while lying temporarily paralysed in the Scottish Military Hospital in Alexandria as a result of a parachuting accident. He and some other members of Number 8 Commando had decided to experiment with jumping out of an ancient biplane while waiting for their future to be resolved. However, they were untrained – and when his parachute caught on the tailplane and ripped, he found himself heading at an alarming speed towards the stony ground. His spine absorbed the shock of the impact, and he also lost his sight for about an hour.

While concentrating on getting some movement back into his legs, he also drew up a detailed memo for the deputy chief of General Staff, General Ritchie. He hoped to see this great man in person, but he was also realistic enough to know that he might have only a few moments to make his case. He was, after all, only a lieutenant.

In the authorized biography written by Alan Hoe, David Stirling recalled:

I suppose it was probably one of the worst pieces of military writing ever submitted to a headquarters. I heavily over-scored sections where I wanted maximum impact; this, I'm told, is never done. I went over it time and again until I reck-oned it could be read and understood in four minutes. Finally, I wrote it in pencil – a cardinal sin when addressing a memo to a senior staff officer. In part there was a sort of subliminal psychology to the memo. I thought the scruffy appearance may have an effect in itself – I may be letting time fool me into thinking that, of course.

Although he was still only semi-mobile, Stirling took a taxi to Middle East Headquarters and tried to bluff his way through without a pass. He was turned back by the sentry – but he had spotted a gap in the barbed-wire fence. While the sentry was otherwise occupied, he abandoned his crutches and crept through. He tried to make himself inconspicuous by joining a party of visitors, but he was spotted as he limped into the build-ing. He burst into the first office that looked suitable – only to find himself face to face with a starchy major who was an old enemy from training days.

The major called the guard, but Stirling managed to stum-ble along the corridor into the office of General Ritchie to make his pitch. Ritchie was intrigued and offered him a seat while he read his proposal. As Stirling recalled:

My clearest memory is of thinking how the hell I was going to manage to stand again. Ritchie read the notes twice, put them down and looked at me, then read them again. I was mentally going over the answers to the questions I knew must be forth-coming, but to my surprise he didn't ask a single one.

Stirling's unorthodox approach paid off. Three days after he had gate-crashed headquarters, he returned by invitation for a meeting with General Claude Auchinleck, Wavell's successor as Commander-in-Chief, Middle East. The Auk, as he was known, promoted Stirling to captain and gave him authority to recruit up to six officers and sixty other ranks. So L Detachment, Special Air Service Brigade, came into being – hardly a brigade, but the name was designed to fool the enemy into thinking a large, fully equipped troop of parachutists had arrived in Africa.

Many of the first volunteers were members of the Number 8 Commando who were being used as ordinary troops and were only too keen to have a taste of the kind of action they had trained for. Johnny Cooper recalled:

> I was in a slit trench with the Scots Guards on the border with Libya, and David Stirling appeared in my slit trench and said: 'I'm going to produce a unit, and are you prepared to come along? You've got to be prepared to parachute.' So I thought, 'Yes,' anything to get out of that slit trench.

Their base was to be at Kabrit, a village about a hundred miles east of Cairo, on the banks of the Suez Canal. Johnny Cooper continued:

> There was a stretch of desert sand about 500 yards by 500 yards and that was our camp. Well, there was one tent that the quartermaster had already set up a store for ammunition and for food and for our arms, but nothing else. So we were all given spades and we had to dig an area that would take a sixteen-pound tent. We had to dig in because the Germans were bombing the Suez Canal every night. We put the sandbags round the sides to protect us in case of any shrapnel or what would come from the bombs, and that night we motored down the road. The New Zealand division camp was almost empty because the New Zealanders were all in action up in the desert, and we went in and we just

collapsed their tents, and we nicked sixteen, I think it was, of these tents. We also nicked a piano, but I don't think anybody ever played it or had the ability to do so. So we set up the camp, and by dawn everything looked as though it had been there for quite a long time. The Kiwis couldn't really put a finger on the fact that we had pinched their tents because they looked as though they had been properly constructed for a long time.

Jimmy Storie recalled:

On the road, we passed by what was their local picture house, which was more or less a cinema made for the Army, and easy chairs were there for officers. We stole the easy chairs and took them back to the camp. And in the next two or three days we had the finest camp in Egypt, because every camp, every hut or tent, I should say, had an easy chair, and we all had folding beds and things like that. And the blankets, I don't know where the blankets came from, but somebody must have stolen them from somewhere. That's where the SAS started up. We stole everything. And after that we were thieves all our days.

Lieutenant Jock Lewes – who had only done one parachute jump himself – was in charge of parachute training. Both the parachute schools then in existence – at Ringway, Manchester, and at Delhi, India – were too hard-pressed to lend instructors. There was also the small matter of a shortage of parachutes – but Jock Lewes solved this by hijacking some equipment that was on its way to India.

Some of the men joked that the 'L' in L Detachment, SAS Brigade, stood for 'learner'. There was a touch of the Heath Robinson about their training, as Jimmy Storie recalled:

Before the parachutes arrived, we had sort of makeshift ideas, and one of them was how to correctly fall, various things like that. So they built platforms, say twelve, fourteen, sixteen feet high, and we used to jump off these and land in different falls, you know, sideways, backwards and all the rest of it. The idea was so that if you did get a parachute and you did fall in high winds and suchlike, you could save your body from getting broken. A few of the lads got broken legs and broken arms during this training.

From this, they graduated to jumping off the back of trucks at increasing speed.

You were all getting knocked and bruised when we were hitting the rocks, and of course you were all swearing in your best English at the same time and calling him [Jock Lewes] this, that and the rest of it, because we thought it was just a lot of rubbish. But that would allow us to fall, and then eventually we got the parachutes. Then again, we got planes... I think their speed was about ninety miles an hour. In fact, you could go outside and use the toilet and come back in and catch them up, that fast they were.

Anyway, we got the planes and we did two or three jumps, the parachutes were opening, everything was going fine. And then there was a new lot of lads came in, and funnily enough two of them were my mates from the Commandos, and they went through the same training as we did.

The plane took off, and I told Joe and this other lad how to fall when you get out of the plane and various things like that. They jumped out, but their 'chutes couldn't open – in those days they only had one 'chute – so anyway they both were killed.

Joe was trying to pull his 'chute open when he hit the ground, and they landed on the other side of the great lake, and we went over to pick up their bodies and they weren't a pretty sight.

When the men jumped, the weight of their bodies pulling on a static wire in the Bombay aircraft was meant to open the parachute. There are differing versions of what exactly went wrong, but the deaths were a potentially serious blow to the men's confidence. In fact, the parachute training school at Ringway had experienced very similar problems. However, lack of communication meant the men in the desert did not know this until later. Jimmy Storie recalled:

> It was wartime, you thought nothing of it, but they were my two mates and I felt it more so than anybody – to the rest they were just two soldiers killed.
>
> Stirling made us all go up in the planes and jump, because if he hadn't done that there would have been a lot of lads that would have said: 'I'm not going to do this because those two were killed.' So we went into the plane, and again, of course, all the 'chutes opened, which should have happened in the first place.

Airpower was decisive in the desert war, as there was so little cover on the ground. The German and Italian air forces outnumbered the British, and the RAF could not deal with them. Their bomber force could not bomb the enemy airfields by day, as they would be seen and shot down. They would not be seen at night – but in the featureless desert it would be hard to find the airfields, let alone bomb them accurately. David Stirling's solution to this problem was simple: he would blow up the aircraft on the ground, together with the trucks, ammunition and fuel dumps that serviced them.

To do this, he needed a lightweight incendiary bomb that could be carried easily in a soldier's backpack – and this is where Jock Lewes came in. Lewes was an Australian and an Oxford rowing blue, who had led his university eight to their first win after a run of Cambridge victories. He was also very inventive. After a series of experiments with a new plastic explosive, he succeeded in perfecting a device that became known as the Lewes bomb. This could be carried in blocks weighing slightly less than a pound, then moulded like putty to be stuck on to a target.

When a senior RAF officer pooh-poohed Stirling's idea of ground raids on aircraft, he took it as a challenge. Stirling made a bet that he could get his men inside an airfield without being spotted – and even told the senior officer when he was going to do it. The result was a cheeky mock attack on the RAF base at Heliopolis, just outside Cairo. No explosives were involved, but each soldier carried an equivalent weight in stones, and minimal water. This made it partly an endurance exercise, as Johnny Cooper recalled:

> The idea was to see how determined we could be. We had two water bottles each, and a pound of dates and some sweets to suck. We had a small piece of camouflaged netting and, by day, as we were laying up, the RAF were looking for us. It took three nights to do the hundred miles, and we attacked Heliopolis airfield and put sticky labels on about fifty aircraft. The RAF was very worried about this, the fact that we had breached their security. They knew we were coming, but we managed to get in without them stopping us.

No planes were destroyed; the stickers simply had drawings of bombs, or messages to the effect that the aircraft had been blown up courtesy of L Detachment, SAS Brigade. But the effect was just as explosive. Jimmy Storie recalled:

> I suppose they thought we were just air force personnel walking about, that's how slack it was. Nobody checked up, nobody stopped you. The guard was walking there with a rifle up and down, but nobody checked uniforms or anything, because there were a certain amount of soldiers there doing guard duty for the RAF. They just thought we were part of the soldiers who were there.

After, of course, the camps became more secure – but then no camp was secure. We proved that later on, what a few men could do.

However, although the attack on Heliopolis proved their capabilities on the ground, it was still generally assumed that the men would reach their targets by parachute. It was only after a disastrous drop on the same November night as the abortive attempt to kill Rommel that this was seriously called into question. Johnny Cooper recalled the background to this first SAS raid:

In 1941 Malta was having a hell of a time. The reason was the fact that the Germans brought in the Messerschmitt 109F, which was a very high-performance fighter, and we were having great problems getting stores and supplies into Malta. David Stirling was asked by a higher command to mount a parachute operation on the two German airfields of Timini and Gazala. That operation meant the requirement of five Bristol Bombay aircraft and the dropping strength of several officers and fifty-two other ranks.

The idea was for them to land about twelve miles south of their targets – but when a weather forecast suggested that wind speeds would be thirty knots or more, Stirling's superiors advised him to abandon the idea. Not only were the men likely to be scattered all over the dropping zone, but they ran the risk of landing very hard and being dragged over the ground. Stirling, however, decided to go ahead.

There were five teams, and the idea was for each to spend the day observing, then to attack simultaneously. The LRDG would pick them up afterwards at a prearranged spot and take them back to base. In the event, the attacks never happened, and many men were lost.

Ernie Bond, who was in a group with Lieutenant Charles Bonnington – father of the mountaineer, Chris Bonnington – described the sequence of events:

It was a disaster. There was a high wind, the rains... the desert was flooded – you wouldn't believe it. Dropping by parachute in those conditions was suicidal, really. Four of the five planes did drop their loads, with disastrous results. A few were killed in the drop, some badly injured, quite a lot taken prisoner. All the equipment was lost, blown all over the place.

His pilot found himself in deep trouble as he tried to locate the airfield at Gazala in the stormy darkness.

He had to come down to 400 feet to make out his target, and in doing so, of course, he attracted all the ground fire from the German ack-ack. One of their shots hit our emergency tank in the middle of the plane, and we lost a lot of petrol. The pilot decided in view of the weather conditions it was suicide to drop us, so he said: 'We'll make back for Cairo.' What he didn't know was that a piece of shrapnel had lodged in the compass binnacle in the aircraft, with the result that the compass needle pointed permanently to the east.

Anyway, he set a course for Cairo, and we'd been flying for hours. I remember one of the lads came back and he said: 'Ever been in a plane that's lost?' I said: 'You're joking.' Eventually, the pilot, Charlie West, said: 'Well, we should be somewhere near Cairo. I'm going down.' So we went down and it was getting dawn, light. We came in over the sea, and I thought, well, there's no sea in Cairo – we're adrift. With a magnificent piece of flying he landed the Bombay intact on the edge of the escarpment, and we sent out a patrol. Would you believe it? We had flown round in a big circle all night, and we landed on the edge of the aerodrome we had set out to attack. When we got through the sand dunes, there it was: Gazala aerodrome with all the aeroplanes, the big black crosses.

We came across an Italian outpost on the edge of the aerodrome. There was a bit of a shoot-up, and we took a young Italian lad prisoner. A quick council of war, and we decided that we would destroy all the papers and plans, get back in the aircraft, take off and try to flop the aircraft in Tobruk harbour, which was then surrounded and ours. We all got aboard and took off. I always remember this little Italian, the young fellow – we stuck him on the top of this petrol tank, which was empty, in the middle of the fuselage and we were sitting on either side. We got up to about 300, 400 feet, and then the ground fire, the ack-ack hit us. Just our luck there was a 109 Messerschmitt fighter coming back from dawn patrol, and he pumped us full of cannon shells and down we went. But it was the skill of the pilot that saved us; he managed to get one wing down which took the shock of the crash, and it cartwheeled over.

I can just remember these cannon shells, big balls of fire coming past me, and I felt as if I were being hit across the back with six-inch nails. I saw this little Italian disappear out the other side of the aircraft, and all the aircraft was disintegrating. When I woke up I was about fifty feet from the aircraft, and there it was, all in a heap. The German staff from Gazala aerodrome had rushed out, and before I passed out again I could see the German officers diving in the wreckage and pulling out the pilot, and we were then well and truly captured.

The second pilot was killed, together with another member of the crew, and several paratroopers were badly injured. Ernie Bond had shrapnel in his back, a broken right ankle and bruises – but despite this, he and the pilot, Charlie West, later tried to escape from the German hospital. They ended up in a German prisoner-of-war camp.

Johnny Cooper, who was in the group commanded by Jock Lewes, recalled the fate of those in the other aircraft:

The night of the parachute drop was horrendous – it was the worst storm for thirty years, and the plane that I was in was caught up by searchlights and we were shot. We were told that we couldn't possibly find our location for dropping, so we had to drop blind. As you left the aircraft the wind took you absolutely miles and miles an hour away. Hitting the ground, unless you could collapse your parachute very quickly, you could be dragged. We had certain people there who were dragged to death.

Of the fifty-seven who actually jumped, only twenty-one managed to survive. Now, the survivors married up for the very, very first time with the Long Range Desert Group. We marched for about a day and a half until at night we could see these two mounds at a distance with these storm lanterns on. We advanced towards them, and my officer – Lieutenant Lewes – said: 'We go forward, and we sing "Roll Out the Barrel" [the prearranged recognition code], and hopefully we shall meet this unit.' We went between the twin pimples and started to sing, and as we came behind the pimples there was our patrol of the Long Range Desert Group commanded by Jake Easonsmith, and we were welcomed with – I'm afraid – mugs and mugs of nice sweet rum.

David Lloyd Owen, interviewed shortly before he died in April 2001, recalled his first meeting with David Stirling after this disastrous drop:

He immediately impressed me, not only because he was not really downhearted by the disaster that had taken place to his force, but he was also already thinking ahead as to how he might do things better the next time. He was a man of immense persuasion. He would convince anyone that black was white and he had very obvious powers of leadership. People were mesmerised, I think to some extent by him.

During discussions between the two men, they talked about the limitations of parachuting – its inaccuracy, its dependency on the weather and availability of aircraft. The LRDG had lost its share of men in actions with the enemy, often having to carry serious casualties hundreds of miles to reach proper medical aid. But it had never experienced the failure that had plagued Layforce and the SAS so far. David Owen recalled:

> After a bit I began to sense that he didn't think parachuting was really the best thing to do, so it suddenly came to me to say to him: 'Look here, why the hell do you want to go and do this chute jumping? We can take you anywhere you like, almost like a taxi. We'll drop you off and you can carry all the equipment you want. You can go and do whatever ghastly deeds you want to do and we will pick you up at the end.'
>
> As David had never operated with us, he didn't know really – although I say it myself – how very efficient we were at operating in the desert. Anyhow, after a bit he left me. He then travelled back to Siwa and he saw Jake Easonsmith, who was quite one of our finest patrol commanders, with his New Zealanders, working in the way that we had learnt to do. I think he was immensely impressed by that – and the fact is, of course, from that moment on, David Stirling never did a parachute raid in the desert.

As Bill Kennedy Shaw explained:

> It was an ideal partnership. We could exploit to the full what was our greatest asset – the ability to deliver a passenger anywhere behind the enemy's lines at any time he asked. And weeks of training for their airborne operations had made the parashots [Kennedy Shaw's name for the SAS] fine artists in getting into – and out of – places at night.

So it was that Libyan Taxis Ltd came to the rescue of the SAS. From the oasis at Jalo, behind the Kalansho Sand Sea, they transported the SAS men to a series of raids on enemy airfields by the Mediterranean coast. One Rhodesian LRDG patrol travelled 350 miles to the north-west, carrying groups led by

Stirling and Paddy Mayne. Blair 'Paddy' Mayne was an Irish Rugby International, a boxer, and something of a maverick. (He had not been able to attend the first meeting of the SAS, as he was under arrest for knocking out his then commanding officer.) He was also a soldier of legendary bravery. By the end of the Second World War he had earned himself four DSOs, making him one of the two most highly decorated officers in the British Army.

The LRDG dropped the two groups within a few miles of their targets, arranging a rendezvous for later. On the way, they had been spotted by an Italian reconnaissance plane, and when Stirling and his men reached their objective they found that the airfield was empty. Mayne and his group were luckier, as Bill Kennedy Shaw described:

> By dusk the parashots were in position on the edge of the airfield, and what a sight for their first attempt! All around the edges were parked the aircraft; at the huts on the western side the unsuspecting aircrews were finishing their evening meal; beyond them on the coast road a little traffic was passing; beyond the road the white sand dunes hid the sea.
>
> For an hour or more Mayne waited and watched; then when all seemed still the party crept up to the huts. Inside, a faint light was burning, and there was a murmur of voices from the few Italians not yet asleep. Quietly, the door was opened and the parashots stepped inside, then a hose-spray from six Tommy guns ensured that there would be no interference from the ground staff in their work. By the time Mayne had finished and was on his way back to the rendezvous the petrol dump and twenty-four aircraft were ablaze.

The story goes that Paddy Mayne ripped out the instrument panel of one aircraft with his bare hands and kept it as a souvenir. The whole raid reportedly took only a quarter of an hour.

Further successful raids meant that by Christmas the SAS could boast that they had destroyed more German and Italian aircraft than any RAF unit in the Middle East. The speed and scale of this destruction were partly due to the combination of the LRDG's navigation and desert-driving skills and partly due to the Commando training of the SAS. However, a vital contribution was also made by the sticky bombs designed by Jock Lewes, as Jimmy Storie recollected:

> These bombs were placed anywhere. When they actually blew up they ignited, just a burst of flame, so we tried to get the bombs near to where they would do the best damage. That was actually where the petrol tanks were on the aircraft. So if they did explode, the petrol would help to destroy the rest. But then we discovered that in some cases they were only blowing off the wing because there wasn't enough plastic explosive. So we used to just blow off wings here and there on different raids.
>
> The Germans were very cute. If we blew up a plane, the left wing and left another plane with that wing and blew the right one, they used that wing and transferred it, so they made one plane out of two planes. So then we started doing all left wings or all right wings.

The fuse for a Lewes bomb was a 'time pencil', a device in which acid from a glass phial ate its way through a fine wire. Choosing the right time rating was important. Too long a delay might give the enemy time to remove the bomb; too short, and the bomb might explode before its placers had finished their job. Jimmy Storie remembered how they developed different uses for the Lewes bomb according to the type of plane:

> The fighters: we used to get the plastic explosive in the hollow tube in the seats, plug it in, just like Plasticine, and then tie a pencil on it. Now, it usually was a twenty-eight-day explosive, the pencil, and the acid ate through slowly, slowly, slowly, slowly, and then when it came to that bit the trigger fired and it ignited the explosive. So if a German happened to

come and take his plane up and he was just flying through the air, the next thing he was left with nothing – he had just blown up in the seat.

So the idea was any planes we left behind that we hadn't got time to blow up, the Germans wouldn't go near them or fly them in case this explosive had been put in them.

The Lewes bomb was thus a vital part of the SAS armoury – but it could be unpredictable, as its inventor discovered to his cost on a raid in December 1941. Jock Lewes had placed a bomb with a half-hour delay fuse on one aircraft, and he was about to place a bomb on the next when the first one exploded prematurely. This left him and the rest of his gang silhouetted against a blaze of light, and they came under heavy fire. They escaped, only to be pursued by relays of aircraft, as Jimmy Storie – who was in the supply truck with Lewes – recalled:

The jeeps were all caught out in the open. We were going round and round this hill, chased by the German planes, and we were getting picked off one at a time. We didn't see this fighter – it must have come over with some other raid – and it caught the back and it opened up, and that's when Jock Lewes was killed. His back was blown to bits with cannon shells, but he was the only one killed out of the five of us that were there. We buried him there. We all went back in one three-ton truck; the jeeps were all destroyed by the Germans.

Of course, we had to go and tell Stirling that Lewes had been killed and that we had buried him. He wasn't very pleased. Oh, no, no, he wanted us to go back and dig up the body and bring the body back. We wouldn't do it, we said no, no, Jock always said that you did what had to be done, it didn't matter who you were, whether a colonel, a captain, a major or a private. He was buried where he wanted to be buried. Funnily enough, he was buried with everything; we didn't take anything off him, no watches, jewellery, nothing.

In February 1942, as the 8th Army came under increasing pressure from the Germans, the LRDG was also forced to retreat. The move from Jalo back to their earlier base at Siwa did not stop them from continuing to act as taxi drivers for the SAS and others. However, in the spring and summer of 1942, their energies were increasingly absorbed with a meticulous road watch behind enemy lines. For five months, the Tripoli–Benghazi road, along which the Axis brought nearly all their armour, supplies and troop reinforcements, was kept under constant observation. Everything was meticulously recorded, and the information fed back to Cairo.

The LRDG's prime spot was near the giant triumphal monument to Mussolini's achievements as leader of the Fascist empire. British soldiers irreverently dubbed it 'Marble Arch'. Bill Kennedy Shaw had noted the year before that this area had more cover than most. He gave the exact latitude and longitude of the best hiding positions and advised arriving in the afternoon, when an onshore wind would be blowing.

Each road watch patrol had to take enormous care to brush out tracks in the sand, and to conceal their trucks using scrub woven into camouflage nets. (One New Zealander remembered how they discovered that the nets used on their own stood out 'like a boil on a baby's bottom' when viewed from the air.) Those not on duty would wait in the *wadi* (a dry watercourse) where the trucks were hidden, swatting flies, listening to the wireless or reading. Shifts were worked in pairs – and Arthur Arger remembered how they had to walk several miles, heavily laden, to reach their observation posts:

> Two of you would go down at dusk. You would have a water bottle, a tin of bully beef and a packet of biscuits, and you could either take a rifle or a revolver. Nothing was going to be much good in any case. Plus, you used to take your greatcoat because it did come in cold, and you got as near to the road as you could. You had binoculars as well, and a notebook, and you lay and watched, the two of you. Maybe one

could have a little kip while the other one was watching, but two of you never kipped at the same time. And you marked down in your little notebook what you saw going up and down that road, what you could see at sea... aircraft flying, or you might see aircraft going back on low loaders, or so-and-so going back to repair units. Everything was marked down that you saw.

The next two would come down at dusk. They would have a rough idea of where you were, but – you have to remember – you had to take your bully beef tin back with you, you never left any evidence. If you got caught short, you had to find somewhere where you could relieve yourself without being spotted, and it could be rather awkward sometimes.

Road watch was not a popular job. As Bill Kennedy Shaw put it:

It was a weary task. Bitterly cold in winter; blowing dust in your face in spring; blistering heat in summer; from dawn at five to dusk at seven was a long, long day. As one watcher said cynically: 'You look at your watch at 11.00 and look again four hours later and it's 11.15.'

In the daytime, it was unsafe for those on road watch to move at all, except perhaps to roll over from their stomach on to their back. At night, however, they walked about to keep warm and to get closer to the road to see better who was using it. Each pair would be armed with recognition pamphlets, and photographs and diagrams of enemy vehicles and tanks. David Lloyd Owen remembered even arranging visits to parks of captured enemy vehicles so they could be more easily identified.

Soldiers were on twenty-four-hour road watch every other day, for a fortnight at a time. This was quite long enough for most – as Alf Saunders remembered:

It was bloody monotonous and it was very nerve-racking. One particular day I was on it, and a load of trucks came up.

I think it was seventeen trucks full of infantry. They were doing their call of nature by the side of the road – and just to one side of us there were three or four gazelles got frightened. There must have been a dozen of these Eyeties got their rifles going on these gazelles. We thought, Jesus, you know, what the hell is going to happen here? We hoped to God they didn't hit one, because that would have come within a few hundred yards of us, and they probably would have seen us. At that time we had been told that Hitler had sent out a directive to his forces in Africa that any Long Range Desert Group or SAS personnel were not to be taken prisoners but to be shot on the spot. If they'd shot one of these animals, probably a dozen of them would have run over to get at the fresh meat and they might have seen us accidentally. We had no chance of running away from them.

The next time we counted seven anti-tank guns coming over the road, and they started firing right over our heads. Only the washerman knew how frightened I was with my underpants, believe you me.

In fact, as they afterwards discovered, the soldiers were doing some target practice, and they happened to be in the line of fire. Whether what they were watching induced fear or anger, road watch patrols were powerless to do anything about it. This was not just because of the risk to themselves, but because of the risk to the vital intelligence they were gathering. David Lloyd Owen recalled:

We were very strictly prohibited from taking any action which might in any way compromise the road watch, at the time or in the future. This made it all the more frustrating when we had to watch motionless as we saw lorry-loads of our own men being taken away from the battle as prisoners of war.

I remember I was doing this duty at the end of June, when Rommel had taken some 80,000 of our men prisoner, and when his front at El Alamein was very nearly 700 miles to the east of us, and that I watched a convoy of them being taken back into captivity. I remember, too, what a lot of self-control it demanded to do absolutely nothing as we heard them defiant to the last and singing lustily as they were driven away past us.

Some of the information supplied by the LRDG road watch could have been obtained from other sources, but much of it could not. At the time, many found the work terrifying and tedious by turns. Now, the survivors are proud to remember the contribution they made. Arthur Arger recalled:

Nobody ever found a road watch, and there was about three or four road watches between Tripoli and Tobruk. In one way it's amazing. Montgomery knew more or less everything, or Cairo knew everything because it was all radioed back into Cairo, and they [the enemy] never even picked up a radio. I think that is why Montgomery was successful at El Alamein. He knew what the Germans had got, so he just let them come on, and then when they had expended themselves he said: 'Well, they haven't got much left now – now it's my turn.'

Appreciation of the LRDG's efforts was reflected in numerous official letters of congratulation. After their last operation in the desert – which was to help the New Zealand Corps beat Rommel back to a tight corner in Tunisia – Montgomery wrote:

Without your careful and reliable reports the launching of the 'left hook' by the New Zealand division would have been a leap in the dark; with the information [the LRDG] produced, the operation could be planned with some certainty and as you know went off without a hitch.

'WHO DARES WINS'

The boy Stirling is mad. Quite, quite mad. However in war there is often a place for mad people.
General Bernard Montgomery

While the LRDG was increasingly occupied with patiently watching in ditches, David Stirling was laying plans that would enable him to reach his targets without the aid of Libyan Taxis Ltd – and would bring him his most dramatic success.

In Alan Hoe's authorized biography, Stirling remembered:

> I was perfectly happy with the LRDG, but we were a burden to them and I was conscious that their support could be withdrawn at any moment; indeed, Colonel Guy Prendergast [commanding LRDG] had expressed concern at the extent of their support to us – not because he disapproved, far from it, but their own vital effort was reduced whilst they escorted us. Under the war conditions of the time, they could be needed more and more by Auchinleck in their reconnaissance and observation role.

Also, the Germans and Italians were getting wise to the sticky bomb ploy. They had started putting a guard on every aircraft.

This meant that David Stirling urgently needed to rethink his tactics in order to recapture that vital element of surprise. Carol Mather – who, along with Stephen Hastings, transferred to the SAS at this time – recalled his next move:

> When I joined, David had managed to collar the first consignment of jeeps to arrive in the Middle East, and so we were equipped with our own transport. The jeeps were a kind of stripped-down vehicle, and for the first time we had machine guns mounted on the passenger seat and the rear seat. This was a novel experiment, actually. These were aircraft Vickers K guns, twin Vickers, so there were four machine guns in the jeep. We had to carry spare tyres, petrol, explosives, ammunition, and our own food and water, so it was quite a load. So although they were the first four-wheel-drive vehicles really in the desert, it was very easy to get bogged down.

The Vickers guns had been designed for the RAF to shoot down aircraft in the air; Stirling's new idea was to use them on the ground, keeping the Lewes bombs in reserve. In July 1942 he and Paddy Mayne experimented with this in a night-time raid on Bagoush airfield, driving through with weapons blazing. They escaped unscathed, leaving behind a trail of destroyed aircraft.

By now, the SAS was a highly trained force of a hundred or more men. But there were still difficulties caused by poor intelligence and lack of communication within the Army. In the authorized biography, Stirling recorded his frustration after he was instructed to abandon a planned raid on El Dhaba airport, as it was supposedly not being used by Rommel. Later, he discovered through some German prisoners that it was not only in use – it was Rommel's most important forward air base. 'I sent a message back to base that could have had me court-martialled under different circumstances. We had missed a glorious opportunity through their bloody negligence.'

For very good reasons, undercover operations behind enemy lines had to be kept secret – but this brought problems of its own. The LRDG had discovered the dangers of friendly fire; David Lloyd Owen's solution had been to construct a plywood circle with a long handle. On one side was painted an RAF roundel, and on the other a swastika. Once the nationality of approaching aircraft had been determined, the sign would be turned the 'right' way up. David Stirling used vehicles with German lookalike paint and recognition insignia. If they were mistakenly fired on by Allied forces, they simply had to try to get out of the way.

As the SAS became involved in increasingly high-risk operations, the toll of men and machines mounted. Stephen Hastings recalled his first expedition with the SAS, when his group lost two out of three jeeps after being attacked by Italian fighter planes. Their one remaining jeep was left with several bullet holes in the radiator, which they plugged with plastic explosive taken from Lewes bombs. There was some uncertainty as to whether or not it would explode when started; luckily for them, it didn't.

Nine men had to scramble on this one rather wounded jeep and drive back to the rendezvous, which was some seventy miles to the west. This was an awkward journey, because it kept overheating, and we'd have to turn it into the wind to cool down. The only way we could manage to keep the thing going was to do a pee in the radiator. That, of course, for biological reasons ran out too. But in the end that gallant jeep got us to within a few miles, and we came back by shanks's pony. You can't say it was very glamorous success, this. Nevertheless, it was a lucky escape.

Escapades like this were expensive on hardware, and Stephen Hastings was one of a small group left waiting – as he put it – 'like rats in holes' in the middle of the desert while David Stirling went back to base to re-equip. Carol Mather, who was also there, recalled the long wait for Stirling and his men to return:

> Stephen Hastings and I, and the doctor [Malcolm Pleydell], were left to the rearguard in this cave. We'd no idea when they were coming back again. The only thing we could do was dream of the day we might spend in Cairo, and we called that 'comfort day'. Every conceivable thing we could think of in the way of food, drink, water and everything else was designed in to this day, and it kept on being elaborated.
>
> Then about a fortnight later, much to our amazement, there was this kind of drumming noise, and this huge army of jeeps arrived, all with fresh equipment, and bristling with these Vickers K guns. And so we were rescued.

The Cairo party had been overdue. Dr Malcolm Pleydell recalled in *Born of the Desert* (written under the pen name Malcolm James) how they had plotted a suitably dramatic reception for their return:

> We discussed how, when eventually they did arrive, some of us would come crawling out on all fours from our cave, croaking, 'Water, master, water! For the love of Allah, water!' whilst others would be feverishly digging holes in the ground with their hands. We would be scrabbling and inarticulate, with the light of fanaticism in our eyes and a mad despair in every gesture. We would be laughing maniacally as each fingered a small piece of dried bully, licking it, nursing it, caressing and crowing over it with possessive pride.
>
> But they came one morning, and it was marvellous to see them. They brought an air of freshness and eagerness with them, of enthusiasm for the next raid; and by no means least important, they brought food and water. Our jaded spirits were revived.

Besides the new batch of twenty new jeeps and much-needed

supplies, Stirling brought ambitious plans for future raids. His idea was that, instead of going – as Carol Mather put it – 'creepy-crawly' up to the aeroplanes, they would simply drive on to the airfield in a U-formation of jeeps, with all guns blazing. He wanted to repeat the success of Bagoush, only on a much larger scale. Carol Mather recalled:

> We did one or two practices driving around the desert at night and keeping exactly in the right order, because it obviously was highly dangerous, with machine guns going off, if any of the vehicles strayed. And we let off our machine guns. It made the most appalling racket.
>
> We had a mixture of ammunition: armour-piercing, incendiary and ordinary bullets. The incendiary bullets, of course, were going to set the aircraft on fire. The fire was directed outwards and forwards, so the idea was to drive round, snake round among the parked aircraft, firing outwards.

Stirling's plan relied on the sheer weight of firepower. Each jeep had a pair of machine guns in the front and a pair in the back, each gun capable of firing 1,200 rounds a minute. The jeeps were to approach the airfield in single file, fanning out into line abreast as they reached the perimeter so they could overwhelm the enemy guard force. Stephen Hastings recalled:

> We had twelve jeeps and their crews, and for the attack there were ten in line and one each side behind, on each flank, to look out for the defences. I remember I was one side, and Carol Mather was the other. The plan was that David would send up a Very [signal] light once we got through the defences of the airfield, and then we would come into a sort of crocodile of two and two so that our guns could bear on either side. We had a full-scale practice of this – we were only about fifty miles south of the coast – with live ammunition. The ammunition consisted of tracer and incendiary bullets exclusively, so you had a sight, but it was night and difficult to

use the thing. The gunners fired by this stream of colour, and as it hit the desert – a shower of sparks – it was a tremendous pyrotechnic display. I was quite nervous that this might have been noticed, but nobody bothered us at all. We had this dress rehearsal on the evening before we set off, and then we had a day to wait, wondering what it would be like. That next evening we set forth.

Their target was to be the airfield at Sidi Haneish in the area of Fuka. This was a staging post for planes approaching or leaving the front, and air reconnaissance had reported that it was constantly busy. In particular, it was known to hold a large number of heavy Junkers transport planes, which were vital to Rommel's supply system. To ensure an element of surprise, Stirling chose a night with a full moon. The sentries would be less likely to expect an attack – and the SAS would be better able to see where they were going. As Carol Mather explained:

Now, it actually worked very well, but we'd had an appalling approach march across the desert. It was only about thirty miles, but we'd had a number of punctures, so we had to stop and mend the punctures. And so instead of arriving at the airfield shortly after midnight, we didn't get there until about three o'clock in the morning, or even later. So we had only about an hour of darkness before the dawn came.

Timing was vital not only for the attack itself, but also for the men's chances of a safe getaway. The plan was for them to split up afterwards and hide from the inevitable air search. This would hardly be possible in daylight. Mike Sadler, who had been poached from the LRDG, was in charge of navigation. He could not do much about the number of punctures suffered by the jeeps – but he could try to ensure they did not waste time getting lost. He remembered Stirling's increasing impatience as the night wore on:

I thought I knew where we were, as it was my job, but it was very bad going, and we were getting awfully late. We nearly always were behind schedule because of the going – you couldn't forecast just how good or bad it was going to be.

He stopped well short of the target to survey their position with a theodolite, and the group then followed a compass course with as little deviation as possible.

David finally became impatient at the rate of progress we were making and stopped and called me up to the front and said, 'How much further is it – and where the hell are we?' I said, 'I think we're about two miles south of the airfield', and just at that moment the runway lights on the airfield were switched on, a German aircraft came in and landed, and they were switched off again. I got a great kick out of it – it was one of my better moments.

Carol Mather recalled what happened next:

We stopped on the edge of the airfield, and David Stirling gave us a bit of a pep talk... 'And now, right – we're off.' So we formed up in a line and opened up, just kind of spraying the area. That sounds rather like the American Army, doesn't it? Then we formed off in our two columns, and set off for the aircraft, which by that time we could see. We simply opened up in the aircraft as we wound round them, and we were very gratified to see them burst into flames pretty quickly.

Stephen Hastings recalled:

It wasn't a perfect formation by any means, but it was working, and Carol and I at the back were the last two jeeps. Then we got into the dispersal area and there were the aircraft on either side and these streams of bullets. You'd see them zipping through the fuselage, and then the plane would glow for a minute and – woof – would go up in flames. We got in among some Stuka dive-bombers, which we feared and disliked particularly, and it was very refreshing to see them go up in flames.

All went well as we went across the airfield until there was a particularly big blazing bomber on our right and we were silhouetted against it. At last they got themselves together, and they shot at us with mortars and one or two big heavy Italian Breda machine guns, and it began to feel not so welcoming.

Johnny Cooper, who had joined the SAS as a teenager and had become David Stirling's navigator and fighting partner, was with him in the leading jeep. He recalled:

We loaded our hundred-round mags on the Vickers Ks with incendiary, armour-piercing and ball, so we had the benefit of penetrating and setting things on fire. As we hit the runway, I was with David in the middle vehicle and the two columns were left and right of us going back. The runway must have been in the region of 1000 yards. David said, 'Put up a red light followed by a green,' which meant we had to turn round and return up the runway.

Halfway back up that runway our jeep stopped. David was driving and he said, 'What the bloody hell is going on?' The bonnet opened, and it was steaming, and of course we had a Breda fifteen-millimetre shell right through the engine. So we bailed out, and on the left-hand side Sandy Scratchley came along and picked us up.

In the back of Sandy's truck was the inert figure of his rear gunner, killed by a bullet through the head. When they reached the open desert, it was to be Johnny Cooper's task to bury this young soldier, who had only recently joined the unit. But for the moment, as he put it: 'There was so much going on, I don't think you had time to be frightened.'

As the columns started to move back down the runway, Paddy Mayne spotted one plane that had been left untouched, and he leaped out of his jeep to attach a sticky bomb. Mike Sadler, who was waiting in the south-east corner of the airfield to pick up any casualties, described it as 'rather like a fireworks show, with the noises as well. It was a magnificent display.' Estimates of the number of planes destroyed varied wildly. Some reckoned as many as forty had gone; Stirling claimed a modest twenty-five. Official records later put the number at thirty-seven.

Having created as much havoc as they could in the shortest possible time, they now had to try to get out equally quickly. This was not easy, as Jimmy Storie remembered:

> We were going right round the 'drome and back again, and when we rode out we had to go through this barbed-wire entanglement, so we had to tow about thirty or forty feet of barbed wire behind us. We had to stop further out and get the wire cutters out and clip them. The lad I was with says to me, 'What will we do now?', and I says, 'Just put your foot down. We'll go like bats out of hell to get out of here. I'll tell you when to stop.'

Mike Sadler waited until the last moment to pick up any stragglers, then had a narrow escape after leaving the airfield:

> After daylight we made our way off, and of course the place was absolutely buzzing at that stage. There was luckily quite a thick mist because we drove off south and we got on to a track which may have been the track that we came up on, I'm not quite sure. We had driven a couple of miles when we ran into a German column which was out looking for us. They didn't expect us to be coming from behind. They were all standing there shivering, because it was a cold morning, and we drove right through and out the other end, and nobody interfered with us at all. I think they must have thought we were a further supply of Germans approaching.

Carol Mather remembered how grateful they were for the cover of the early morning mist. This prevented any remaining aircraft from taking off to look for them, as well as helping to conceal them.

> We were able to drive under cover of mist for some time. Then when daylight came we had to stop and hide ourselves as best we could. And, of course, this was absolutely flat desert, with occasional clumps of scrub. The only thing we could do was to camouflage up the jeeps with the net, get as far away from them as possible ourselves, and make ourselves as inconspicuous as we could, which was very difficult.
>
> We were extremely elated, obviously, that the thing had been successful. Seeing all these aircraft burning was a marvellous sight to our eyes. But then the hard work began, because we were being chased, and it was very hot. We had a bush about two feet high, which we were trying to shelter behind. Then we heard these aircraft droning around, droning around. Eventually, they'd spot one of our vehicles, or spot one of us, and – probably Stukas or the Italian Macchis – they'd dive down, machine-gunning. Much to our dismay, one vehicle after another burst into flames and exploded.

For years afterwards, Carol Mather – like many other survivors of such desert attacks – had nightmares about being machine-gunned by dive-bombers. Once they had been spotted, they were sitting targets. There was very little they could do about it, except wait for darkness and hope that the planes would run out of ammunition.

> Our small party, which I think had three jeeps, was left with one jeep, without any tyres. So we drove on the rims, with about twelve men up, when dusk came, heading – we hoped – in the right direction.

They joined up with the rest of their group and started the exhausting journey back through the desolate Qattara Depression to the rendezvous. Progress was painfully slow, and they frequently became bogged down. At one point they suddenly found to their horror that they were missing ten vehicles. After an hour's search, they found all ten of them, with the drivers slumped asleep over their steering wheels. They were so dead tired they had all gone to sleep at the last halt; the engine noise and cries of 'Start up!' had failed to waken them.

Meanwhile, the other patrols had returned safely to the rendezvous. There was only one casualty – a Frenchman, André Zirnheld, who had been killed in an air attack. Stirling himself had been summoned back to Cairo for briefing on an operation planned by Middle East Headquarters. It was a summons he obeyed only reluctantly. As he told his biographer: 'They still hadn't got the message. The only persons who would plan SAS operations were SAS officers.'

In the short term, Stirling's instincts were proved right. The operation planned for September 1942 was a full-scale raid on Benghazi town and harbour, with air and naval support. It was difficult to maintain security with so many people involved. The Germans turned out to be expecting the attack, and the SAS was forced to withdraw. By the end of the raid, Stirling had lost a quarter of his men, either killed, wounded, captured or missing. At the same time, the LRDG successfully attacked Barce airfield, using classic SAS tactics to destroy thirty-two aircraft. This only served to reinforce Stirling's conviction that Commando units operated better independently.

In the long term, however, the summons back to Cairo operated in Stirling's favour. It brought him a valuable meeting with Winston Churchill, who had heard colourful stories of SAS exploits from his son, Randolph. (Randolph Churchill had been on one raid with David Stirling and had been deeply impressed – even though after the raid he had badly injured his back in one of Stirling's many car crashes.)

Churchill gave orders that Stirling (Churchill called him the Scarlet Pimpernel) should have a free hand. He was promoted to lieutenant-colonel and given permission to recruit up to full regimental strength. For someone who was still only twenty-five and considered by many to be a bit of a maverick, this was recognition indeed.

As Stirling's reputation grew, he did not have to look far for talented recruits. Wilfred Thesiger, who was later to become a distinguished travel writer, was then serving with the Special Operations Executive. Frustrated by lack of action, he visited Stirling in Cairo. Stirling took an instant liking to him, and a quick phone call to a handy brigadier secured his transfer.

However, in his rush to build up his regiment, Stirling ran up against General Bernard Montgomery, who strongly objected to his plans to poach fighters already trained in desert warfare, reasoning that he needed them just as much, if not more. The 8th Army was at this point preparing for the offensive which was to lead to the Battle of El Alamein on 23 October 1942.

Stirling was left with the prospect of a greatly enlarged but only half-trained regiment. He had an ambitious scheme to support the Allied offensive – but he could not see how he could carry it out with raw recruits. His solution was to divide the regiment into two squadrons. Major Paddy Mayne, with the more experienced soldiers, was sent to establish a forward base from which to attack targets along the coast. He himself was to take charge of training the other squadron.

He also took over the Greek Sacred Regiment, formed by Greek Army officers who had escaped from Greece after the German invasion. As Stirling himself put it: 'They were a proud bunch and based their battle traditions on the wives' farewells to the ancient Thebans: "Return – with your shield or on it".'

The desert was filling up with maverick groups such as that led by Vladimir Peniakoff. Officially his group was called Number 1 Long Range Demolition Squadron; unofficially it was known as Popski's Private Army. With so many groups operating on their own initiative, it became important to have some sort of central control. There had been occasions when SAS raids had alerted enemy patrols, putting LRDG road watch teams in jeopardy. A friendly rivalry had developed between the long-established desert specialists and the 'parashots', and the territory was carved up between them. The LRDG was to concentrate on reconnaissance and long-range attacks, the SAS on short-range.

David Stirling spent a period in hospital with severe desert sores – but he simply carried on directing things from his hospital bed. In particular, he made sure the SAS continued to have a high profile among those who mattered. His success in this is illustrated by comments made by General Montgomery at a dinner, and quoted in the authorized biography of Stirling:

> The boy Stirling is mad. Quite, quite mad. However in war there is often a place for mad people. Now take this scheme of his. Penetrating miles behind the enemy lines. Attacking the coastal road on a 400-mile front. Who but the boy Stirling could think up such a plan? Yet if it comes off I don't mind saying it could have a really decisive effect on my forthcoming offensive.

Over Christmas 1942, which the SAS spent holed up in a *wadi*, Montgomery sent a bottle of whisky and 500 cigarettes for each of Stirling's men. He also sent a personal message to say that the force had, since Alamein, done more than any other division for the war effort.

Stephen Hastings only served under Stirling for nine months, as he was forced to leave the SAS through illness. However, during that time he developed an enormous respect for him, as he recalled:

> If you had to find a character out of British history – although he was a seaman, as opposed to a land soldier – the one nearest to him that I can think of is Sir Francis Drake, whose brilliant raids on the Spaniards were such that when they thought of the British Navy, they simply

thought of Drake. He was extremely effective when he was raiding on his own with his own ships; he was not so effective when he was placed under orders in the Armada. He was a man who succeeded in the front; he was not so good when it came to the planning and the administration and the rest, which had to be done by others.

David Lloyd Owen suggested that Stirling lost his effectiveness once he became independent of the LRDG, because he had to concern himself with the mechanics of administration:

David Stirling was a magnificent fighting leader, but the tedious business of worrying where the food, the ammunition, the communications, the fuel and water were to come from was something with which he did not want to concern himself. Up until then the LRDG had done all that for him.

Carol Mather's account of Stirling's planning – or lack of it – for the trip that led to his capture in the desert confirms this:

The idea was that we would have a jeep patrol every ten miles between the back of the Alamein line and Tripoli. These patrols would operate against German and Italian transport during the night, and the RAF would look after this transport during the day, because it was just this single ribbon, single one road, which had to take everything. Because it was quite near the coast, it was quite difficult moving off the road, because of the danger of mines. So we set off and had a kind of base area where we all congregated. We had some good cover there: thorn trees and things.

As luck would have it, I drew the short straw and found myself on the Tripoli end. That was about 400 miles away, across unknown desert. Then it turned out it wasn't really desert. It was very rough country, deep *wadis* and gorges, and quite a lot of farming going on there too, and villages, this kind of thing, which we hadn't been used to at all.

We were about to set out, so I said to David, 'Well, you reckon I might have to stay about a month in my hideout near the Tripoli end, but I've only got enough food for a week, and water for about four days, so what am I going to do then?' 'Oh,' he said, 'don't worry about that. I mean, you'll be able to raid these Italian houses, and they'll have hams hanging up on the ceiling, and just take a few of those, you know. You'll find it quite easy to live.'

So as I drove away on this expedition, I just imagined myself raiding this Italian farmhouse as the family were sitting down to dinner, and dashing in and seizing their plates, or ham off the rafters. Of course, it didn't work out like that. We had terrific delays, because we had to take everything, water, petrol, ammunition, explosives, and so we were very heavily laden. It was very difficult getting across country. And we ran out of water after about four days. Fortunately, it had been raining quite hard, so we managed to get enough water out of the puddles.

Eventually, they reached what they thought was the right point (it was). The idea was that they would dismantle their vehicles at night and hide them in a cave so the Italians would not find them. However, things did not turn out quite that simply.

We did a kind of recce the first night – we still had our vehicles – and we found ourselves passing a fort. That was all quiet. Then we came into a small town with a roadblock and sentries, and the only thing we could do was just drive straight for this roadblock and drive through it, and then get out of the other side of the town and get into the country again. But this time the show had been rather given away.

The next morning they concealed their vehicles and hid in a cave in a deep *wadi*. What they did not realize was that they were right next to the desert equivalent of a main road.

From about seven o'clock in the morning there were donkeys and camels, and goodness knows what else passing. And, of course, everyone took a great interest in where we were, having our breakfast in this cave. Just as we were about to eat our scrambled egg – we'd got some eggs from there – an Italian patrol came down the valley and so it was impossible to stay in the cave. We got out, clambered up the cliff on to the top of the *wadi*, and then they came rushing down to this cave, very excited, all poured in, and saw our breakfast lying there. We opened fire on them, and I think we must have done some damage because later in the day they wanted to put us up against the wall and shoot us.

We spent the day playing hide-and-seek among olive groves, and all the dogs barked, every village, they were standing on the roof pointing out where we were. Eventually, we ran out of what little ammunition we had, and they came in with grenades, so we got out of our ditch and put our hands up, and that was that.

A similar fate was to overtake Stirling himself. As the SAS had expanded, he had managed to carve out a second regiment, which operated on the 1st Army front in Tunisia. His plan was to carry out raids in northern Tunisia, and eventually to link up with the 2nd SAS Regiment, which was commanded by his brother, Bill. There was a lot of ground still between the 1st and 8th Armies in North Africa, and his ultimate dream was for the SAS to be the means by which they could meet.

His route took him through an area known as the Gabes Gap, which was full of German and Italian troops. He had been given direct orders to go around the Gap, not through it, as intelligence reports had suggested this would be too dangerous. However, they were short of fuel – and, as David Lloyd Owen put it: 'David was always a man in a hurry, and this was the quickest route to where he wanted to go.'

Realizing that they might be seen in daylight, Stirling and his group decided to catch up on some much-needed sleep. It was early morning, and they had been travelling for forty-eight hours. They had driven over an enemy airfield and bluffed their way through a group of sleepy German soldiers, and they were now so exhausted they did not even mount a guard.

Mike Sadler, who was with Johnny Cooper in the leading jeep, recalled the sequence of events:

> When we got near the hills, we were just looking along to see if there was somewhere we could get in, and we saw this opening and very gratefully drove into it. It seemed to be perfectly OK at that stage. We did camouflage the vehicles – that's why we were caught out, in a way. We made quite a good job of camouflage with a tarpaulin over the whole thing, and then a scrim netting over the top of that, so there was no way one could have got at the guns and everything underneath.

They collapsed into their sleeping bags with their boots on. The next thing they knew was that they were being kicked, and they each woke up to find themselves looking down the barrel of a German automatic weapon. As Mike Sadler put it, with masterly understatement: 'It was a pretty nasty surprise. I looked round and saw Johnny looking out of his bag, and I just think we both looked rather depressed.'

The Germans went to get reinforcements and they made a break for it. Johnny Cooper recalled:

> Mike dived into the Jeep to get the codes, because obviously they were very, very important. If they had been picked up they could have picked up other parties who were coming behind us. Then we made a break up the *wadi* together, running, and at some stage Freddy Taxis, the French sergeant from the Free French forces, tagged on behind us, and we went up and up and up and up, until we were so exhausted we collapsed into a little sort of hole in the ground.

They were lucky to find themselves some mobile camouflage in the form of a flock of sheep and goats. They heard the sounds of a search, but were not found. However, their troubles were not over. On the first stage of their long march to meet up with the 1st Army, they were stoned by Arabs, as Johnny Cooper recalled:

> Being stoned was not a very nice experience. There were about four young boys aged about ten to twelve round me, and they were throwing stones and then one clobbered me [on the forehead] and of course I couldn't see because the blood went straight into my eyes, and I shouted, 'Help.' Mike and Freddie came down and they got one side, one the other, and ran me away. I couldn't see because the blood was filling me up. It wasn't a big cut, but the blood was all over the place.

Since they had boots, and the Arabs did not, they were able to escape by running over a stony area. They then faced the long and painful walk of a hundred or so miles to rejoin the SAS. They were picked up by an American armoured patrol, but their bearded, dusty and generally dishevelled appearance led them to be handcuffed and treated as spies. However, they were released once they had told their survival story and their identities had been confirmed. Mike Sadler's navigation talents were later called on in the very area that he had just left. He was asked to help the LRDG guide the New Zealand Division in their left-hook approach to the Mareth line, an approach that was to prove vital in Rommel's retreat.

Their commander, however, was not so lucky. Stirling had been awoken by a nervous German holding a Luger pistol (the nervous German turned out later to be the unit dentist). He emerged to find a whole company of Germans outside. He managed to escape under cover of darkness that evening and stayed the next day with a friendly Arab. When darkness fell, he set off again – but was fatally delayed by a boyish impulse, as he recalled in his biography:

> I was a bloody fool. I noticed an aerodrome which I did not recognize and like an idiot I went to recce it. I should have moved at all possible speed towards the RV [rendezvous] at Bir Soltane but I couldn't resist a check to see whether it was a worthwhile job for the boys. I was convinced I was going to make it back, you see. There were lots of planes, Junkers, it would be an easy target from my assessment of the defences. The trouble was it took me about three hours to sneak around the place.

Progress after this little diversion was painfully slow; he had underestimated how long it would take him to cross the difficult terrain. As daylight came, he found himself some cover and slept. He awoke to find a young Arab who offered to get him food and water – and led him straight into the arms of the Italians. He was taken, heavily guarded, to the nearest headquarters.

Alan Hoe, Stirling's official biographer, speculates that the Italians did not immediately know of the importance of their prisoner. As he put it:

> The Italians knew they had captured one of the SAS (he still had his cap with its badge) but it is equally certain that they did not initially realize that in their hands they had the Phantom Major. They probably imagined the latter to be eight feet tall with huge shoulders, bristling with machine guns and aggression. This quiet, stooping fellow could be of little consequence, but he may have information and must be sent off without delay.

Ironically, the aircraft in which he was dispatched to Italy took off from the very airfield he had chosen for his recce. As a prisoner, it was not long before Stirling made his presence felt in numerous escape attempts. These were eventually to land him in the notorious German prison camp for serial escapers – Colditz. There, he was to share a cell with another legend of military history – the legless fighter pilot, Douglas Bader.

David Lloyd Owen commented on his capture:

What a tragedy it was that he was caught when the end in North Africa was so near! He had done such a lot, and put everything that he had towards achieving this great victory, which before Alamein seemed impossible. His contribution to the final defeat of the Axis in North Africa is not easy to assess, for I believe that after he began to expand the SAS the balance sheet showed too great an excess of expenditure over achievement. But before that time Paddy Mayne, for instance, on his own destroyed far more enemy aircraft than did any of the great fighter aces on either side.

Paddy Mayne was an obvious choice to take over command of the SAS, but Stirling was a hard act to follow. Quite apart from his personal charisma, there was a practical difficulty: he never wrote things down. After his capture, at the end of January 1943, no one had much idea about what his future plans had been. Indeed, there was some haziness about his present ones.

The greatest testament to his worth came from his enemy. Rommel wrote in his diary: 'Thus the British lost the very able and adaptable commander of the desert group which had caused us more damage than any other unit of equal strength.'

The long-lasting value of the organization founded by Stirling became increasingly clear in the second part of the twentieth century, as Sir Stephen Hastings pointed out in his autobiography, *The Drums of Memory*:

Since the war of course the SAS Regiment has evolved. It is no exaggeration to say they have become an essential arm of defence in this wretched age of cowardly terrorism. Their expertise is legendary and their operational range immense. Probably there is no other unit in the Western world which possesses this combination of exhaustive training, daring and ubiquitous resource. By comparison with their present competence, the early desert operations must seem strangely amateur. They were. But the principles were already established and without David Stirling's imagination and inspiration this essential and extraordinary regiment would never have existed.

Amateurish or not, the dedication and daring of both the LRDG and the SAS have ensured them a place in military history. The information provided by members of the LRDG as they holed up in their dry and dusty *wadis* was crucial in determining the course of the war in Africa. They transported agents, wounded soldiers and themselves hundreds of miles through the deepest desert with the modest efficiency of London taxi drivers.

Handfuls of SAS men, armed with nothing more sophisticated than sticky bombs and machine guns, managed to clock up individual tallies of destroyed aircraft greater than any RAF fighter ace. Perhaps most important, the unpredictable raids of both units tied down thousands of Italian and German troops, keeping them constantly guessing as to where these phantom forces would surface next.

PART FOUR

A Leap in the Dark

THE RINGWAY CIRCUS

Before the war, people would pay to see stunt parachutists jump from the wings of aeroplanes – but it was not until Hitler's spectacular successes with his *fallschirmjaeger* (elite paratroopers) that it was taken seriously as a way of going to war.

Both the Russians and the Germans had had trained troops of parachutists since 1936 – and British generals who had regarded them as simply a way of giving a crowd a cheap thrill were to pay for their complacency. In June 1940 Churchill directed that 5,000 parachute troops should be prepared. This was a hopelessly ambitious total. Equipment was primitive or nonexistent. The RAF was used to the idea of emergency escape chutes – but very few people in Britain had actually made a parachute jump.

The guinea pigs for this new technology had to be brave men, temperamentally suited to taking a leap in the dark. They underwent the same selection and basic training as other Commando units; if they could master the art of parachuting, it would be an ideal way to take them behind enemy lines.

Ernie Chinnery, who had joined the Army at the age of fourteen, was one of the last to train by horseback – and one of the first to train by parachute. Yet he had never even been in an aircraft before he joined Number 2 Commando. He recalled:

Having been in the Army for twelve years, I didn't want to be in the training regiment for the next twelve. I knew absolutely nothing about parachuting because I had never been in an aircraft before. Any rate, I wanted something different and I thought to myself I might as well go over to France and fight over there as let Jerry come over here and do his fighting here.

Nobody had thought of parachuting before the war. We never heard anything about what Germany was doing, but what we did know was Max Schmelling, the world heavyweight champion at one time, was in the German paras. It didn't alter my intention, though, because I had done a bit of boxing myself. I got the middleweight belt two years out of three when I was serving in India, so I was ready for a fight at any time.

Harry Pexton, a painter and decorator in civilian life, recalled his reasons for joining this mystery unit:

I was attached to the South Staffordshire Regiment, and we used to have to stand to in the morning at dawn and again at night, in fear of an invasion that never happened, and it got to be very trying. I think most of us volunteered for it to get away from the boredom, which was getting a bit much.

After five interviews in five different places, he was selected – but what he had been selected for remained unclear.

I asked the officer what it consisted of, and he said, 'Well, you're either going to be a seaborne commando or an airborne commando.' So I said, knowing what a seaborne commando did, 'Well, what does an airborne commando do?' He said, 'You'll be jumping out of aeroplanes.' Well, I didn't think a great lot to that at the time, but he said, 'I like the look of you, son. You're going to be with me – you're going to be an airborne commando.' I was committed, and he later became my boss.

I think most of us that turned up at this place hadn't a clue what was going on. They sent some instructors out of the Army, who didn't know any more than we did. It was the lame leading the blind; they were as wise as we were about what to do next, and we spent a fair bit of time just hanging about.

At the beginning of June 1940, in anticipation of Churchill's orders, the RAF had established a parachute training centre at Ringway (now Manchester Airport), ten miles south of Manchester. They had four ageing Whitley bombers, twenty-eight parachutes, permission to use the grounds of nearby Tatton Park as a drop zone, and little else. Members of the RAF, who had some experience in training pilots to bale out of aircraft in emergencies, were joined by PT instructors from the Army. They were expert in teaching forward rolls – but not exactly used to dealing with aeroplanes.

Before the would-be parachutists even set foot on an aeroplane, they used primitive jumping platforms and dummy fuselages to practise landing from a height. Their nickname for this apparatus was to be 'Kilkenny's circus', after its RAF inventor. This may have helped them learn how to avoid broken legs and ankles – but not even the most sophisticated mock-up could prepare them for the real thing.

Although members of Number 2 Commando had been carefully picked for their bravery and willingness to have a go at the enemy, there was no way of telling in advance whether or not they would have the guts to jump out of an aeroplane. The only test was to take them up into the skies and try it.

First for the high jump were the officers, some of whom had been acting as parachute instructors without having ever tried it themselves. They jumped from the rear end of a Whitley bomber that had had its nest of machine guns removed. This meant standing where the rear gunner was meant to stand, pulling the ripcord of the parachute, and being ejected like a pilot from a plane in distress. Quite apart from the fact that this was such an alarming experience, it was clearly impractical for dropping large numbers. The decision was made to use bombers with a hole cut in the floor, and the men practised the art of jumping through this – first on the ground, then in the air.

The hole in the aircraft fuselage was shaped like a plant pot – big at the top, small at the bottom – and making an exit without hitting the side of the hole was a fine art, as Ernie Chinnery recalled:

> The pack you carried was at least six to eight inches deep. You were sitting with your legs in the hole, and the other side of the hole was about a yard away, so you'd jump forward far enough to clear the pack from the back of the hole. If you jumped far enough away you'd go down straight, as though at attention. If you didn't, the pack would hit the side and your head would go forward and you would hit the other side. So unless you cleared the back of the hole, you would hit your face.

When journalists were eventually allowed to write about parachuting, they coined the phrase the 'Whitley kiss' for this particular occupational hazard. The Whitley was a bomber, never originally designed for parachuting, and even the smallest of men could not stand up inside. As Ernie Chinnery put it: 'When you were travelling, it was like the bloody London Underground, with no windows.'

In those early days, each individual parachutist jumped with a static line. One end was clipped to a bar next to the hole in the aircraft; the other was attached to the ripcord. When each man jumped, the weight of his body automatically used the static line to open the parachute. The signal to jump was given by a dispatcher, who knelt by the hole.

Harry Pexton remembered every detail of his first parachute jump:

> It was like stepping off a bus, but it was far more frightening. There was a dispatcher, an RAF warrant officer who

said, 'When I tap you on the shoulder, you go.' But he felt as though he had a hand about the size of a dustbin lid, and when he tapped you on the shoulder, if you'd have hung on to the aircraft you would have pulled it over. But you went, and you just shut your eyes and hoped for the best.

Eventually, we got into the habit of parachuting, and we used to sneak in for an extra jump. But initially I have never been more frightened in my life, because from 800 feet houses look about the size of a matchbox, and cows and sheep look about the size of small flea. It looked 800 miles, never mind 800 feet, but it was OK. In the end, I daresay it was enjoyable because you knew what was going to happen.

Parachutists jumped singly, the aircraft flying round in a circle to drop each one in the same area. The first jump, with the officers, had been on 13 July; the first fatality came within a fortnight, on 25 July. A parachutist named Evans was killed when his rigging lines and canopy formed a hopeless tangle.

Ernie Chinnery had been next in line to make his fourth jump when the accident happened. He recalled:

Once you were inside the Whitley, you couldn't see outside, except through the hole – and, don't forget, the hole was moving forward with the aeroplane. We were flying round, and I was getting into position ready to do my jump, and the dispatcher said, 'We've had a red light from the ground. We're going back to Ringway. Somebody has been hurt.'

So we went back to Ringway, and when we got there we were assembled in the lecture room, and we were told that Evans had been killed, and that jumping had been suspended. Then we just marched back to our billets, and we were told a couple of days later that we were being sent up to Scotland. I suppose the reason why we were being sent up there was to get us out of the way while they were trying to devise something a bit safer.

Harry Pexton recalled how he heard about the accident:

> We were at a meeting in the gym at Ringway, and some big wheel was telling us how safe and easy parachuting was, and someone came in and whispered in his ear, and he said, 'Oh, I'm sorry to tell you that a man has just been killed.' And he was two or three minutes before telling us how safe it was.

They went to Lord Lovat's estate near Fort William, where they had six intensive weeks of Commando training – including an encounter with the Shanghai unarmed combat instructors, Fairburn and Sykes. Harry Pexton gave this description of them:

> They were lethal. They had loops inside their coats with knuckle-dusters and knives and hand grenades and sawn-off revolvers. They were a terrible pair of men, but very nice men. They could teach you all sorts of very nasty ways to kill people. Fortunately, I suppose we never had need to practise them properly, but they were there just in case.

Dave Struthers found the lessons he learned from Fairburn and Sykes very useful in later life, as he recalled:

> I quite often had a deal with them on a Sunday, instead of going to church, I'm afraid. They had invented what was called the Fairburn and Sykes fighting knife, and that was one of our issues. They taught us unarmed combat, knife-fighting and close-quarter pistol-shooting. By close quarter I mean from about three yards to twelve, fifteen yards. My recollection is that when I had finished that training I could fire five shots in two seconds, irrespective of whether it was half-dark or what the lighting was, at a man-sized target.
> They taught us hand-to-hand fighting. In fact, this was very useful to me. I was a policeman for most of my life after the war, but at night I never troubled carrying a baton,

because I had the confidence that if I had anyone to deal with
I didn't require a baton.

The regime was tough, but it paid dividends in improved
fitness. Harry Pexton again:

> We lived in tents, and we were out as soon as it became light
> until it went dark – and, of course, it rained most of the time,
> as it does in Scotland. But we were hardened up then, and
> we all put weight on. It wasn't fat, it was muscle weight, and
> it was quite a good thing.

If they were trained to be tough, they were also trained to be
self-reliant – as Harry Pexton found to his cost when he injured
an ankle near the summit of Ben Nevis. His comrades were not
allowed to help him – and drivers of army vehicles in the area
had been told not to stop for soldiers. He was left to scramble
his way down the mountainside, eventually hitching a lift with
a ration lorry.

An incident on the way back south demonstrated that the
force was now one to be reckoned with. Harry Pexton:

> Coming back on the train from Fort William to Manchester,
> somebody had got hold of an automatic rifle and they were
> firing it through the window, and there was a lot of trouble
> over that. When we got into Glasgow, changing trains, there
> was a gang of redcaps, military policemen, waiting for us.
> Eventually, of course, we had a dust-up with them, and we
> all arrived in Knutsford with black eyes, thick lips. But it was
> worth it against the redcaps.

They arrived back at the training school to discover that the
parachute packing bags had been redesigned, and parachutes were now being specially made for them. As Ernie
Chinnery recalled, each man had a special relationship with
his parachute:

The unpacked parachutes were kept in the lecture room while we were under training. We used to go over, pick up a parachute, and in the hangar there were two long tables. We were told which one to put them on, and we would hand it over to these chaps and then they would pack it. They showed us what they were doing, and when they had packed it, they'd say, 'Are you satisfied with it?' We'd say, 'Yeah.' Actually, we knew no bloody different; what they told us was good, God's truth. And then when they had packed it they handed it over to you and you would keep that. You would stick to that like shit to a blanket, never leave go of it. You saw it packed, and it was going to save your life.

As the unit expanded, female parachute packers were brought in. Their training left them in no doubt of the responsibility of their job, as Anne Davenport remembered:

They explained everything about the parachute and what it entailed, and that was when you got the word that if anything happened to the 'chute you would be brought up for manslaughter. They stressed that, because there were one or two finished the course and they didn't want to be a parachute packer after that.

Olive 'Snowy' Quayle remembered the parachutists visiting with their instructors to watch their chutes being packed:

They used to all get around the table – it was a bit nerve-racking, but we managed it – and they said, 'What happens if our 'chute doesn't open?' We said, 'Well, you can always come back for another one.' We had a logbook for each parachute, so we had to sign it, and so did the chap who had the 'chute. If a 'chute was packed wrong, they knew exactly who had done it.

Anne Davenport recalled the dreadful moment when one of the packers was taken away after a man died when a parachute she had packed turned into a Roman candle. This was their euphemism for a parachute which failed to open properly. The streaming canopy would look like a candle flame as it fell.

> We didn't know about it until they stopped us packing, and word got round in the section that a parachute hadn't opened … some redcaps came in and took this lady away.

Both Anne and Olive were grateful that this never happened to them, although Olive received a stark reminder of the risks of parachuting when she was taken to watch a jump:

> I only went once, and then this Polish paratrooper had a Roman candle. It wasn't the fault of the 'chute, of the parachute packer. I don't know what it was – but he went into the ground and dug his own grave. We were very sorry, but they wouldn't let us go again. They said, 'Oh, no, you're not going to watch them.' I could see them from my house at home, you could see them jumping out of the plane, and a lot of them went into the lake.

She also remembered being chatted up by the parachutists:

> We used to go in the YMCA and they'd all come in from the jump – some of them with split lips, big noses, you know – they'd hit the side of the plane. A lot of them used to come in and thank us.

Parachutists had to make five jumps before they could receive their wings. All were volunteers, and there was no disgrace in backing out during the training – but they could be put on a charge if they refused to jump after they were qualified.

Doug Russell, who had originally worked at the London Stock Exchange, arrived at Ringway some three months after the first intake. He recalled:

I had a fellow who came with me from the rifle brigade in the early days, and when we did our first drop, he came home back to the digs in the evening and he said, 'I couldn't do it' – and he just automatically went back. You weren't penalized for it; he just went back to his unit. I only saw two or three like that. I don't think there were many refusals.

I thought it was much easier to get out of that hole or out of the door, or whatever you were doing, than to refuse to do it. It would take a lot of guts to refuse to go – it was easier to go.

He recalled how they gained confidence from the instructors – one of the most colourful of whom was Harry Ward. Nicknamed the Yorkshire Birdman, he had made his name with stunt parachute jumps before the war, as part of Alan Cobham's Flying Circus. He had also helped to introduce parachutes to aircrews after the First World War.

I remember somebody saying, 'That's Harry Ward', and we said, 'Well, exactly who is Harry Ward?' They said, 'Well, he's done 156 jumps.' We were just going to do our first one, and we thought, Oh, my God, he must be good.

Harry Ward himself never counted the number of jumps he had done, but his estimate was nearer 2,000. Harry Pexton recalled:

He was not a big fellow – he was normal size, probably five and a half feet, or something like that. He was very good in telling you what was going to happen. He never seemed to get excited; he seemed to take things very casually, and it gave you the same feeling. He was older than any of us, and it's the thing about 'If this guy can do it, I can,' you know?

However, leaving aside the fear factor, not everyone was suited to parachuting, as Len Shepherd recalled:

I always feel that it was very sad, because you had a lot of competent soldiers who were RTUd – returned to their units – because they just didn't have the muscle co-ordination. It wasn't easy, even for a small man like myself. For the big chaps it was much more difficult to sit on the floor and move up to the hole and jump through, bearing in mind you had a parachute on your back.

Len Shepherd was an example of an instructor who was teaching and learning at the same time, and he remembered the relief after his first drop:

After landing, the other chaps and myself on the DZ [drop zone], we were reasonably excited, and the men that smoked went for their cigarettes. I was offered one, but I thought, 'Oh, I don't smoke,' and refused. I think if I had taken a cigarette at the time I would have been a smoker, a real hardened smoker by now. We were all pretty buoyed up, and it was a good confidence booster.

We had to sign a book, to put down anything that might have gone haywire, or not been right, but it was quite something – a great feeling.

Christopher Lea, a Sandhurst-trained officer who came from a military family, was just twenty-two when he arrived at Ringway. He had taken part in the advance into Belgium and the retreat to Dunkirk. Like many others, he had volunteered for the Commandos so he could stay in the thick of the action. He recalled:

My first jump was out of a Bombay aircraft. We jumped not through the hole, like we did in the Whitley, but through the door – which had in fact been taken off its hinges. So you simply stood with your hands each side of the door waiting to be told to jump.

I had with me however many it was... about twelve,

thirteen, fourteen people altogether, all of whom I had been a party to recruiting. There were these men whom I had helped recruit sitting there watching me, who was expected to go first.

The person I felt sorry for was the person who was last, who would be on his own. The aircraft was going to have to do another circuit and come round again over the dropping zone. I remember thinking of that man – I can't remember his name now – but he had got to be really rather brave, I think. The temptation when you're on your own, and there is nobody watching you... As I stood by that door before that jump, I would have jumped without a parachute with all those eyes watching me. There was no way I would not have jumped. But that man on his own, in hindsight I felt sorry for him.

In the early days, a parachutist had only a pilot-type leather helmet for head protection, as Ernie Chinnery recalled:

They issued us with sorbo rubber pads to put round our knees and round our backside. They also gave us a jock-strap, which I assumed was to protect your wedding tackle, but they gave you nothing to protect your head. Your knees, your backside and the wedding tackle – that's all you were worth, I think.

The first casualty was by no means the last experienced by the training school, and fully trained parachutists got danger money along with their wings. This was four shillings a day above normal pay for officers, and two shillings for other ranks. A lot of this found its way into the tills of nearby bars, with some riotous results, as Len Shepherd recalled:

Sometimes things got a little bit out of hand. The habit was to put the money in the centre of the table and what was left paid for the breakages, put it that way.

Partly in recognition of their special status, the parachutists were billeted with families in nearby Wythenshawe, Benchill, and Knutsford, rather than having to stay in barracks. Since most of the soldiers were very young, they were treated like family. Dave Struthers is still in touch with the son, then only eight, of the family he stayed with in Knutsford. Doug Russell remembered coming up against an unexpected problem with his first landlady:

> There was two of us staying there, and she used to say, 'Now which one of you is going to take me out to the pictures, and who is going to stay in with my husband?' This got a bit too much; we didn't go much on this idea at all. So I got out and I moved down the road, and there was a lovely lady there, a Mrs Brooks – old enough to be my mother. She looked after us; she was marvellous. They treated us like kids. You used to come in and you'd get your food on the table, and all your washing done for you, and I used to be out pretty late in those days – we all were. I'd come in about two in the morning, and in the oven was a cup of cocoa. It was always there. I didn't really want the cocoa, but I used to drink it. I didn't want to upset her.

Morning parades were fairly haphazard affairs as Doug Russell recalled:

> You see, we were all in civilian houses. It wasn't like the Army, where bugles wake them up and all this sort of thing. You got up when your landlady called you. We could not parade too early in the morning because it upset the breakfast situation. So anyway, we used to parade at nine o'clock. People would get to the end of the road and they would form up in some sort of semblance of an army. My friend, he was there one day – and he wasn't the only one – he had put his battledress over his pyjamas. Of course, his collar was undone and he'd got his blue striped pyjamas underneath.

Harry Pexton recalled:

> I think we worked on the premise that it was going to be a short life but a good one, and the George Hotel in Knutsford was our main watering hole. I always say that it was the birthplace of the Parachute Regiment, because during opening hours if you wanted any of the officers you went to the George. We had a house in Knutsford which was the official headquarters, but the George Hotel was the unofficial headquarters. If you wanted the medical officer or the orderly officer, you went to the George. The landlord was a gentleman of the first order. Mind you, we spent all our money there, so I suppose he had just cause to be that. All our wages went into the George. Nobody went very far away.

Meanwhile, they were coping with the everyday hazards of parachute practice; Harry Pexton:

> The RAF lads, they were quite good, but they weren't always dead accurate at dropping you. I remember dropping into the middle of the road outside the boundaries of Tatton Park, and I just managed to get my parachute gathered up as a lorry came thundering round the corner – it was just one of those things. The RAF were learning to drop us as we were learning to drop.

As the parachutists – and their instructors – increased in confidence, they started doing drops at night as well as by day. Harry Pexton recalled:

> In the daytime, we did it into Tatton Park, but at night we did it on the airport. Now, the officer then in charge who did a parachute jump had a battery-driven lamp fastened to his uniform, so that he could see his way down – but when it came to the lads jumping there were no lamps. You had to hope for the best.

I remember once looking down on a night jump, and I could see a big hole underneath me, and I thought, I'm going to land in that hole. So I guided my parachute the best I could away from it, but when I looked down again it was still there. It was a moonlit night – and it was the shadow of my parachute, and I thought it was a hole in the ground. I was beginning to get a bit panicky, but I hit the deck and everything was OK.

They also experimented with landing in different territory, including water – not an attractive prospect in the depths of a northern winter:

Invariably they would say, 'You're night jumping tonight', and you'd say, 'OK.' About three or four o'clock in the morning you'd be dragged out, still half-asleep, and bunged into an aircraft and away you went. You were dropped into Rostherne Mere, which is reputed to be one of the deepest meres in the country. They used to say that when you get six feet from the water, you will release your parachute and drop into the water. Well, I never trusted that. I used to wait until it was about thirty feet from the water and I would release. I would be swimming long before I hit the water, because I didn't want the parachute to come over me like a plastic bag. Then there was a couple of guys in a dinghy with an outboard motor, I think it had, that used to come and drag you in and bring you ashore.

After a night on the lemonade the last thing you wanted to do was a night jump into water, but you had to do it. When you came out of the water you were stone-cold sober, no messing.

At least one parachutist drowned after landing in water – but this was within the grounds of Tatton Park, in a shallow mere. Cecily Paget-Bowman, who drove an ambulance, recalled the story:

The water wasn't more than about four feet deep – it was nothing, really – and they waded in and got him, but he was dead. The strange thing was that they found a letter he had written to his mother saying he knew he was going to die, and nobody knows why he died. He wasn't drowned – his lungs were completely clear.

Like many others, Cecily Paget-Bowman had to learn her skills on the job. Her original training was as an actress:

I was in Edinburgh, in rep, and it was when France fell, and I thought, I must get out of this. My mother was alone in London and I was miles away. They thought we would be invaded, and I didn't want to be at one end of the British Isles and she alone in the other. So I said, 'I'm afraid I must leave and go back to London.' So I did, and then, of course, all the theatres closed down.

My sister-in-law knew one of these groups of ATS that had been formed in France during the past winter, and had got out of France, come back to England, and re-formed themselves into BVACs, they called them – British Volunteer Ambulance Corps – and they were going to be stationed up in Western Command, Chester being the headquarters.

While I was there at the hospital in Chester, they asked for an ambulance driver to go to Knutsford to join these parachutists. I think they had all had a pretty harrowing time in France, and I was the new girl, so they said, 'This is a job you can do, because you'll probably have to go out to manoeuvres in the Welsh mountains, and it will be pretty tough.'

She had been promised both mechanical and medical training, but in the event neither materialized.

When I joined the corps I said, 'I'm an actress. I don't know these things.' So they said, 'Don't worry. When you get to the hospital you will be taught.' I said, 'Oh, lovely', but, of course, nothing happened at all. So I just had to pick things up as I went along, and with the MO I picked up a lot because he used to talk to me about the cases. Of course, I pretended I knew a lot, but I didn't know a thing.

One incident, which happened within the first few weeks of her time with the parachutists, stood out in her mind:

They had had grenade practice. One of the grenades didn't go off, so it was left there, and nothing happened and nothing happened, and one man – an officer – went forward to pick it up and chuck it out, and it exploded in his face. As he bent down to pick it up it exploded, and one of his eyes blew out, which was not very nice, and I had to cope with that. But there was nothing I could do except get him to hospital as quickly as I could.

He lost it, but he was back within a week with a black patch over one eye, and he was kept on – a very, very brave man, he was. Unfortunately, he was killed in Africa.

One of her main duties was standing by with her ambulance on a drop zone; the men knew her as 'Miss Bowman and her blood tub', and she became something of a mascot. She was even offered a Commando knife as protection in case of an invasion.

One of the chaps, a funny little cockney man, said, 'You'll be driving along, and they'll stop you in your ambulance, and they'll come and put their hands on your driving door.' So he said, 'I'm giving you this, which is my Commando knife, and if they do that you just cut their hands off.' I said, 'That's very kind of you, but I don't think I ever would.' Can you imagine slicing people's hands off? But that was their feeling – they wanted to protect me, which was very sweet.

As parachute training developed, men were dropped in 'sticks', or groups of eight. Cecily Paget-Bowman had a vivid

memory of watching a man plunge to his death as she stood by
with her ambulance:

> They just dropped the stick of men, and the final one came
> out, and I thought it was a roll of overcoats, which they used
> to throw down at the end. Then suddenly I saw his hands
> coming up, groping for the rope, and of course it wasn't there,
> because the parachute had never opened. He came down
> absolutely like a stone and went into the ground – oh, about
> ten or twelve inches. But he was completely dead; his neck
> was broken. He looked quite peaceful, so I picked him up and
> put him in the ambulance and took him to the mortuary.

She described her time there as 'rather like living with ghosts', a
constant feeling that things were temporary because of the
numbers of young men passing through on their way to unknown
destinations.

> One knew the hazards of their job, and of course so many
> were killed, so many. New recruits kept on coming along,
> but it was a strange feeling. You never knew whether you
> were going to be there yourself the next day because of the
> raids. We suffered from the Manchester raids a lot because
> they dropped bombs on us.
>   I hated air-raid shelters, because one thing I was really
> frightened of was being buried alive. I felt much happier with
> a tin hat on, even if shrapnel was bouncing about on it.

A favourite phrase with parachute instructors is that parachuting is 'safer than crossing the road' – a cliché that was only too
true on wartime roads at night. Cecily Paget-Bowman had to
deal with victims of the blackout – and she herself had to cope
with the hazards of driving when it was impossible to see where
you were going.

> I was lucky. I could see pretty well in the dark. But the most

difficult thing was finding your way about, because we were in a strange part of the country and there were no signposts. They took every signpost down. You were just suddenly told to go to such and such a road, and somebody would be there to help you, but to find the road was very difficult.

The [ambulance] lights were turned down on to the road immediately below you. So you were looking into darkness, you couldn't see lights at all. The only wonderful thing was the catseyes on the roads. The chap who invented those catseyes really deserved everything, because you could just get a reflection.

Soon after she arrived at Knutsford, she was called out to go and pick up a soldier who had been on night manoeuvres when fog came down. They were marching back in single file when a lorry came along and hit a soldier on the back of the head with its side mirror.

He had very bad injuries to his skull, and he had been taken to the cottage hospital in Knutsford. The MO and I followed him there and the MO examined him and said, 'He must go to hospital; he's got very bad injuries.' It was a dreadful night, freezing fog, and the road was ice, and they thought it wasn't very safe for me to drive. They asked the CO's driver, who was a Scot, and he refused point-blank. So we set off. It was a dreadful drive. I managed to get the turning off the main road, and then the fog came down – I could not see a hand in front of me, I didn't know where I was. Suddenly we saw a dim, dim blue light, which was the police station. The MO got out and went in to say, where were we? Actually, I had missed the hospital by one turning.

I remember the orderly said to me, 'Do hurry up, miss, I think he's going.' I managed to turn round – it was very diffi-cult in this thick fog, you couldn't see anything coming either way. Anyway, all was well. We went back, and we got to the hospital. I've never been so glad in my life.

I waited there, oh, it must have been an hour, an hour and a half – it was about three in the morning by this time – and the MO came and said, 'Well, they can't operate tonight, but they'll operate first thing in the morning.' So we went out of the hospital and there was clear starlight, the fog had lifted. Oh, it was wonderful. But sadly, the poor man died the next day, before they could even operate.

Obviously, those living near the airfield – not to mention drinkers at the George Hotel in Knutsford – knew about the parachutists' presence. But officially their activities were still secret. When, in November 1940, they were deemed ready to demonstrate their skills before an invited audience of pressmen and VIPs, it was only on the understanding that this was a private viewing. The articles the journalists wrote that day were not published until a year later – after the first parachute operation had taken place.

Salisbury Plain was chosen as the venue for this public relations exercise, as Harry Pexton recalled:

They got the whole of Southern Command troops surrounding a village, and they gave us the task of taking the village. Taking it was signified by a flag on the church flagpole. Well, when we jumped there was a mass of brass – colonels and that were ten a penny. There were masses of Allied troops to see the first public effort by airborne troops.

We were trained to – if we wanted to – nick a car. Well, there was one pointing our way, and it was a big thing, so my officer stuck a gun in this guy's ear and said, 'You're going to drive us, aren't you?' and he said, 'Yes, sir.' So we piled into it and drove into the village and eventually, within three-quarters of an hour of jumping, we had put the flag up and that signified that we had taken it.

Mind you, it was a typical British Army effort. They were going down one side of the road and we were going down the other side and we were waving at each other, you know. They didn't know whether we were the enemy or they were.

We took up defensive positions, and mine was outside a pub – not by choice, but I was put there.

While he was standing there, he had two conversations, one with an impressive-looking gentleman who spoke perfect English, the other with a general. Both went into the pub after speaking to him – and some while later the landlady came out with two pints: one for him, and the other for his mate on the other side of the road.

Well, the car they [the gentleman and the general] came up in, the driver came up to us and said, 'Did you nick a car?' So we said, 'Yes.' He said, 'You know who it belongs to, do you?' I said, 'No, not a clue. It was going our way, so we borrowed it.' He said, 'Well, it belongs to Crown Prince Olav of Norway, and that was him you were talking to.'

After the two pints incident, whenever I saw him on television I used to say to the wife, 'There's my boozing mate, Olav', because, of course, later on he became King Olav.

Buoyed up with their success, they went back to Knutsford. They had trained hard for months; they had demonstrated their skills. Now they were ready for action. In January 1941 their chance came. Harry Pexton recalled:

We all fell in one day opposite where we were billeted in Knutsford. The officer then came and said, 'There is going to be an operation, and we want volunteers for it. Will any volunteers step forward,' which is the usual procedure, and everybody stepped forward. You normally only see that in American films and things like that, but this was quite true. We all stepped forward, because we were getting edgy – time we did something.

Faced with such a plethora of volunteers, they picked a number of officers, and each officer had to pick his quota. A total of thirty-six were needed, but some extra were taken as reserves. Members of X Troop, as it was called, had to leave their civilian quarters and hole up in barracks at Ringway. The men joked that 'X' stood for the unknown; they had little clue what they had let themselves in for as Harry Pexton remembered:

> We didn't know what was going on. We didn't know until the last minute where we were going. We knew within reason what we were going to do because we had trained for it in Tatton Park, but where it was we hadn't a clue.
>
> We were carted off to Ringway and put in a wooden shed, and there we lived for another month at least. Running round Ringway at 6.30 in the morning in January 1941, in the rain and the snow... it wasn't something you would look forward to, but we still had to do it.

Harry Pexton recalled that the men slept on the floor of the shed wrapped in blankets:

> It wasn't exactly the Savoy Hotel by any means. But we were tough; we were hardened to it. We had been sleeping in tents in Scotland, which wasn't one of my favourite occupations, because it was wet and cold and miserable, and it was raining, and the river was flooding. So to live in a wooden shed was quite a relief, in spite of the fact that aircraft were taking off over you day and night.

They were kept well occupied during the day, as Dave Struthers recalled:

> I think with the benefit of hindsight, the forward planning was excellent. For one thing, they got us training together, so we knew one another exceptionally well. I was most impressed by our leaders, our officers, how they achieved this.

We were doing shooting to improve our shooting skills at close quarters, and we were doing a lot of short... I would call them runs more than marches, to keep us fit. My recollection is that we could keep up six miles per hour across almost any kind of country.

In theory, the men were not allowed out in the evenings, but they still managed to find their way to a source of 'lemonade'. Harry Pexton again:

While we were confined to barracks in Ringway, we still used to go out at night on a bus. Each of us chipped in a tip for the bus driver, and when he got so far, he would switch his lights out, and – providing there was nobody else on the bus but us – he would drop us off at this watering hole. Then we used to have to walk back at night, of course, and that was quite an experience.

Each individual was impressed with the importance of secrecy – but in fact they had little to be secret about. They knew they were going to demolish some kind of structure. About half the group had explosives experience, and they practised laying charges on a forty-foot model of a bridge which had been erected behind Lord Egerton's house in Tatton Park. This was guarded night and day. Maps of Abyssinia had also been casually left lying around, but those were the only clues to what their great expedition was to be. In fact, the maps of Abyssinia were a blind, and the bridge only part of the story.

While the men were practising jumping, laying charges and marching with heavy loads, high-level meetings were being held to work out the details of this first major operation. Cecily Paget-Bowman recalled the reaction when she admitted she had overheard part of the discussions, which were meant to be secret.

There was a meeting at Ringway, and the MO that I drove was at this meeting. I was sitting in the background, not supposed to hear anything that was going on, but of course I did – I couldn't help it. They were discussing tablets for airsickness, and there weren't very many in those days. I had tried some for seasickness about a year before. I had gone over to Ireland, and I'm not a good sailor, so I had tried these pills, which were very, very efficient. I can't even remember the name of them now, it's so long ago. Anyway, driving home I said to him about these pills, and he was furious. He said: 'You heard! You weren't supposed to hear anything.' I said: 'I know I'm not, but I couldn't help it. I was there and I heard it, and I'll just tell you what I've had myself, and they were very efficient.' So I told him about these pills, and apparently they used them, and they were very good. So that was one small job that was quite useful.

Before they set off, they carried out a final night drop on the wooden bridge in Tatton Park. This was disastrous, as Harry Pexton recalled:

The wind came up, and in those days, if the wind was over about sixteen miles an hour we didn't jump: it was considered it could be nasty. But in taking off and flying around wasting time up the Welsh coast, the wind came up to something like thirty miles an hour – but it was the final dress rehearsal, so it had to go ahead. We baled out into a thirty-mile-an-hour wind and you were all over the place, scattered about like sheaves of corn. We gathered eventually – the fire brigade had to come out and get some out of trees and things like that, but there were only one or two accidents. There was an ambulance standing by – one or two went into the ambulance – but it had to go on, you see. It was getting to the end of the time we should have been heading out.

The high wind meant that even those who managed to escape being tangled up in trees found themselves being dragged across the ground. Dave Struthers narrowly escaped serious injury after a tussle with his parachute, as he recalled:

> It was such a gale that my parachute harness got slightly entangled at the release box, and I found myself bouncing along the ground towards a railway sleeper fence. There was no railway anywhere near, just a solid fence made of railway sleepers. I thought to myself, well, we were lucky we cleared this, but the parachute went over the top and I didn't. I hit the wooden fence. I was black and blue for a couple of weeks after, and demolished the fence.

There is a saying in the theatre that a bad dress rehearsal makes a good performance. X Troop had yet to discover whether this old superstition held good.

PIONEERS –
OR GUINEA PIGS?

Operation Colossus was the grandiose title given to the raid that was to be the big test for the Ringway parachutists. Seven months of intensive training had brought them to a peak of fitness. They had shown off their skills to generals and cabinet ministers, and now they were ready to use them for real behind enemy lines.

In February 1941 members of X Troop paraded at RAF Mildenhall in Suffolk, to be inspected by Admiral Sir Roger Keyes, Chief of Combined Operations. They still did not know where they were going – but the atmosphere left them in no doubt about the riskiness of the venture.

The men formed two ranks on either side of the door of an aircraft hangar. The admiral, a veteran of the First World War who walked on two sticks, shook hands with each man in turn. There was some polite conversation. Then he gave a short talk, after which he drew himself up and saluted *them*. Harry Pexton recalled:

> As he was going out, my mates and I heard him say, 'It's a pity, it's a pity', and my mate said, 'What do you think he meant?' I said, 'I have no idea', until a few days later when

there was a guy with a machine gun stuffed up our nose, and I said, 'This is what he meant.'

Christopher Lea also had a vivid memory of the scene:

We paraded in front of him, and he said the usual sort of words. I didn't hear him say, 'What a pity'; I only read about that in a book by somebody. But I do remember a really rather embarrassing scene for everybody when he saluted us. Now, if you can picture two lines of men and their officers lined up in front of him... well, we didn't know what to do. So we rather slowly and unmilitarily, I think, sort of raised our hands and saluted him. It was quite an emotional moment. I think he had perhaps a rather better understanding of our likely fate than we had.

The men had been told in general terms that it might be difficult to extract survivors – and some had taken this more seriously than others. One had married his Knutsford sweetheart; others had mentioned perhaps a little too casually who to contact if anything happened to them. A late addition to the group was a small, Fascist-hating Italian called Fortunato Picchi, who was to act as an interpreter. In civilian life, Fortunato had been a banqueting manager at the Savoy Hotel. Before he got on the plane at RAF Mildenhall, he made sure that he had written out a will.

Their destination was an aqueduct in southern Italy – a target originally suggested by the London engineering firm that had helped to build it. They had detailed construction plans and were only too well aware that if the parachutists succeeded in destroying it, it would cut off the water supply for some two million Italians. This could have a devastating effect on morale, particularly since it was a showpiece of engineering of which Mussolini was particularly proud. The destruction of the aqueduct would also prove to ordinary Italian people that they were not immune from the effects of war; up to this point, most of the action had been abroad.

The aqueduct ran across the Tragino creek, in the shadow of the Apennine mountains. Its inaccessibility was one of its attractions for the generals who planned the raid, which would be a test of the RAF's skill in accurate dropping – and of the parachutists' ability to operate deep in enemy territory. However, the choice of such a remote target also reduced any hope of rescue. All those who jumped would be wearing uniform, but if they were captured they would most likely be treated as spies.

In freezing cold on the evening of 7 February, members of X Troop were taken by truck to the Whitley bombers that were to fly them to Malta on the first stage of their journey to Italy. They did not walk to the runway, as snow on their boots would have increased the danger of frostbite on the long, chilly journey. Their flight of nearly 1,000 miles took them over occupied France, where they had to run the gauntlet of enemy anti-aircraft fire. Harry Pexton recalled a narrow escape:

> We were the last but one to take off. Our pilot was called Ennis, and his nickname in the RAF was Ennis the Menace. He didn't believe in going round when he could go across. He said: 'We'll be there first.' Actually, we were second. We were picked on by a German night fighter over the Mediterranean, and he came down, straight down almost on to the water, to get away from him. Everybody slid forward, because we were lying in the belly of the aircraft – we just laid in sleeping bags dispersed about the aircraft. I finished up looking between the pilot and the co-pilot – I had slid right down.

Christopher Lea almost didn't join the group, as he had injured a knee after a road accident on his last leave. A reserve had been organized and was ready to go in his place. But as he said: 'I think it's unnecessary to say that I was determined to go. My knee got better, and I went.' His main memory of the flight was the effect of the altitude:

I remember lying on the floor of this Whitley, and it was a tremendous effort to lift your head because we were flying at about 17-, 18,000 feet with no oxygen, and it was very cold. It was quite interesting, because I told somebody that that was the kind of height we were flying at, and he said: 'Were you alive when you got to Malta?' I said: 'I think we were – more or less.'

When they arrived at Malta, they were forced to circle for an hour. There had been a German bombing raid overnight, and some potholes had to be filled in before the runway was safe enough for landing. Tony Deane-Drummond was there to meet them. He had gone out by Sunderland flying boat, some forty-eight hours before, to carry orders, prepare provisions and fix up suitably secure sleeping quarters. These were in an old quarantine hospital, on Manuel Island, which had been taken over as a naval base. Harry Pexton recalled:

The Navy looked after us very well, except living in hammocks didn't go down all that well. None of us were conversant with getting in and out of the hammocks, and as you got in one side so you fell out the other.

The day we left, they cooked up what we thought was half a lamb, but in fact it was half a goat on a big platter. We had a fill of that. Then they brought on a steamed spotted dick, which was about three feet long and nine inches round. I had two helpings of that. Everybody had gone, and I was still stuck into the second helping. That was the last steamed pudding I had in several years, but it was beautiful.

They paraded for inspection by the Governor of Malta, General Dobbie. With much packing and patching up of aeroplanes, and a favourable weather report, they were ready by teatime on 10 February. It was not until then – just as they were about to set off – that the men were finally told that their destination was Italy, not Abyssinia or anywhere else. A cheer went up, and Dave Struthers remembered the widely shared relief at this piece of news:

> I think those of us who had had dealings with the Germans felt, 'Oh, well, this should be much easier than dealing with the German troops.' Not that we were too worried about the Germans. We had a very good esprit de corps.

Major Trevor (T. A. G.) Pritchard – nicknamed Tag after his initials – briefed the five other officers with details of the rendezvous after the raid, and when and where they were supposed to be picked up. They had to know, in case the groups became separated. Then he addressed the whole troop, telling them: 'You are pioneers or guinea pigs – you can choose which word you prefer.'

After a meal of hard-boiled eggs and hot, sweet tea – which few were in the mood to eat – the men boarded the aircraft that were to take them on the short hop from Malta to southern Italy. A total of eight Whitley bombers took off in the early evening – two for a diversionary bombing raid, six for the drop on the aqueduct. The officers had studied a model made from a construction photograph of their intended target – but it was not until the eve of their departure that they realized the model was inaccurate. RAF reconnaissance photographs showed that there were two aqueducts in the area, not one. They decided to go for the larger of the two.

Each man had rations intended to last for six days. Their uniforms had a small hacksaw blade hidden in a seam above the left breast pocket, with 50,000 lire in notes sewn into the lining. This was hidden in different places, so that if a group was captured, all the money would not automatically be discovered. The lining of the sleeves contained two silk maps – one of northern, the other of southern Italy. A particularly deft touch was a metal collar stud that concealed a tiny compass.

All had a Commando knife strapped to one leg, a pistol in a holster, and a battledress lined with chamois leather so they could carry hand grenades. (The extra padding prevented them from going off accidentally.) Those designated as sappers had also to be prepared to jump with a tin containing cotton wool and a dozen detonators in a breast pocket.

The troop was divided into a covering party, and those with Royal Engineers training who would deal with the explosives. Captain Gerry Daly was meant to lead the explosives group, but his aeroplane took off last, minus one man who had felt sick at the last minute.

On the journey to Italy, the men slept, played cards or sang. They made up new words to an old tune, with the refrain: 'Oh, what a surprise for the Duce, the Duce!' As Harry Pexton put it: 'The feeling was one of "Let's go now – we're on our way – let's go and make a job of it."'

There was some flak over Sicily, and the pilots had to make wide circles to avoid anti-aircraft fire as they flew over the coast of the mainland. The final approach involved some tricky navigating as they had to take their lumbering bombers down to 400 feet over the dropping zone by the village of Calitri. Since they were flying through mountains, some of which were as high as 4,000 feet, this was skilful stuff.

After a flight of more than three hours, the men in each aircraft took up their prearranged positions by the hole. The usual last-minute tension before a drop was made worse in one plane by communication problems. Tony Deane-Drummond recalled:

> The intercom in our plane failed, and the tail gunner – who was a nice little man – came back through the fuselage and said: 'Come on – you're just about to jump out.' So we opened everything up and we were ready in a few seconds – and, blow me down, we saw the Calitri lights go underneath, then the river, and then came the green light, and we landed just bang on. Well done, the RAF.

In fact, five of the six aeroplanes dropped their parachutists more or less on target. Harry Pexton, who arrived after Tony Deane-Drummond's group, landed in a tree and had to cut himself free with his Commando knife. He recalled:

> It was a beautiful moonlit night – I have never seen a moon so close. I thought they had laid on one especially for us. I just landed in this tree, only about three feet from the ground, and I was in my harness and I couldn't really think that there was a war on. I'm thinking, what am I doing here? It just didn't seem right that we were there to commit an act of war.

As the first to arrive – their aeroplane had been meant to drop third – Tony Deane-Drummond and his group had some half an hour of anxious waiting as they speculated about what had happened to everybody else. As he put it in his autobiography, *Return Ticket*:

> I remember having a rather funny feeling somewhere inside me when it occurred to me that perhaps all the other planes had lost their way and ours was the only one to arrive. I think we all had the same thought. Then we saw the parachutes idly floating down in the silent night.

He had come down in a ploughed field on a hill only a hundred yards away from the aqueduct; the arms and explosives containers from his aeroplane had landed nearby. Using the prearranged password – 'Heil, Hitler!' – and the reply – 'Viva Duce' – he quickly gathered his group together. One man, Harry Boulter, was missing; as they were later to discover, he had crash-landed and broken his ankle. Tony Deane-Drummond ordered his men to clear the nearby houses of people and bring them to him at the aqueduct. To his relief, he found this was unguarded.

Closer inspection of the structure suggested that it was made of concrete, not brick, as they had been led to believe. This would be much harder to destroy – a prospect not helped by the fact that much of the explosive had not made it to the drop zone.

Some twenty-eight hundredweight of explosive had been loaded up as they left Malta – but only around eight hundredweight were dropped. The release mechanism on one plane had failed to function, leaving the containers stuck in the plane as it headed back to Malta. The group containing the senior engineer, Gerry Daly, was dropped in the wrong valley altogether – too far away to be of any use.

However, the planning had allowed for all these eventualities. The planes had been loaded up with far more explosives than were actually needed – and all the men had been trained to fill in for each other in case of accident. When it became obvious that Gerry Daly was not going to arrive in time, a Canadian officer, George Patterson, took his place.

Meanwhile, some two dozen men, women and children had been rounded up from nearby houses. All but one – a soldier – were civilians, and the men were pressed into helping to carry the heavy blocks of gun cotton (an acid-sealed explosive compound) up the valley. (One planeload had been dropped by the river, about a mile away.) It was heavy going, as the ground was covered with mud and melting snow. When the stationmaster from nearby Calitri arrived, he, too, was roped into this job. Christopher Lea recalled:

> He said: 'Well, first of all I must get a certificate to say that I am being forced to do this under duress.' So I said: 'Yes, well, that will be quite all right. I will sign a certificate. If you produce it for me, I will sign it.' I can't really remember whether I signed it or not, but, anyway, the chap then turned himself into a porter and helped bring this gun cotton up to the bridge. He was rather a good porter, but it was rather beneath him to do it.

The families of the men who were helping to carry the explosives were locked inside houses a safe distance away from the aqueduct. Two Italian women who still remember the events of that night are Francesca and Angela Galgano. They still live very close to the site of the house from which they were captured, although the original building has been demolished.

Francesca Galgano – who was just ten years old at the time of the raid – remembered the sequence of events:

> It was a calm night with a full moon – no breeze. It was very tranquil. We heard a very loud sound of aeroplanes – the planes seemed to be on the roof. We opened the window. We saw the plane dropping parachutists, and while I was looking a parachutist landed right on the roof. We were face to face – I was very scared. They knocked on the door and said, 'Open up!' My father opened the door, and they asked us to go with them. There was me, my mother, my father and my sister – four of us.

The children were crying, and the soldiers offered them some chocolate. Their mother – perhaps afraid that it might be poisoned – told them not to eat it. The soldiers broke off pieces, swallowed them to show that it was safe, then handed it back.

> While we were walking, my mother said: 'We're coming with you, but who are you?' They replied: 'We're English – Italy's friend.' My mother quietly said: 'They've taken us prisoners.' They understood and told my mother to walk in front. So slowly, slowly, we arrived at the house, and they locked us inside.
>
> We thought bad things – bad things – they'd locked us in the house. They shut the door and placed a soldier with a gun there.

With the local people safely locked away, an eerie calm descended on the valley. The place was full of soldiers, heavily armed and trained to deal with the enemy – but there was no enemy in sight. Meanwhile, the sappers were busy laying charges. Using two portable ladders, they ran a steel cable around the main column of the aqueduct and suspended the charges on the wire. Anti-slip brackets were fixed to each corner, the cord was tightened, and eventually the whole column was encircled with eighty-pound charges of gun cotton. Some explosive was also put at the point where the aqueduct joined the land. Tony Deane-Drummond, who was guarding a bridge further up the valley, put a surplus pack of gun cotton underneath this.

At half-past midnight, all was ready. Tag Pritchard fired a warning signal for all but the demolition party to withdraw, then lit the sixty-second fuse. He and George Patterson took cover behind a rock. After what they thought had been the right length of time, nothing seemed to have happened. They re-emerged, but had taken only a few steps when there was an almighty explosion, shortly followed by a smaller one.

Harry Pexton recalled:

> There was a rumble, and it gathered momentum, and eventually it reached a crescendo where it just flew, you know. There were about 8- or 900 pounds of high explosive all going off in one bundle.

Tony Deane-Drummond recalled the moment his bridge went up:

> I remember very well that down on the top of the roofs [of the nearby houses] came thuds of bits of concrete. The poor people inside rushed out shouting, 'Mama mia!' They weren't hurt, but they were very worried indeed by the bits and pieces coming down on the roof, and I don't blame them.

He went over to inspect the damage and found that the bridge had been cut, and one end lay in the stream. Meanwhile, Tag Pritchard and George Patterson were inspecting the aqueduct, while everyone else waited at the assembly point a couple of hundred yards away. In *Return Ticket*, Tony Deane-Drummond recalled the suspense:

Impatiently we awaited their return, all wondering what on earth we should do if there was no damage. We had been keyed up for this moment for the past six weeks and failure would have been unbearable.

Tag and Pat [George Patterson] came back without a smile on their faces. Was it a fiasco? Tag put up his hand and everybody stopped talking. All he said was, 'Listen!' We all strained our ears, and sure enough we heard the sound of a great waterfall. It was a success. How we cheered and cheered! We could hardly imagine that we were in enemy country. Those British cheers must have been heard a good mile or two away.

Harry Pexton recalled:

There was water pouring out all over the place. Old Tag Pritchard was doing an Irish jig or something like that in the water – he was so relieved that we had actually achieved what we set out to do, not knowing what was to come later on. It was a beautiful bang. I've seen a few bangs since, but that was the best.

Dave Struthers was more low-key about his and his fellow sappers' success. He admitted that the sound of the running water was 'bliss' – but, as he put it: 'You have to accept that we weren't surprised, though, because we did it in our training. We couldn't see it not working.'

It was only now, having achieved what they had set out to do, that their troubles began. Tag Pritchard gathered everyone together and explained the rescue plan. They were to split up into small parties, each of which was to make its own way to the coast, where a submarine was due to meet them all. It was a sixty-mile journey through cold, mountainous and difficult terrain, and they had four nights in which to do it.

They left behind them the sapper equipment and heavier guns, which were taken to bits and pushed into the mud. They also left behind the injured Harry Boulter, armed with chocolate, cigarettes and a gun. Tony Deane-Drummond recalled:

> He was philosophical about it. He had been told that this was possible: if anybody does hurt themselves you can't expect the rest of the party to stay and look after you. He knew that, and we all knew that. If it had happened to me, it would have been the same thing. He insisted on having a Bren gun with him, and he was quite determined to use it. He was a nice guy. It was a great pity – but it didn't make any difference in the end.

Boulter was to be captured and taken by train to Naples prison, where he would meet up with his comrades again. However, first he had to face the wrath of the Italians single-handedly. Angela Galgano, the younger of the two Italian sisters who witnessed the raid, recalled:

> When the Italians found him they beat him. A lady who owned a vineyard near here had just returned from Calitri, and she went up to them and said: 'Leave him alone! What are you doing to the poor boy? The English have sent him – he didn't come by choice to blow the bridge up.' So they took him away as prisoner.

He was interrogated – but, as instructed, disclosed nothing that would give away the rest of his company's plans.

Meanwhile, the three escape parties had been making their different ways up the mountain behind the aqueduct. The hard reality of the task before them struck home very quickly, as Christopher Lea recalled:

> When we started off, we were immediately climbing through mud because we were trying to go across country to begin with, and there weren't any tracks. It was just at the time when the snow was melting; you were just below the snow

line, and everything was sodden. If you had to climb up a hill, you know, you slid back again. It was very, very hard going, and so a feeling of anticlimax, I think, for most of us crept in pretty quick.

Tag Pritchard's group, which had set off first, at 1.30 a.m., included Tony Deane-Drummond and two Italian inter-preters: Fortunato Picchi and a cockney Italian, Nicol Nastri. They had to make wide detours to avoid deep snow-filled gorges. Even resting every three-quarters of an hour, they were soon exhausted. By the time daylight came, they had travelled no more than five miles of the sixty they needed to cover. The next night, they started by following a goat track. Eventually, however, desperation tempted them on to the apparently deserted road. For five or six miles they tramped along happily, then they heard the sound of horses' hooves. There was no time to make a run for it, so Tag instructed Nicol Nastri to call out the step in Italian. They put on a pass-able imitation of marching Italian soldiers for their audience of one: an old lady, who turned out to be fast asleep inside her vegetable-laden pony cart.

They headed for an area that was marked on the map as being covered with trees, only to discover that the trees hid a farmhouse. Tony Deane-Drummond, who had pictured the countryside as being an Italian version of the Scottish Highlands, recalled:

My main disappointment was to discover that there were so many farms scattered over the hillsides. If it had been like Scotland, we could have got straight through to the coast.

Too worn out to walk very much further, they found some temporary hiding places and fell asleep. Tony Deane-Drummond awoke after an hour's sleep to find a peasant standing not a hundred yards away, looking intently at them. Tag dispatched Fortunato Picchi to try to convince him they were only German and Italian troops on manoeuvres. However, they had also been spotted by several women and children. What happened next is described in *Return Ticket*:

> Some half-naked and filthy Italian children with a few mongrel dogs were our first spectators. They sat down about a hundred yards away from us, sucking their dirty thumbs and gazing at us as if we were men from the moon. A minute or two later a peasant appeared with pointers and a shotgun from over the hill just above our position. He seemed very frightened as he pointed his shotgun straight at Tag and kept up a running commentary, which of course was unintelligible to us.

The children's mothers arrived, and the crowd swelled. Eventually, it emerged that the man who was waving his shotgun wanted them to lay down their arms. In normal circumstances, they might have thrown a few grenades and tried to make a run for it. However, faced with this army of women and children, Tag Pritchard ordered his men not to fight. Tony Deane-Drummond recalled Tag's response when he told him he disagreed:

> 'All right, Tony,' he said, 'you throw a grenade at those people on the right and I will throw mine over there.'
> At that moment I realized I could not do it. Women, children and unarmed peasants were everywhere, and we would not be able to avoid casualties among them. All we could achieve were a few extra hours of freedom at the price of a particularly odious and inglorious action.

They dropped their pistols and were immediately surrounded and stripped of all their equipment. As Tony Deane-Drummond put it: 'I have never felt so ashamed before or since, that we should have surrendered to a lot of practically unarmed Italian peasants.'

The *carabinieri* arrived, and all except Tag Pritchard were chained together. There was one practical problem, however. One of the grenades had a broken pin and could go off at any moment. Tag Pritchard tried to explain this, but the nervous Italian sergeant, perhaps thinking this was some English trick, put a pistol to his head. Eventually, he calmed down, and the grenade was thrown safely away from the crowd. As the prisoners were taken down the hillside, their humiliation was made complete by the fact that they not only had handcuffs with chains around their wrists, but they were dragging heavy iron balls, like old-fashioned convicts.

Meanwhile, Christopher Lea's group was facing very similar difficulties. The winter had been the most severe for many years. Mountain streams had become torrents, and rivers were swollen with melted snow. As they waded across one particularly fast-flowing river, a soldier was almost swept away. A six-foot-tall Scot known as Big Jock grabbed him just in time and hauled him back into line.

On another occasion, they bedded down in what they thought was a dry river bed in a tree-covered ravine – only to wake up and discover that their kit was floating. They heard spotter planes and the sound of distant trucks – and there were other near misses, as Dave Struthers recalled:

> We slept during the day and walked at night. Through February, there was quite a number of hours of darkness, and I remember on one occasion I was with my chum under some bramble bushes just on the outskirts of a large mansion house, and we heard children singing not far from us. We only went to sleep one at a time. We always had someone awake because a danger was that someone would snore too loud.
>
> Our main problem, as we saw it, was dogs, and towards the end we carried quite a large amount of black pepper, which was virtually unobtainable in Britain at that time. When we were doing a change of direction we put down some black pepper so that if any bloodhounds came after us they wouldn't follow that scent any longer.

Harry Pexton recalled:

> We had three mountain ranges to climb over, and when you
> came into a valley, dogs were barking. I've never liked dogs
> since, because as one dog started you could hear it going
> right through the valley – they all started. The Italians told us
> later on that they listened to the dogs barking and followed
> us from that.

Normally cheerful and extrovert, even Harry Pexton sometimes
found it difficult to live up to the reputation that had led his
mates to nickname him 'Lucky'. The exhausting walking conditions meant that they had to stop and rest every two hours – but
they could not have a hot drink in case the light of their stoves
gave them away. Only when daylight came could they brew up tea
and make porridge. The latter was supposed to be made with
added pemmican, a concentrated, greasy meat extract. However,
according to Harry Pexton, this was definitely an acquired taste:

> It was a square block like a large Oxo cube, and you were
> supposed to break some off and put it in your porridge. It
> melted – or was supposed to – but it was like a ceramic tile;
> you couldn't break any off, so we slung that.

Christopher Lea recalled:

> Of all the wrong things to give people in that kind of climate,
> even though it was winter, you simply can't imagine. I mean,
> the person who decided we ought to have pemmican was a
> charming, charming man, an Arctic explorer, but it was
> dreadful – none of my people could stomach it.

He himself had an additional problem. The road accident,
which nearly cost him his place on the expedition in the first
place, had meant that he had not had time to wear in his new
army boots.

I did have terrible trouble, because the back of the boots that we had broke in the wrong place, so it was pressing on my Achilles tendon, and I was getting horribly lame. So either the first night out or the next one, I got my Commando knife, which I hadn't used for anything else, and cut a sort of U-shape thing out of the back of the boot.

Eventually – like Tony Deane-Drummond's group before them – they decided that they would have to risk marching on the road if they were to have any chance of making the rendezvous on time. After slithering through a mass of mud, they at last had solid ground beneath their feet. Christopher Lea recalled:

To be able to walk on tarmac was wonderful. So we made several kilometres quite successfully and came to a bridge going over one of these ravines. We didn't like the look of a bridge [where] you were hemmed in very much, so I said to my chaps: 'You stay there, and I'll go across and see whether it's safe to go.' So I walked across with my pistol in my hand. Everything was absolutely quiet, absolutely still, and I did actually have a kind of feeling that it was too quiet. But there it was, nothing happened. You couldn't believe that a crowd of people would keep sufficiently quiet for me not to hear them, or move, or do something. So I went back and waved the rest of them on, at which they came across and there we were pinned by a mob of people, *carabinieri*, civilians, women, both behind us and in front of us. We were absolutely neatly ambushed.

The *carabinieri* had firearms, and the rest of the crowd had a motley assortment of guns, sticks, scythes and the like. Some of the men were keen to try to fight it out. However, faced with the prospect of being shot or clubbed to death themselves, and injuring civilians in the process, Christopher Lea felt they had no choice but to surrender. It was an emotional moment, and one that still brings tears to his eyes today when he recalls it:

I can seldom remember a more ghastly moment in my life. There I was, I had recruited these people, we were making for a rendezvous, we had failed. I was sitting there just mixed with tiredness and, quite honestly, despair, and Lance-Corporals Pexton and Derek... I've forgotten his name now, it's gone... came along, and they sat one each side of me. Harry Pexton said: 'We think you made the right decision, sir.' They sat beside me for a bit longer, then made some excuse to go back again. That made a lot of difference – I've always remembered that.

Dave Struthers recalled:

My Irish colleague, when these people appeared and we were really ambushed good and proper, he wanted to shoot it out, he had a Thompson sub-machine gun. I can't say I heard Lea tell him not to, but common sense dictated there was no point.

The majority were civilians, but they were armed with different types of weapons, including shotguns. When I was captured, the one who was delegated to look after me had a double-barrelled old-fashioned shotgun with outside hammers, and I thought both hammers were back. He had this jabbed under my right ear. I wasn't too happy with his antics at all, in case he pulled the trigger, but I thought to myself, 'At least it will be quick.'

Handcuffed and chained together, they were loaded on to mule carts and taken cross-country to Calitri Station. Here, they found Tag Pritchard and his group already locked up in the waiting room. They were constantly threatened with being shot – but, as Dave Struthers put it: 'They were Italians. We kept our fingers crossed.'

Not long afterwards, members of the third and smallest group were brought to the station. They had been captured after a battle with armed troops, during which two Italians were killed and several more wounded. The deaths enraged the Italians, and, after the British soldiers eventually surrendered, they narrowly escaped being executed on the spot.

For two days the men remained under heavy guard in the station waiting room, not knowing whether they were going to be shot as spies or treated as ordinary prisoners of war. Harry Pexton picked up the story:

> Then they took us to Naples jail, a long train journey – well, it seemed a long time, anyway – and at each station the local population was out shouting at us, and threatening us with death.
>
> We asked for a bath, because we were covered in mud, and they gave us a bath, one bath in cold water, and we all had to bath in it. If you were at the end, you were scooping the mud off the top of the water to get your bath.

In prison they met up with the group who had originally been dropped in the wrong valley. They had managed to travel further than anybody else before walking straight into a company of Italian soldiers taking a rest on a routemarch. Their leader, Gerry Daly, in fact escaped from the jail by the simple expedient of opening the lock on his wooden cell door from the inside, using a conveniently sited hole. However, he was later recaptured after he slipped and knocked himself unconscious while trying to jump aboard a goods train.

Naples Military Prison was not a comfortable place, as Tony Deane-Drummond recalled:

> A high wall surrounded the prison into which a sentry box was built at each corner. The sentries were able to walk along the top of it and look down into the passage that surrounded the main prison building itself. My cell was about ten feet long and five feet broad. Along one side there was a large concrete block about two feet off the ground and about six feet long. On this was scattered a little straw,

which had obviously been used before and had become damp from condensation in the cell. A very small square pane of glass high up in the end of the cell gave the only light. The door was heavily barred and bolted, with a small peephole for the sentry stationed in the corridor.

Every night for three weeks, their guards told them they would be shot the next day. Every morning, they woke up relieved to be still alive. Harry Pexton remembered how, throughout their stay, they made sure they caused as much aggravation as possible:

> We used to wake up in the middle of the night when all the Italian squaddies were sleeping, or trying to sleep, creating all sorts of noise and rattling our mugs against the iron bars on the cell gate. In the old days, in American prison films like *Alcatraz*, all the prisoners seemed to have a tin mug which they rattled up and down the cage – 'Let me out! I'm too young to die!' – and we would be doing all that. They brought us this psychiatrist, but he decided that we weren't drugged or we weren't barmy – not completely, anyway.

Eventually, they were taken into the main compound, where they encountered other British captives. It became clear that they were to be treated as prisoners of war. All were interrogated, some showing themselves experts in the art of the inventively obstructive answer. Harry Pexton recalled:

> One of the aircrew, who was captured with us virtually, when he was interrogated, they asked him what sort of an aircraft he was in. He said, 'I'm sorry, I can't tell you.' So they said, you know, the usual things – they said it to me – 'It will go no further, you needn't worry.' So Butch – his name was Butch, Butch Allenby – said it was a Heinz 57. Apparently, they had a big book there of aircraft of the world, and they were going through it looking for a Heinz 57. Of course, there wasn't one, so they decided it was a secret aircraft.

Then they asked him how many were with him, and he said, 'Well, we were number eighty. As we took off, there were seventy-nine in front of us.' So, of course, that added extra consternation, and then they asked him what sort of engines the Heinz 57 had. So he said they were very secret, they were Crosse and Blackwell's. Again, they had a book of engines and aircraft and things like that, and they were look-ing for Crosse and Blackwell engines, and of course there weren't any.

You know, with hindsight, we gave them a dog's life, because they were on pins and needles. We could scratch a little hole out near a wall. The next morning, when they came and saw it there, they thought we had been trying to escape through, underneath the wall, and they would have a gang of squaddies digging to find out how we had got through, and of course we hadn't. I mean, we had just gone down about a foot or something like that, but that didn't mean anything. They were frightened to death that we would escape.

They had good reason to be frightened. Each soldier had been well provided with escape aids – to such an extent that they were later to wonder whether this was not a sign that the authorities knew perfectly well they were unlikely to make a safe return home without being captured.

One soldier, who had been shot in the arm, was in hospital. While he was there, his guards went through his uniform:

We had sealed maps in the cuff of our battledress jackets, files and things like that across the top of the battledress pocket, and money. Well, instead of waiting until they found everything, they found things one at a time, and each time they found something they would come into the [other pris-oners'] cells looking for it. By that time, of course, we had got wind of it, and we hid them in the holes in the walls, and things like that. 'Where is the money you had?' 'Oh, the civil-ians took it off us when they captured us.'

> We all had 3,000 lire, for bribery. Well, obviously, we
> didn't get anywhere to bribe. The prison sergeant used to
> come to us and ask if we wanted any shopping doing. So we
> used to send out for baskets of fruit and bars of chocolate
> and things like that.

Most of those who had volunteered for X Troop were young,
enthusiastic and keen to see some action. Accomplishing the
mission had seemed more important than what happened
afterwards. As Christopher Lea put it:

> Being the age I was, I didn't bother about it very much. I think
> we expected either to be dead or safe back home, frankly. I
> don't think we had ever anticipated that we'd be attacked and
> caught by their people, who were the sort of rabble.

What they did not know – and perhaps it was just as well – was
that even if they had made it to the arranged rendezvous, there
would have been no submarine there to meet them. The plan
had been for HMS *Triumph* to pick them up at the mouth of the
River Sele four nights after the attack. However, by pure bad
luck, one of the aeroplanes that had accompanied X Troop on
a diversionary bombing raid had developed engine trouble. It
was forced to ditch at exactly the same spot as the agreed
rendezvous – and the pilot had sent a message in very basic
code giving his location. Fearing that the code might be
cracked, and the area would be full of enemy soldiers looking
for the crew of the Whitley, the submarine's orders were
cancelled. No alternative rendezvous had been planned – so
even if the aqueduct raiders had made it to the coast, they
would have been stranded.

Reflecting on this now, some of the survivors of the aqueduct
raid are surprisingly philosophical. In the harsh economics of
war, thirty-odd men were more dispensable than a submarine –
especially a new one such as HMS *Triumph*. As Dave Struthers put
it: 'It was common sense to put the submarine first.'

Harry Pexton felt the whole exercise was purely a psychological one to see if they could get troops in. No one had seriously considered the practicalities of how they were to get out again.

> I mean, sixty-two miles... They gave us [under] a week to get back to the mouth of the River Sele. Well, if they'd given us a month under the conditions that we were in, we wouldn't have got back to the coast. I think it was bad planning. I don't think they thought it through thoroughly, you know. Since then, of course, we have all become experts in what should have happened and what didn't happen.

Among the questions raised by such postmortems on the raid is a very simple one: why did they have to go so far south, and so far inland, to prove a point? Clearly, the inaccessibility of the location made it a test of the skill of pilots and parachutists alike. The aqueduct would have been difficult to bomb accurately, and as the area it served included the naval base at Taranto, and other strategically important ports, it was an obviously attractive target. However, if the authorities had hoped to cause major disruption, they were to be disappointed. Dave Struthers:

> I think it proved one thing: that it forced the Italians to put a lot of men to guard all the vulnerable points down through Italy, and that would tie up thousands of soldiers or policemen. I think that was one of the objectives. The Italians were very good civil engineers, and they had the aqueduct, I believe, back functioning within five or six days. But it was really a morale-damaging exercise. I'm not sure whether Bari, Brindisi and Taranto were all affected in their water supply, but I think from the morale point of view it was very efficient.

The War Office, which would not even officially admit the existence of parachutists, kept the raid secret in Britain. The news filtered through only via Italian newspapers three days after the event. However, when the story emerged, the headlines had undoubted propaganda value.

Most of the parachutists themselves, however, were destined to spend the rest of the war in captivity. They were taken away from jail in Naples and transported to prison camp in Sulmona. All, that is, except one. Fortunato Picchi, the Savoy waiter whose name meant 'Little Fortune', ran out of luck in the Naples jail. His dark Italian looks led his interrogators to see through his French alias. The man who had travelled as Pierre Dupont was quickly revealed as a native-born Italian, and thus deemed to be a spy and traitor to his country. He disappeared after his interrogation, and on Palm Sunday 1941 he was executed. Under the headline SAVOY'S PICCHI DIES FOR US, the *Daily Express* described him as 'a hero in dress clothes'. The newspaper carried a full-length front-page picture of him with the caption: 'Fortunato Picchi. Gave up a job that was sometimes worth £60 a week.'

Meanwhile, his one-time comrades-at-arms continued to make life as difficult as possible for their captors. Harry Pexton recalled:

> I think they were glad to see the back of us in Naples jail when we left. Then they took us to Sulmona, and it was bucketing down with rain. Now these *carabinieri* officers, they were always elegantly dressed. They had long black coats with a red silk lining, and they were escorting us. Of course, there were mud and puddles, and as you got near a puddle with a *carabinieri* officer at the side of you, you happened to put your foot down a bit harder. They were glad to see the back of us as well.

For the first two months of their time in the *Campo di Concentramento*, the X Troop prisoners were isolated in two walled-off compounds: one for the officers, and one for the men. To be locked up with no glimpse of the outside world except the sky above was torture to these men, used as they were to leading such an active life. They complained to a visiting American military attaché and were eventually 'promoted' to the main camp. Tony Deane-Drummond recalled:

> At last the great day arrived and we were led up to the top compound. I remember we were held up for about twenty minutes before being let in. We grouped together and sang 'God Save the King'. It sounds odd now, long after the event, but it shows how tense and worked up we must have been.

Their new living quarters meant not only that they could at last have some exercise, but that they could get together to hatch escape plans. Tag Pritchard set up an escape committee. There was a failed attempt at a tunnel. Tony Deane-Drummond also had the idea of going out with the rubbish – but the day before he was due to go the guards started spearing it with swords and bayonets.

Eventually, he and Christopher Lea – another keen would-be escaper – decided to take advantage of a break in the wire:

> There were three wires that went right round the camp, and a break where it ended up at a wall and then started again higher up. The wall was about ten feet high, and the Italians had in fact got a spotlight looking down on this particular ledge. We said: 'How on earth could we get there? First of all, obviously, to put out the light – and, secondly, to sidle along this edge until we got to the point where we could drop down outside.'

Eventually, they decided to pretend to be Italian electricians. One rainy night – deliberately chosen in the hope that the sentry would be less likely to emerge from his box – they headed for the series of walls which they hoped would lead to freedom. They were armed with an electric light bulb, some coils of flex, and a ladder cobbled together from a split plank, with pieces of firewood and chairs for rungs. Tony Deane-Drummond remembered that night:

> We came down, picked the ladder up, and having dropped down over the second wall, which was covered with glass so that it was not entirely comfortable, we dropped down. Then we marched through the guardroom with our ladder, looking straight ahead. Just outside, there was a sentry box with another sleepy sentry in it. They didn't challenge us. We crossed about 2- or 300 yards to where this light was shining down on this ledge, and we put the ladder up.

Tony Deane-Drummond climbed up the ladder and unscrewed the bulb. When the inevitable challenge came from the sentry, he just shouted back '*Lampa*', in the hope that the sentry would not stop to wonder why they were replacing a perfectly good bulb. However, the ruse did not work. Christopher Lea picked up the story:

> Tony jumped down, and just as I was jumping this chap fired a shot. What I hadn't calculated on was that they were going to use dumdum bullets. I collected about five different pieces of metal in me which went through either a main vein in my leg or an artery – I don't know which. At any rate, I couldn't move, and I lay there bleeding and eventually was brought in – I gather, at the instigation of an English doctor who got to know what was happening. Otherwise, I think they were going to leave me, so I was told – that's purely hearsay. I was carried in to the doctor's room in the camp, and I do remember them undressing one and finding these various maps and so on strapped to one's leg in a suitable place to keep them out of sight. I remember thinking that my left leg was going to slip off the table. I knew it was; there was nothing I could do about it, except just point a finger. Fortunately, the English doctor saw what was going to happen, because I had just

gone with my leg, as it were, and he got hold of my leg and pulled me back on the table.

Besides the injuries to his leg, he had slashed a finger on the glass on top of the wall. (This was to leave him with no sensation in the fingertip for years afterwards.) However, despite his clearly weakened state, he was heavily guarded until he was well enough to leave hospital and return to the prison camp.

When they were originally making plans for their escape, Christopher had favoured trying to hitch a ride on a goods train. Tony wanted to try the more brazen approach of simply walking on to the station and buying a ticket. For this reason – and to increase their chances of success – they had each agreed to go their separate ways once outside. So although Tony Deane-Drummond felt a shot go past his cheek, he did not realize that his companion had been hit. He disappeared as fast as he could once safely over the wall.

Walking at night, and hiding during the daytime, he timed his arrival at Pescara Station for just ten minutes before the Milan train was due to leave. As he recalled:

> I got hold of the ticket, no problem, and passed the military inspectors. I got on to the train and – blow me down! – right behind me were two or three *carabinieri*. They came in after me, and I thought, 'Oh, God, what's going to happen next?' But in fact they sat down each side of me, and for the next fourteen hours I was on my way to Milan. These *carabinieri* in fact came off the train a few stations beyond, and at one place I bought a *cestina*, which was a little cardboard box with a leg of chicken and an orange, and it was wonderful.

Arriving late at night in Milan, he missed the last train to Como. He decided to risk an overnight hotel stay – but to his horror was confronted by a hotel receptionist who spoke perfect German. (He had covered up for his halting Italian by pretending he was a German.) He made some excuse and went back to the station, sleeping in the waiting room until morning. Eventually, he arrived in Como, and was walking towards the Swiss frontier when he was confronted by a party of guards.

> My instinct at the time was: should I turn and go backwards? I thought that would be too obvious, so anyhow I decided to brazen it out. After all, I had passed lots of people who had all had a look at me, and they didn't seem to think I was abnormal at all. These chaps, they went past, and then the NCO [Non-Commissioned Officer] in charge called me back and said: 'We want to see your papers.' I gave them some fairly bogus papers that had been manufactured in Sulmona, and I was taken off to the camp where these people were based, given some wine and a leg of chicken. Then they said, 'We'll take you down to Chiasso,' where there was an interpreter. Of course, I was taken down there, and they soon discovered who I was. My name was actually on the list of people who had escaped, so that was the end of that – for the time being.

However, Tony Deane-Drummond did eventually make a successful escape – by jumping out of a window from Florence Military Hospital, where he had been taken after complaining of severe earache. Travelling openly by train as before, he made his way to a different section of the frontier with Switzerland. He got through by the simple expedient of scraping a hole under the fence and crawling underneath. He was guided across France with the aid of the French Resistance, and travelled from Marseilles to Gibraltar on a fishing boat full of Polish refugees. Eventually, he reached England in July 1942. He was the first member of X Troop to return home, although he was not the only one to escape from captivity. Others, too, were to find their way to Allied troops or groups of partisans and continue to play an active part in the war.

Although every man who took part in Operation Colossus had been captured, and one executed, the exercise was successful in that it disconcerted the enemy. Fighting a war is never straightforward, but it does help if you know where the battle lines are. Just as the LRDG and the SAS made vast tracts of desert into potential battlegrounds, so the activities of X Troop forced the Italians to tie up money and manpower in protecting their own back yard.

The way the Italians treated the *paracadutisti* as dangerous prisoners was, in fact, a backhanded compliment. It was a testament to their potential value, and foreshadowed the increasingly important role they were to play.

THE ROAD TO ARNHEM

The raid on the Tragino aqueduct had shown that British pilots could drop parachutists accurately deep into enemy territory. However, it also demonstrated that there was still a lot to learn – not least, how to get them out again.

The generals were acutely aware that they had been slow off the mark in the parachute stakes. That this was a source of embarrassment is suggested by the fact that five years after the war ended, the official RAF publication on the history of airborne forces was still marked 'restricted'. On the shelves of the Imperial War Museum library is Air Publication 3231, a thin, harmless-looking volume, issued by the Air Ministry in 1950. It details what the anonymous author describes as the 'leisurely pace' at which RAF officials investigated this new phenomenon.

In 1936 a British Military Mission, led by General – later Field Marshal – Archie Wavell, had attended Red Army manoeuvres near Minsk, and had seen the dropping of 1,500 troops by parachute. The Mission's report remarked that, although this had been a spectacular performance, the use of parachutists was 'of doubtful tactical value'.

The same year as the Soviet Army's demonstration, the Germans had opened an Air Landing Training School. In July

1939 a 1,000-strong battalion landed by parachute on a single dropping zone. By the time the war started, the Germans had two whole parachute battalions ready for action.

Meanwhile, the French had two companies of *L'Infanterie de l'Air*, with an estimated total strength of 300. In April 1939 negotiations were started for two British officers to go and visit them to study their technique. However, progress was so slow that they had still not finalized arrangements by the time war was declared. In October 1939 the visit was cancelled.

In June 1940, when Hitler was sweeping all before him in Europe, Churchill's memo demanding the instant recruitment of 1,000s of parachutists showed that he recognized their importance. However, Britain had a long way to go to catch up. By May the following year, when Hitler's elite airborne forces descended to victory in Crete, Britain still had only 500 men at Knutsford. However, this was set to change.

Many of the early parachutists were colourful individualists, attracted not only by the challenge but by the chance to be themselves. They could live in ordinary houses with families, instead of in army barracks, and there was very little regimental discipline. Doug Russell recalled the story of a soldier called Izzie Goldstein:

> He was on parade wearing suede shoes. So the platoon commander said: 'Goldstein, if you can't come on parade in anything other than suede shoes, you had better stay off.' So he did – for a fortnight; nothing happened to him.

Once they felt they had mastered the art of parachuting, many treated it as routine. An example was a night-time balloon jump that happened to coincide with a dinner:

> We had one officer who was from a very classy regiment in Northern Ireland, the North Irish Horse. He had his full regalia on, all his blue uniform, his spurs and his dog, a little

dog. He went up and jumped with his dog in his arms and came wandering back to the George... Quite amusing.

It got to the point where exercises at night – which took a couple of hours and frequently involved an 'attack' on a pub – were treated as simply an interruption in the evening's entertainment. Doug Russell recalled:

We'd get to the pub, we'd have the operation, we'd take the pub and then we'd all go inside and drink. Very simple. There was very little discipline in those days. Obviously, you had to go on parade and you had to do as you were told, but I really think we were very slack.

I think that the powers that be realized, too, that we were very slack, because they sent a colonel up, a Colonel Down. He was going to take over the battalion, he said, and we had to meet in Knutsford Town Hall. He stood up on the stage and everybody booed, including all the officers – senior officers as well. Anyway, he told us that we were only profiteering, getting two shillings a day for parachuting, and – what was it? – six and eight a day ration allowance, and he would stop that. After all, going to war by parachute or lorry or bus or walking didn't make any difference – it's what you did when you got on the ground.

Oh, we didn't like that very much at all, being told this, but he was quite right. He took command of that battalion, and he was the most respected officer of that time. But it took a little while for it to happen. He sent us all over to Bury, and it poured with rain. We had to all fire a [weapons] course. If you didn't fire a first-class course, you were out. Then you had to go back to Ringway and drop over the Pennines. It was pouring with rain – awful – then you had to make your way back. And that just about saw the fortnight off, which was to give us an idea of what we were going to have to do in future.

Then he said: 'Right, everybody get kitted up and we're

going to march back to Knutsford.' We marched from Bury to Knutsford, not very far really, but it was in those days cobbled stones all through Salford. It was the hottest day of the year, all the rain had gone and it was beautiful sunshine. And we got to Knutsford and that was about it. From there on, we moved into barracks, into Chesterfield, and we became a disciplined troop – which is what we should have been in the first place, but we weren't.

The move to new headquarters at Hardwick Hall came in late 1941. According to Doug Russell, 'Every landlady in Knutsford was at the station, and half of them were in tears.' Not everyone was willing to go, as he recalled:

A lot said they didn't want to put up with the Army now if it was going to be like this – regimental; they'd just as well go back where they came from. So an awful lot went back to their units; they got rid of a lot like that. Well, some of them were no good. On the other hand, we had a very nice chap, I think his name was Cheery. He spoke about six languages fluently, but because he didn't pass the rifle course they chucked him out. We thought he might have been a very useful asset to anybody, which he was.

All would-be parachutists, whatever their rank, now had to go through a tough selection fortnight at Hardwick Hall. This involved jumping from fuselages, swinging from trapezes – and being swung for twenty minutes in a stretcher suspended by ropes to see if they got airsick. Army PT instructors scrutinized their every move; everything had to be done at the double. Operation Colossus had inspired many thousands of British soldiers to volunteer for parachute training – but, not surprisingly, there was a high dropout rate.

Increasingly, parachutists were to be trained to take their part in much larger infantry operations. In heavily occupied Northern Europe, there were limited opportunities for them to carry out Commando raids behind enemy lines. It was easier simply to bomb from the air. However, sometimes there was no substitute for the carefully targeted raid as opposed to the indiscriminate destruction involved in bombing.

German radar developments contributed to huge losses among RAF bomber crews, and scientists wanted to see what the Germans were up to in this field. Plans were laid for a raid by parachutists – but since this was a smash-and-grab raid, rather than straightforward sabotage, getting them out was to be just as important as getting them in.

Radar – Radio Direction and Ranging – had been discovered by Britain and Germany independently in the 1930s. During the Second World War, the battle in the skies was matched by a battle in the laboratories, as each side competed to produce ever more sophisticated versions. The British had learned how to jam conventional early warning systems – but had no defence against a new radar called the *Würzburg*. This could tell the altitude of British bombers, enabling anti-aircraft guns and night fighters to home in on their targets with deadly accuracy.

RAF reconnaissance crews had photographed a *Würzburg* radar dish on a clifftop at Bruneval, near Le Havre. However, this gave no indication of how it worked. Lord Louis Mountbatten, Chief of Combined Operations, authorized a raid by paratroops, who would steal selected parts of the *Würzburg* and return to Britain by sea.

The raiders were chosen from C Company of the Second Parachute Battalion – a company made up of volunteers from the Scots regiments. A group of six officers and 113 men were to be joined by nine sappers, four signallers, 'Private Newman' – an anti-Fascist German who would act as interpreter – and an RAF radar mechanic. Charles Cox was one of the best radar technicians in Britain. He came from East Anglia and, in civilian life, had been a cinema projectionist and radio ham. Before he joined the RAF in 1940, he had never been in a ship, let alone an aeroplane. He had just under a fortnight to complete his parachute training before joining the rest of the group for fitness exercises.

Tom Hill, a member of C Company, recalled their training regime:

> We had a spell in Scotland on Loch Fyne. We lived for a while on what had previously been a ferry across the Channel, the *Prince Albert*, and we practised with assault barges. The bargers had to get into the habit of getting us on quickly and taking off quickly. It was all a question of efficiency and speed in doing things.
>
> We went on to Dartmoor; we would live in tents to practise manoeuvring quickly through hills and mud and whatever came up. Then we were told we would have to do a demonstration for the War Office. We went down to a little camp at Tilshead [on Salisbury Plain]. It was only a Nissen hut camp, and it was going to be a demonstration of what could be done on cliffs. We didn't know what it was all leading up to at the time.

Every evening, at about 6 p.m., they would set off for the South Coast for a cold night's practice going up and down the cliffs. They would then head back for camp, a meal and bed, only to repeat the same process the next night.

> Then one day we were told that the demonstration was off – but there would be a raid. From then on the camp was sealed, nobody unauthorized could come into the camp, nobody could leave. That's when I was told they had a little job for me, and I was taken down to a little hut about 150 yards away from any of the other huts, given all these maps and a tray of sand and told: 'Right, make a model.'

With the help of two other men, he painstakingly marked out squares of the sand tray with string. He then translated information from photographs, and maps of the French coast, into a contoured scale model in wet sand. Since the raid was to take place by moonlight, it was important that everyone concerned had a proper mental map.

The dress rehearsal was held on the night of 23 February 1942. The parachuting part of the operation went smoothly, but the landing craft became firmly grounded sixty yards offshore. As with Operation Colossus, the men were left simply hoping that it would be all right on the night.

Operation Biting, as it was code-named, was set for some point during the four days between 24 and 27 February. Only then would there be a full moon and a rising tide, which would enable the landing craft to evacuate the troops from the beach at Bruneval. Tom Hill recalled:

> The first three evenings we would be all ready to go in the camp, and then we were told, no, the raid was off because of weather conditions. That happened three nights in a row. Then on the last night they said, 'The raid is on', and so it was off to the airfield, to assemble and be off.

To the accompaniment of bagpipes playing Scottish regimental tunes, the men and weapons containers were loaded into waiting Whitley bombers at Thruxton aerodrome for the chilly journey across the Channel.

> Whitleys were always cold – there was no heating in them at all, and it was midwinter. But our uniforms were warm; we were well clad. We were fit, which helped a lot – you can stand a lot of cold if you're fit.

Intelligence had suggested that there could be up to 200 Germans in the area around the radar. If this was true, the raiding force would be outnumbered – but the British would have the advantage of surprise. The radar was well protected from assault by sea, but the guards would be unlikely to expect a parachute invasion.

The raiders were to be split into several groups. Three groups, which included the sappers, were to capture the radar site and dismantle the machinery. Tom Hill's group was to clear the enemy defences.

Our man [the pilot] was slightly confused, and we were dropped some three miles from where we should have been. Now, this was in country we didn't know the slightest thing about. We didn't know we were three miles away to start with – he just gave us the green light and we dropped. There was no sign of any other aircraft dropping anyone, so the lieutenant – he was a very bright fellow – got us all together. He knew immediately what was happening. 'Right,' he said, 'the moon must be somewhere out towards the coast at the moment – we'll head for the moon.'

However, it had been snowing, and their dark camouflage meant they were clearly visible in the moonlight.

We had to stick to hedgerows and woodland; otherwise we would be so obvious. We were about halfway back to the beach, and the platoon officer was in the lead. There were ten of us from that particular stick. I was at the tail end, and quite suddenly this voice behind me spoke in German. Now, there was snow on the ground, and everything was quiet, but we didn't hear him somehow. I don't know how he suddenly joined us. He just spoke in a normal voice, thinking, I should imagine, that he had joined a section of his own people.

I started to turn, but I saw Gibby [the platoon officer] turning as well, so I thought the best thing I can do is duck... Gibby swung round like lightning, turned and shot him. Thinking sensibly about it, there was nothing else you could do. We would all have died.

The group charged with preventing a German counter-attack landed right on target. Among them was Richard Scott, who remembered how he was hit by an ammunition container as he parachuted down:

> I was number six, and you were supposed to come out: one, two, three, four, five, container, six. That was me – but I must have got out too soon, and I came down with the container. It hit me first, and it took my knife – it was stitched to the trousers, and it ripped right off. So my knife was left for a souvenir for the Jerries – but I was OK apart from that.

The radar station was on a clifftop, near an isolated villa. Inside the villa, Major Johnny Frost and his company met only one enemy soldier, who had opened fire from an upstairs window. At the radar site itself, they captured two prisoners, who told them that there were German reinforcements inland.

Meanwhile, Charles Cox and his team battled to dismantle the radar. Despite the meticulous planning of the raid, they did not have a screwdriver long enough to remove a part. When they used a crowbar to break it off, it came away complete with its frame. This later turned out to be a stroke of luck, as the frame contained the aerial switching unit, which was a vital part of the design.

Just as firing from nearby German positions was getting stronger, the group that was meant to be knocking out the defences arrived. Tom Hill recalled:

> We were told that they still had the beach defences. We didn't know whether they were occupied or not. The most simple method was, where you had a dugout with an entrance at each end, just roll a hand grenade in at one end and see who comes out the other. I think there were maybe three German soldiers, but they all came out and gave themselves up immediately, and we took them down to the beach. I think they were probably quite happy to get out of the war. We took them back to England with us for questioning.

With sounds of vehicles moving in woodlands behind the cliffs, the radar parts were loaded on to a specially built trolley and hurried down to the evacuation beach. The idea was that they would be taken off by landing craft, then transferred to gunboats for the journey back to England. However, when they got down to the beach, there was no sign of the craft. Tom Hill:

We had been given some new radios, new on the market, and they didn't work. We were all standing on the beach, watching for these landing craft coming... no sign... We knew that by now German forces must have been alerted, and in desperation the CO fired a Very pistol into the air. The boats we were waiting for were about three miles out, and fortunately one of them saw this Very flare, and they came in on that.

They hadn't come in earlier, apparently, because three German E boats had passed them in the vicinity. They hadn't spotted them, fortunately, but they had to wait until they were clear before they could come in and take us off. They did come in finally, and so off we scrambled into these boats, and back to the gunboats.

That was an amusing – well, hardly amusing – journey back. A gunboat had a crew of probably about six, and there were twenty of us getting on to each gunboat, so it was rather crowded. We went down into the little cabin area, and one man on the crew was opening tins of soup as fast as he could. It didn't matter what it was – it all went into the one big pot. They gave us all a mug of hot soup and a mug of rum, and this was in a gunboat which, because it was towing, could only go at a speed of about six knots. On deck, you were holding on to the rail and looking at the sky one moment, and you could put your hand in the water the next, it was rocking and rolling so much about. So with hot soup and rum, it was quite a trek up and down to the rail every so often. There was quite a lot of seasickness.

The original plan had been for the beach to be evacuated in phases, but all six landing craft moved in at the same time. There were a few nasty moments when the men on the landing craft started shooting at their own soldiers on the clifftop defences, but agonized shouts from the beach made them realize their mistake. The radar team and their trophies were loaded into the first boat. However, the withdrawal after that was chaotic, as Richard Scott recalled:

> I was the very last man, because when we withdrew they put me on top of the cliff to give them covering fire. I had to wait there while the wounded came in, and they just gave me a shout to come down. I got into the boat, and a silly seaman forgot to put the door up, and we got swamped. We were standing in about three feet of water, and all these people who were wounded, they were a bit noisy, they were in pain. I tried to bail out, but the wind blew it back at you, so it wasn't very cosy.

In the general confusion, there was no time to check everyone was on board.

> When we left, there was a signalman who was bringing the boats in just by a torch. When we got out to sea I looked back and I could see this signal flash, and I tried to tell the seaman. I said: 'The signalman – we've left the signalman behind.' He wouldn't turn back for him, so the poor devil got killed – that was the same name as me, a fellow called Scott. I often think of him. It should never have happened.

On the way back across the Channel, they were escorted by Spitfires and Navy destroyers, and they were filmed as they arrived safely back in Portsmouth with their booty. Two men had been killed and several wounded – but the operation was judged a success. The German prisoners included the radar operator, and studying the parts that had been brought back helped scientists understand how German radar worked. Technology moves fast in war – but at the time the raid had enormous impact. As Tom Hill put it:

> We seemed to be losing everything up to that stage, and then we'd been off on an extremely successful raid. According to all the accounts, it was a great morale-booster. Everyone you met who could talk about it seemed highly delighted that we had done something that was a real smack at the enemy.

The Bruneval raid had been meticulously planned, with the help of intelligence from the French Resistance. This meant that they knew in advance that the beach would not be mined, and they knew on the night of the drop that it was snowing in France. Unlike Operation Colossus, carried out almost exactly a year before, every stage had been rehearsed and thought through. The result was that most of the highly skilled soldiers who took part returned home safely.

Despite this spectacular success, only a limited number of raids involved individuals taking a 'smack at the enemy'. Increasingly, parachutists were to find themselves taking part in much larger operations. Their numbers grew dramatically, and their distinctive role was symbolized by the red beret that they adopted from the middle of 1942. Legend has it that the colour was chosen by the novelist Daphne du Maurier, who was married to the paratroop commander, Major General Frederick 'Boy' Browning; however, she always denied this.

Paratroopers took part in attacks in North Africa (where they had to learn how to jump from USAF Dakotas), Sicily and Italy. They fought in Normandy from D-Day onwards, with a total of 821 men killed from June to September 1944. The SAS had their own role in France, arming and training the French Resistance and locating targets for the RAF. They also continued to mount aggressive operations on their own, using armed jeeps dropped by glider. However, much to their chagrin, they were forced to exchange their sand-coloured berets for airborne maroon ones.

Arnhem, in September 1944, was typical of the scale of parachute operations now being mounted. Code-named Market Garden, this was an ambitious attempt to establish a bridgehead across the lower Rhine at the Dutch town of Arnhem. The operation was divided into two parts: Market, using airborne troops to seize bridges across eight water barriers, and Garden, the advance of infantry across them. If it had been successful, it could have brought the war to an early close. However, it turned out to be a bridge too far.

To capture the bridges, some 16,500 paratroopers from both British and US divisions were dropped, and 3,500 conventional troops landed in gliders. Pictures taken from the air afterwards show the dropping zone – heathland eight miles west of Arnhem – littered with abandoned parachutes.

Among those dropped was Tony Deane-Drummond, who had first gone into action as a parachutist in Operation Colossus. Following his spectacular escape from prison camp in Italy, he had continued to take an active part in the war, and was now deputy commander of the First Airborne Signals. His first task was to stay in the rear and keep up communications – but when they lost touch with the First Parachute Brigade, only five miles away, he was asked by his colonel to go forward and see what the trouble was.

The trouble – although they did not realize it at the time – was that two SS Panzer divisions happened to be refitting close to Arnhem. The Dutch Resistance had sent a message warning about this, but it had been too late to affect the plan. To make matters worse, the Panzers had just completed an exercise on how to repel an airborne landing. When the parachutists had dropped, they had been seen by a German field marshal, who was able immediately to order armoured reinforcements.

It took four hours for British paratroopers to reach the bridges on foot, by which time the Germans were ready for them. Tony Deane-Drummond caught up with a group whose commander had just been killed, and found himself taking over. There followed some messy street fighting, after which he and the twenty men who remained of the company split up into groups and holed up in houses by the river. They were running out of ammunition, and were surrounded by Germans. They had little choice but to try to sneak out at night – swimming across the river, if need be – to rejoin the British forces.

In *Return Ticket*, Tony Deane-Drummond described what happened next:

> We were just looking out of the window on the other side of the house when I heard somebody, obviously a German, trying to get into the front door of the house. I thought it most unlikely that we had been seen, and so we all dived into the lavatory and locked the door on the inside.
>
> Eventually, he broke in through the door, and to our dismay a section of about ten German soldiers followed him in and on upstairs. From the sounds of tile removing and furniture shifting, the house was being converted into a strong point in the German defensive position.

For the following three nights and three days, they took it in turns to sit on the lavatory seat. The Germans would come and try the door but, finding it locked, would go away again. They had eaten nothing except some apples from a cellar, which they would creep out and raid at night. On the fourth night they decided to break out. Tony Deane-Drummond was swept downstream as he swam across the river and became separated from the rest of his party. He was just scrambling up a railway embankment when he fell into a slit trench containing a sleepy German. Once more, he was a prisoner.

When he met up with others who had been captured, he found out what a failure the whole operation had been. This did not affect his determination to escape again. Some 500 prisoners were crammed into a house in a suburb of Arnhem, and he decided his best chance lay in hiding up before the guards could take a roll call. He found a suitable cupboard, changed the lock round so he could open and shut it from the inside, and holed up with his water bottle, a one-pound tin of lard and half a loaf of bread. As he put it:

> Little did I think that I would be confined to my cramped little cupboard for thirteen days and nights before getting out. I thought that the limit of my endurance would be reached after three or four days, because I did not start off in the best condition for an endurance test.
>
> There was no room to sit down because the cupboard was too shallow. I managed to sleep all right although occasionally my knees would give way and would drop forward against the door, making a hammer-like noise. Every bone in my body ached, and I felt quite light-headed from lack of food, water and rest.

By day, the room was used for interrogation, and he had to listen in silence as two British prisoners gave away secrets. By night, it was turned into sleeping quarters for the German guard. As his water ran out and cramp became unbearable, he decided to make a break for it. Taking advantage of the room being empty, he slipped out of the window, hid in a shrubbery until it became dark, then crept away. He was helped by sympathetic Dutch people, until finally he arrived back in England by aeroplane, landing at the same Lincolnshire airfield from which he had taken off some six weeks before.

Arnhem illustrates just how much parachuting had changed since its early use as a way of getting small groups of raiders behind enemy lines. With the larger numbers involved, the crucial elements of surprise and speed had been lost. However, the story of Tony Deane-Drummond's escape shows that the spirit which had led to the creation of such elite fighting forces was still very much alive.

CONCLUSION

*Nothing throws a clearer light upon the characteristics of
a nation than the way it goes to war, and what is revealed
there is likely to be reflected to some degree in everything
else it does.*

General Sir John Hackett's comment, in his foreword to David
Lloyd Owen's history of the Long Range Desert Group, throws
an interesting light on the story of the elite troops whose activities have filled these pages. For, despite some spectacular
successes, only one – the SAS – has survived in something like
its original form. Could this be because they threatened a
conservative military establishment?

Of course, there are practical reasons why generals – with
men and equipment in short supply – might be reluctant to go
for the high-risk Commando approach. Those who volunteered for such raids tend even now, with the wisdom of hindsight, to gloss over the difficulties. It is all too easy to forget just
how dangerous it all was.

Most of the raids which are the focus for this book took
place behind enemy lines between 1940 and 1942. That is not
to say that all Commando activity stopped after that – but,
increasingly, they were used as part of larger-scale assaults. The

parachutists earned their nickname, *Rote Teufel* – the Red Devils – while fighting in Tunisia in 1942–3. As we have seen, they also played a key role at Arnhem. The Army Commandos fought alongside nearly 5,000 Canadian troops in a disastrous attempted raid on German-occupied Dieppe in August 1942. The Commando Association Battle Honours Flag in Westminster Abbey lists thirty-eight engagements – only four of which were not part of combined operations with other forces.

The LRDG served with distinction in the Balkans as well as the desert, and proved to be a highly cost-effective force. They had hoped to go on to fight in the Far East, but were disbanded in June 1945. Individual generals supported what they did. However, despite the skills they had developed as pirates of the sand seas, they were all too often treated simply as ordinary soldiers. As Archie Gibson put it:

> We lost good people... you have no control over these clowns who run things from the back yard. There are all these fat pompous little bastards who think they know better. We were being used as infantry – we weren't infantry; we were specialists.

Throughout its history, the SAS fought similar battles against military planners who mistrusted their somewhat maverick approach. In the later stages of the war, they resisted attempts to use them for short-term raids, and held out for a distinctive role in occupied France. The effectiveness of their sabotage and work with the French Resistance justified their determination. In September 1944 General Frederick Browning told them: 'The operations you have carried out have had more effect in hastening the disintegration of the German 7th and 5th Armies than any other single effort in the Army.' After the war, the SAS was disbanded, but resurfaced to develop a high-profile role in the fight against terrorism.

Small-scale organizations, which soldiers have to drop rank to join, threaten the normal Army hierarchy. The SAS, with its units of four – the number of men who can fit into a jeep – was an essentially democratic organization. Each individual would be trained to carry out the general duties expected of an SAS soldier – but each would also have a particular expertise. David Stirling was keen to eliminate barriers of class and rank, and saw self-discipline as more important than regimental discipline. This undercut the idea of a leader in the conventional sense – although, of course, he himself demonstrated what could be achieved by individual charisma. It is perhaps not surprising that the stuffier elements of the Army found his ideas hard to take.

Those on raids behind enemy lines experienced a very different war from those who served in larger regiments. Stephen Hastings, who saw service in both the Brigade of Guards and the SAS, summed this up:

A raid demands a pretty cool head, but it didn't always go on for very long, a matter of an hour or two. Generally speaking, the pattern was that you went and hit and then you came out and that was that. You could relax – at least for a bit. It was certainly extremely exciting. You often had the priceless advantage of surprise, which is a tremendous morale-booster, very different from digging your slit trench in the desert in the full knowledge that the 15th Panzer Division are going to come and you've just got to sit there and wait. I think the lot of the infantry soldier overall was probably in a way a harder one – that's not to say the SAS was a soft touch, for goodness' sake, but it was different.

In a regular battalion in the line, then it was a question of week after week, month after month, obeying orders that you probably often didn't understand, in positions which you maybe wouldn't have chosen, but in any case couldn't abandon.

The Commando experience was also very different according to the theatre of war, as he recalled:

If we're talking about the desert campaign, we respected our German enemy, the Afrika Korps. They were fine soldiers. They treated our prisoners and wounded, particularly under Rommel, with courtesy, exactly the same as we treated them. There was no sense of knowledge among us young men of the horrors of Europe. It wasn't until much later on, when I was parachuted into the Italian mountains to do my best to arm and help the Italian partisans that one saw what was really happening – the villages burned, people murdered, and all that beastliness of German occupation. That was a very different matter altogether.

Despite the bloodthirstiness of some aspects of their training, the vast majority of those who volunteered for raiding units were simply ordinary young men with a taste for adventure. Michael Burn, whose experiences in one of the early Commandos turned him against war, recalled:

Most were people who wanted to get away from the routine of drills and things of that kind. Probably some of them thought, as I did, that the sooner we could bring the war to an end the better, and that by volunteering for this kind of thing we might help. They were adventurous, they were imaginative, very independent, and their independence was brought out by the kind of training we had. They were not thugs – the last thing they were were thugs – but they were tough, of course.

New Zealander Alf Saunders, of the Long Range Desert Group, recalled:

We knew that shells would kill you and bullets could kill you and bombs could kill you, but... well, we didn't realize what could happen, and that's probably why we survived it. I think if you were going to go into a thing like that and you knew beforehand, it would drive you mad, wouldn't it? It did drive a lot of people mad – it did in the First World War. They just deserted, and all sorts of things.

No, I never thought about it – just a sense of adventure, a bunch of good jokers – it makes it so simple, doesn't it? That's why they'll always get armies, because the young ignorant youth can't get there quick enough.

Buster Gibb, also a New Zealander, summed up the personal cost of war:

You talk to most returned men and they never talk about the actual grim wartime; they talk about the games and the fun and the jokes, and all the things they got up to. But when it comes to the actual warfare part of it, they seem to shut it from their minds. I'd never talk to my family about some of the things I've done, the times you've shot somebody. It doesn't give you a feeling of elation or anything like that – it gives you a feeling of depression.

The survivors of these raids came back to a world that could not hope to understand exactly what they had been through. Many whose words appear in this book continued to serve as soldiers, several rising to the rank of brigadier. Some found nothing in ordinary life could match up to the excitement they had experienced in wartime. John Durnford-Slater, the first commando, died under the wheels of the Brighton train near Haywards Heath in 1972. Some simply went back to what they had been doing before; others went on to become prominent members of the community. Carol Mather and Stephen Hastings were both elected as Conservative MPs. Christopher Lea studied law while a prisoner of war, rose to become a judge, then became an ordained minister.

In the year 2000, members of the St Nazaire Society made their last pilgrimage to the cemetery where their comrades are buried. Michael Burn described his feelings as one of the inevitably dwindling numbers of survivors:

I think it's natural to feel that you've survived from luck. But a lot of people who have been through the war feel that there was some purpose in it which you have to go on with afterwards. It sounds ridiculous and very vain to say that you were saved for some purpose, but the war was fought to some purpose, and one must not forget that. It isn't only through reunions and exchanging reminiscences that you can do that – it is through continuing the purposes for which the war was fought.

These men fought in the enemy's back yard under conditions sometimes more like those of Stone Age warriors than twentieth-century soldiers. Their feats of bravery and endurance should not be forgotten.

SOURCES

Cooper, Johnny, *One of the Originals*, Pan Books, London, 1991

Deane-Drummond, Anthony, *Return Ticket*, Fontana Books, London, 1955

Durnford-Slater, John, *Commando*, William Kimber & Co., London, 1953

Harclerode, Peter, *Para! Fifty Years of the Parachute Regiment*, Cassell, London, 1992

Hastings, Stephen, *The Drums of Memory*, Leo Cooper, Barnsley, 1994

Hearn, Peter, *The Sky People*, Airlife Publishing, Shrewsbury, 1990

Hoe, Alan, *David Stirling: The Authorized Biography of the Creator of the SAS*, Little, Brown, London, 1992

James, Malcolm, *Born of the Desert*, Collins, London, 1945

Kennedy Shaw, Bill, *The Long Range Desert Group*, Collins, London, 1945; reprinted Greenhill Books, London, 2000

Lucas Phillips, C.E., *The Greatest Raid of All*, Heinemann, London, 1958

O'Carroll, Brendan, *Kiwi Scorpions*, Token Publishing, Honiton, 2000

Owen, David Lloyd, *Providence Their Guide*, Harrap, London, 1980

Parker, John, *Commandos*, Headline, London, 2000

Ranfurly, Countess of, *To War with Whitaker: The Wartime Diaries of the Countess of Ranfurly 1939–1945*, Arrow Books, London, 1998

Thompson, Julian, *War Behind Enemy Lines*, Sidgwick & Jackson, London, 1998

MAGAZINES

After the Battle, ed. Winston G. Ramsey. No. 32: *Operation Ambassador*; No. 59: *The Raid on St-Nazaire*; No. 81: *Tragino Paratroop Raid*; No. 109: *The Vaagso Commando Raid*. Battle of Britain Prints, London

INDEX